LIFE IS LOCAL

The history of

Johnston Press plc

by Edward Riley

Johnston Press plc

Published in 2006 by Johnston Press plc
53 Manor Place, Edinburgh EH3 7EG

A CIP record for this book is
available from the British Library

ISBN-10: 0-9551729-0-X
ISBN-13: 978-0-9551729-0-8

Designed by Robin Turton Design & Illustration Ltd, Leeds
Printed by The Amadeus Press, Cleckheaton

Contents

Foreword

I am writing this brief foreword to the updated history of Johnston Press – the first account was published in 1925 – 238 years after Patrick Mair's printing works, which had shadowy beginnings in Glasgow a few years previously, was established in Falkirk. Patrick Mair was my great-great-great grandfather.

The company is unusual in that it has lasted for well over two centuries without changing hands. It still has the same registered number that it received on its incorporation as a limited company in 1928. The founding family retain a significant shareholding. The present chairman, Roger Parry, is only the fourth holder of this office since 1882.

I believe that despite this long history Johnston Press has remained forward looking. It is now the second largest regional newspaper publisher in Britain and one of the 200 largest quoted companies on the London Stock Exchange. It has enjoyed considerable financial success and this in turn has underpinned its development and made everything else possible.

But profitability, though vital, is not everything. We have also tried to produce decent, responsible newspapers, which adequately reflect the life of the communities which we serve, and to consider the interests of our workforce, which now numbers many thousands.

We are aware that we live in a changing world. We are investing for the future, with substantial sums being spent on new printing plants in Sheffield and Portsmouth, and significant efforts are being made to develop our interests in digital media.

Yet we have not forgotten our roots in Falkirk and I hope we never shall. The past is of vital importance to us but we are not obsessed with it. We regard its real importance as providing the gateway to the future.

Freddy Johnston
Chairman, 1973–2001
March 2006

Introduction

In the space of a little over 150 years Johnston Press plc grew from modest beginnings in small-town Scotland to become the second largest provincial newspaper publisher in the British Isles.

And for most of that time there were generations of Johnstons at the helm to keep the business on a steady course of growth and consolidation in Scotland, followed by expansion into England.

Today Johnston Press is a publicly quoted company and has not been a family-controlled firm since 1988, when it obtained a full listing on the London Stock Exchange and changed its name from F. Johnston and Co Ltd to Johnston Press plc.

But even after going public the Johnston family influence remained substantial, and in 2006 family members held 20 per cent of the company's 286.7 million shares, which were capitalised at approximately £1.3 billion. At flotation in 1988 the family had owned 59 per cent of the company, when it was valued at £29 million. This, of course, was diluted by subsequent share issues, but the family has never been sellers of shares in any substantial way.

For many years the principal family shareholders were Freddy Johnston and his wife Ann, his brothers Harry and Jim, the trustees of Harry's two daughters, and Freddy's two sons Michael and Robert.

Despite the new demands from the City and institutional investors the company retained much of its family character, and this was largely due to the diversity of its component parts – newspapers that prior to acquisition were in many cases themselves family-run enterprises with the same sort of people as the Johnstons in charge.

It was a proud heritage of mainly local publications built up over many years and handed on for safe keeping to new custodians.

Indeed, the local emphasis is central to the Johnston Press ethos. It always has been and it is highly unlikely that this will change. When the slogan "Life is Local" was adopted it was a simple but effective way of expressing how the group conducts its business.

Chief Executive Tim Bowdler neatly summed up the character of the company when he said:

"Our business depends on the local nature of our markets, and our publishing activities are a reflection of numerous local economies across the United Kingdom and, in turn, the behaviour of local consumers and advertisers.

"It is this dependence on local markets which differentiates the regional and local press from so many other branches of the media.

"This focus on meeting the needs of local market places is the cornerstone of the group's business strategy."

Chairman Roger Parry struck a similar theme in his introduction to the 2002 annual report and accounts, reflecting that while Britain is well served by national media it was the role of Johnston Press to understand and meet the needs of people in the areas where they live, work and play.

Four years later, and with more than 300 regional newspaper titles and specialist publications and more than 250 related websites, the group remains closely focused on community publishing in the UK and Ireland – a strategy that is supported by extensive research that was commissioned by the Newspaper Society, the industry's trade association. It confirmed the intensely local focus of people's lives covering a wide spectrum of activities including occupation, shopping, leisure and socialising.

The fact that this strategy was implemented so successfully meant that Johnston Press could rightly claim its place among the newspaper publishing elite. In many ways its own development is the story of how the provincial newspaper industry in the United Kingdom and Ireland has evolved over the years – from scores of individual enterprises to concentration into a cluster of larger and more powerful groups with real financial clout and a profound influence on communities the length and breadth of the British Isles.

The company statistics tell that same story in a clinical, matter of fact way that only numbers can, for by their very nature they are devoid of feeling and emotion. But they are a reflection of the considerable effort, dedication and pride of those who helped to create them – in Johnston Press's case more than 9,000 employees – and, as we shall see, people, committed people, are at the very heart of producing successful newspapers.

The Johnston Press story is one of years of almost continuous progress and expansion through organic growth and acquisitions. In turn this has been reflected in the increasing profitability of the company to a level that would not have seemed possible only a decade ago.

The six financial years 2000 to 2005 epitomised this trend: group turnover up from £292.2 million to £520.2 million, operating profit on ordinary activities up from £84.3 million to £180.3 million, operating profit margin up from 28.8 per cent to 34.7 per cent, underlying earnings per share up from 20.97p to 38.62p.

By 2006 the group was publishing and distributing around 535 million newspapers each year with an average weekly readership of more than 22 million people – local people loyal to small circulation papers such as the Hebden Bridge Times, in West Yorkshire, with a weekly sale of 3,600; local people who turn to a big circulation evening title like The News, Portsmouth, with about 60,000 daily sales; local people who receive a copy of the 100,800 free distribution newspaper the Milton Keynes Citizen.

The extent of the group's penetration into the British domestic market was confirmed by The Newspaper Society, when in 2001 it ranked Johnston Press fourth out of 96 regional publishers, and that position was consolidated with the biggest acquisition in the group's history, the £560 million purchase of Regional Independent Media in 2002. But by 2006 Johnston Press had moved up to second place following a series of deals during 2005 – a record year for new acquisitions. Mid-year the Celtic publishing group, Score Press, was added to the portfolio, giving the company a presence in Northern Ireland and the Irish Republic for the first time.

As the year drew to a close a further 18 titles in Northern Ireland and Eire joined the group. The addition of the newspaper publishing interests of the Leinster Leader, based in Naas in the Republic, and the Local Press Group, centered on Belfast but with cross-border interests, meant that Johnston had become the largest regional newspaper business on the Emerald Isle. Finally, in 2005 the Johnston directors delivered a gift-wrapped Christmas present to shareholders – the prestigious Scottish morning newspaper, The Scotsman, along with the Edinburgh Evening News, Scotland on Sunday and Herald and Post free newspaper series.

In early 2006 when the Newspaper Society issued a new league table it looked like this:

Group	Titles	Weekly circ.
Trinity Mirror	230	14,356,106
Johnston Press	283	10,195,565
Newsquest	216	10,156,153
Northcliffe	113	8,738,425

Johnston Press has grown into a vibrant, robust, forward-looking company with what was once described as "a single-minded focus." The fact that it has achieved so much is all the more remarkable given the way in which the public perception of the media, and the printed word in particular, has changed over recent years. As if increased competition and a slow but remorseless decline in evening newspaper circulations were not enough, Johnston Press has seen its high editorial standards under scrutiny as a result of the seemingly falling standards displayed by some sectors of the national press. Sadly, many readers fail to make the distinction between the two.

Moving with the times and keeping pace with the latest technical innovations have been key factors that have enabled the company to remain competitive, efficient and profitable. In recent times advances in computer technology have allowed Johnston Press to develop an integrated communications and IT structure and take full advantage of the greatest phenomenon of the age – the internet.

Business is no longer restricted to the printed word. Online publishing through a network of local websites is delivering news, information and advertising to a new and diverse audience. Rather than regard the internet as a threat, the company skillfully avoided the excesses of the dotcom boom and bust and took a postitive decision to complement is traditional newspaper publishing activities with locally focused digital media development. Now that is set to become a major part of the group's commercial activities.

What the founding fathers of Johnston Press would have made of this is anyone's guess. But one thing is for sure, the belief that Life is Local has never changed, no matter how that message is delivered.

Edward Riley,
March 2006

Chapter One

Sowing the seeds

Johnston Press has come a long way from its formative years, so far in fact that it would be unrecognisable to those who planted the first seeds in 18th century Scotland. Little did they realise how those seeds would take root and flourish.

Growth just for the sake of it, as former chairman Freddy Johnston was at pains to insist, was never the sole reason for being in business. There were periods when economic conditions in Scotland meant that little development took place and acquisitions have always been structured and thoroughly considered, but good fortune played a part on occasions.

"We've never been in the business of collecting newspapers," stated Johnston, although under his leadership the group enjoyed probably the most vigorous period of expansion and acquisition in its history.

So what would Patrick Mair have made of all this?

It is to him that the very existence of the company is generally credited. It was his ambition to be a successful printer that prompted him to start out in business and so, indirectly, give birth to Britain's longest surviving newspaper dynasty.

In the Johnston family the name of Mair has never been forgotten and from time to time has been included as an additional Christian name for male children, Freddy Johnston among them.

Mair's roots were in West Lothian, where his forbears were among the smaller lairds who for generations had farmed their own patrimonial lands. But although he was expected to inherit the family holdings his father decided that instead he should learn a trade, and for seven years he was apprenticed to a printer in Glasgow.

Qualified and raring to succeed, Patrick set up his own printing business in Glasgow in 1764 – "in the second close above Bell's Wynd" – and found a popular line reprinting ministers' sermons.

Three years later he moved to Falkirk and continued in the printing trade for a further 30 years until his retirement, specialising in religious titles.

And it was then that he handed over his business to his son-in-law Thomas Johnston, who was descended from old-established

Thomas Johnston, whose move into the printing trade laid the foundations for Johnston Press

For the very first time the printed word, once the privilege of the intellectual and the gentry, was being made available to the uneducated, working classes

Linlithgowshire stock, the family having farmed lands at Ballencrief, near Bathgate, for many years. His marriage to Mair's daughter, Margaret, in 1785 linked these two old Scottish families.

Thomas Johnston made the momentous decision not to follow in the family farming tradition and instead joined Patrick Mair to learn the printing trade. As subsequent events were to prove, this was a significant step. So, too, was the way in which he set about developing the business.

Like his father-in-law, Johnston was deeply religious and enthusiastically continued the publication of works of divinity, for which there was a strong demand in Scotland at the time. But he also branched out into lighter literature – cheaply produced, so-called "chap books" that were distributed even into the most remote areas by packmen and pedlars, where they were eagerly bought by the local populace.

The chap books were infinite in their variety, from romances, sermons and ballads to the lives of heroes, history and exciting tales of travel and adventure. For the very first time the printed word, once the privilege of the intellectual and the gentry, was being made available to the uneducated, working classes on a scale never seen before.

The very titles of the books had an air of excitement about them that had readers queuing up for more – "The Life and Exploits of Rob Roy Macgregor", "The Surprising Life and Sufferings of Peter Williamson, who was carried off from Aberdeen in his infancy and sold as a slave in North America", and "The History and Adventures of that famous Negro robber, Three-fingered Jack, the Terror of Jamaica."

It was, it would seem, a logical next step to exploit this new-found thirst for knowledge by expanding into newspapers, but that important decision was left to the next generation of the Johnston family.

After Thomas Johnston's death in 1831 the running of the printing business was taken over by his youngest son, Archibald, who was only 21 at the time. Fourteen years later – by then an experienced printer and well respected in the community – he summoned up enough courage to take over the Falkirk Herald, which had first appeared on August 14, 1845.

Legend has it that that was in settlement of an outstanding debt for printing work undertaken for the paper's owners at the time.

In those days the paper was known as the Falkirk Herald and

Stirlingshire Monthly Advertiser and it was to have several other name changes over the years – Falkirk Herald and General Advertiser, Falkirk Herald and Linlithgow Journal, Falkirk Herald and Scottish Midlands Journal . . .

The paper had been founded by local lawyer Alexander Hedderwick – later to meet an untimely end in a railway accident – backed by other local businessmen, and printed in Glasgow. It came about as a result of growing dissatisfaction at the inefficient and wasteful way in which the town was being run and an upsurge of public opinion in favour of reform.

But it was to be another 14 years, and after a fiercely fought Parliamentary Bill, that the Herald's constant prompting produced results and local government was at last placed on a sound footing.

After a long and painful adolescence the new burgh was set fair for a period of prolonged prosperity and the Herald had been the catalyst.

Archibald Johnston, who found solace from the pressures of business by cultivating flowers and entering them in horticultural society shows, was also looking to the future.

Within a year he moved the Herald from Glasgow to its natural home in Falkirk and the paper was printed there for the first time on August 13, 1846. It has been produced in the town ever since – the very epitome of what a local newspaper is all about.

Years later his great grandson, Freddy Johnston, was to applaud that decision. When the paper celebrated its 150th anniversary he wrote: "Falkirk is the ideal place for local newspaper publication.

"It is at the very nerve centre of the country and, despite many changes in recent years, the local economy has remained diverse and dynamic.

"The company . . . is still deeply rooted in its Falkirk origins. The Falkirk Herald and the Falkirk community remain inextricable."

As a small, monthly sheet sold for twopence a copy the infant Herald found instant appeal among the people of the burgeoning town. Six years on, having already gone weekly, Archibald Johnston increased the size to broadsheet and raised the cover price to fourpence halfpenny.

But oppressive taxation – the so-called tax on knowledge – was a severe restraint to progress, a barrier that even the enterprising Johnston could not overcome.

Total sales, for example, in the first three years of the 1850s amounted to 106,000 copies – roughly what the paper sells now in

The Falkirk Herald is the very epitome of what a local newspaper is all about

11

only three weeks.

Relief came in 1853 when the advertisement duty, a particularly irksome imposition, was abolished. This was welcome news, not only for the company but also for local businesses anxious to put their message across to a wider audience.

Such was the demand for advertising that news had already been removed from the front page and it was not until 1968 – 123 years into the newspaper's life – that it was restored there. Colour appeared in the paper for the first time in 1969.

Two years after the abolition of advertisement duty the stamp duty on newspapers, levied at the rate of a penny on every copy printed, was also removed and the cover price of the Herald was reduced to three pence.

Now at last Archibald Johnston could begin to look ahead with confidence and he wasted little time in planning his next move. In November, 1857, the Falkirk Herald became bi-weekly, a Saturday edition priced at just one penny, joining the established Thursday edition.

Next the Thursday paper, which was especially popular with the professional, landed, agricultural and business fraternity, was enlarged to eight pages.

Sales increased significantly and were given an additional boost in 1861 when the tax on paper – the last of the obnoxious burdens on the dissemination of information – was removed and the cover price was further reduced to two pence.

But in due course the weekend edition prevailed while the circulation of the midweek paper declined to a few thousand. The final issue was printed in the early 1960s, but not without incident. As copies were being parcelled up for newsagents it was noticed that the back page imprint – a section including the publisher's name and address – was missing. All the papers were recalled and a new print run ordered.

Under Archibald Johnston's determined leadership the Falkirk Herald had exceeded his wildest expectations, but inevitably questions were asked about its future viability when he died in 1877 at the family home, Woodville.

Doubts about the suitability of his successor were all too quickly justified.

Command was passed to his fourth son, James – a bachelor with a reputation as a rake who was more interested in the pleasures of life than running a newspaper.

Archibald Johnston, Thomas' youngest son, took over the running of the Falkirk Herald

Inevitably the business began to suffer and there is little doubt that under James's profligate lifestyle the Johnston company was heading for financial ruin.

After only five years he was persuaded to hand over control to his youngest brother Frederick (always known as Fred), who not only pulled the firm back from the brink but was to remain directing principal of the family business for an amazing 53 years until his death in 1936. For much of that time he combined the roles of general manager and editor and became a prominent public figure in Falkirk and the wider Stirlingshire area.

James, meanwhile, sought a new life in the Colonies and settled for a time in New Zealand, where he continued his rakish behaviour. Letters from ministers of religion and other worthies to his brother Fred talk of James's "outrageous lifestyle." He was in his nineties when he died – a disfigured face, as a result of a fight, a reminder of his earlier profligacy.

Another bachelor brother, Tom, was of similar disposition and showed no interest in the family business. Instead he also took himself abroad and it was while in Canada in 1884-85 that he became involved in the last Native North American rebellion known as the Red River Rising. Exactly what happened to him there is not

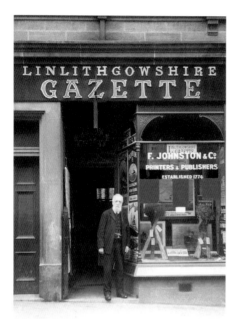

Offices of the
Linlithgowshire
Gazette and the
Falkirk Herald

recorded, but when he returned to Scotland the experience had affected him so profoundly that he never settled down to a steady job for the rest of his long life.

One of Frederick's strategic decisions, in 1883, was to switch publication of the Herald to Wednesdays, not only to nicely split the week but also an inevitable consequence of changing trading conditions in the area.

The ancient Falkirk grain market, held on Thursdays for as long as anyone could remember, was in decline and soon destined to close. The crowds of people from the surrounding districts who once flocked to the market no longer did so – evidence of the end of Falkirk as an essentially agricultural community and a symptom of the emergence of the new Falkirk as a manufacturing centre, especially of light iron castings.

Falkirk was about to move in a new direction and, as you would expect from a socially aware newspaper, the Herald also moved with the times.

It is not just for his longevity in office that "Uncle" Fred Johnston is remembered. He was famous for his appeals – he launched a fundraising appeal for Belgian refugees during the First World War that raised £3,000 and earned a thank-you from the King of Belgium. When disaster struck Redding mine in 1923 he called on readers of the Herald to rally to the cause. That appeal raised a staggering £63,000, equivalent to several million pounds today.

A great raconteur and Burns fan, there was one story he loved to repeat – of the night he and the Sheriff had attended a Burns supper in Stirling. Slightly worse for drink, and desperate to obey the call of nature, the pair pulled off the road on the way back home and in relieving themselves doused one of the car's oil lamps.

They were later stopped by the police and Fred was charged with failing to properly illuminate a motor vehicle.

Fred duly appeared before the court where he was warned: "This is a most serious offence which must be stamped out. There's been altogether too much of this lately. Fined £2."

When the pair next met up in the nearby Royal Hotel they proceeded to bemoan the state of justice in the nation.

Johnston embraced new technology that kept his paper at the cutting edge at the time, and no sooner had he taken over the running of the business than new founts of type and machinery were purchased and print works equipment re-conditioned.

Such was the increase in circulation that the old flatbed press – slow, laborious and prone to annoying breakdowns – was unable to cope. Johnston invested heavily in the company's first stereo rotary press in 1898. Print capacity increased from 1,500 to 8,000 copies per hour – and that must have seemed like a phenomenal achievement at the time. A mere 14 years later an even faster rotary press was purchased.

For all of its life in Falkirk the Herald had operated out of small premises erected in 1805 but these, too, were proving inadequate. Frederick Johnston bought a prime town centre plot of land and in 1908 opened the new Herald Office in High Street. Today the building, with its distinctive arched frontage, is occupied by W.H. Smith but a small, carved shield with the entwined, carved letters "F.J. and Co" is a reminder of its original use.

As the newspaper's influence grew so did the need for branch offices in the wider area it served. The first branch office was opened in 1883 – such an interesting year – in Linlithglow, followed by offices in Bo'ness in 1884, Denny in 1897, Grangemouth in 1900 and Bathgate in 1903.

Such was the Herald's success in Linlithgow, famous as the birthplace of Mary Queen of Scots, that it soon became obvious that this pretty, largely rural town six miles east of Falkirk, deserved its own paper. On April 11, 1891, the first edition of the Linlithgowshire Gazette appeared. It has been in continuous publication ever since and now sells a little over 8,000 copies a week.

By the time of Fred's death in 1936 the weekly sale of the weekend Herald had gone up from 7,000 to 15,000. He was so greatly loved and respected in the Falkirk community that large crowds turned out for his funeral and to mourn as the crystal-windowed hearse, drawn by a team of great black Belgian horses with waving white plumes brought in from Edinburgh, passed by.

Standing on the pavement among the crowds was Tom Mackie, proprietor of the rival Falkirk Mail, a bit of a dandy in a shabby, faded sort of way but always with a ready wit.

As the funeral procession drew to a close a coal cart pulled in directly behind. "Aye," said Mackie. "There goes old Fred, aye prepared!"

In his time at the helm Johnston had also overseen the incorporation of the business as F. Johnston and Company Ltd in 1928 – an event of considerable significance which formalised it on a new legal and financial footing. Until then the company had been run as a private business without limited liability and with Johnston as controlling shareholder and operating principal.

Incorporation and the restrictions associated with this influenced the nature of the company for the next 60 years, when it was floated on the London Stock Exchange. Although a simple transfer of shares between family members, their spouses and descendants was permitted the sale of shares to anyone outside the family required board approval, but as a matter of principle they always refused to sanction this. For example, when a family shareholder, Miss Eva Burns, bequeathed Johnston shares to someone who was not a relation the directors blocked the registration, so rigorous was their policy.

Another effect of the rules was that even when shares were sold or transferred within the tight-knit family group this did not reflect their true market value – indeed, it was the company auditor who usually decided what the sale price should be. If the take-up of the shares was oversubscribed they were then allocated on a pro rata basis.

With no children of his own to carry on the family firm, Fred Johnston's nephew, Frederick Mair Johnston, took over as chairman and managing director, and in due course we shall see how he expanded the company's influence in other parts of Scotland.

His legacy of 72 per cent of the company had been agreed shortly after his birth in 1903 when the childless Fred Johnston travelled to Leith to visit his sister-in-law Grace, the infant's mother. "If you call him Fred I will make him my heir," promised the child's uncle. And so the line of succession was assured.

After a brief spell as a reporter at Falkirk, nephew Frederick had moved on to Dumfries and then to Evesham, where he was managing editor of one of the Worcestershire town's weekly papers, The Evesham Journal. His next move, in 1929, was to Edinburgh, where he became a reporter on The Scotsman, and then in 1934 he joined his uncle in Falkirk.

Those who worked with "Young Fred" remember him as a quiet and unassuming man, keen to uphold traditional values and not prone to making change simply for change's sake. But he had a fun-loving side to his character, too, and the annual staff parties were the occasions when the chairman threw off his inhibitions. Most of his time was spent mingling with the younger employees and demonstrating what he thought were his considerable dancing skills to any office girl or typist he invited to join him for a quickstep or a rousing Gay Gordons.

Never one to blow his own trumpet, Johnston was unenthusiastic to celebrate the Herald's centenary and there was considerable debate whether that should be in 1945 or 1946. Other factors were the dire shortage of newsprint and the absence of staff to carry out

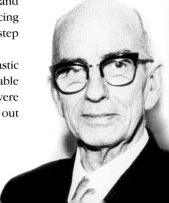

the necessary research.

In the end far more significant world events proved to be the deciding factor. Just three days before the Herald's centenary issue was due to hit the streets in August, 1945, Japan surrendered to the Allies and thus brought an end to the Second World War.

Needless to say, that week's paper was almost exclusively devoted to the news. Acknowledgement that the Herald had reached such an important milestone had to be confined to a single column of editorial and a few pictures of old Falkirk.

The following August the paper recorded its acquisition by Archibald Johnston exactly 100 years before. As a special treat the staff went on a trip to Balloch, on what was known as a Wayse Goose, or a printers' day out.

It was also a special day for Fred Johnston's secretary, Iris Brown, the daughter of Linlithgow Gazette editor Arthur Brown. During the outing her boyfriend Tom McGowran, a reporter on the Herald, proposed to her and the couple were married in December. McGowran went on to become managing editor and managing director of the company and played a key role in its subsequent development.

Johnston was in no mood to celebrate in 1967 when the 200th anniversary of Patrick Mair's move from Glasgow to Falkirk was reached. A suggestion that a commemorative booklet should be published met with an unenthusiastic response: "Forget it – let's just concentrate on the next 200."

Frederick Johnston was a well-respected figure in the newspaper world and it came as no surprise when he was invited to become a founder member of the Press Council – the predecessor of the present day Press Complaints Commission – and to adjudicate on moral and ethical issues and complaints against newspapers.

That was almost to provide him with one of his most embarrassing moments when the Falkirk Herald itself was reported to the Press Council in 1969 following the newspaper's leaked story of plans to merge Falkirk and Grangemouth to form an enlarged burgh.

Johnston promptly declared an interest and concentrated his energies on helping editor Neil Burnett and chief reporter Ken Waddell defend the complaint, which they did successfully. On one occasion Waddell recalls leaving Johnston's house at three o'clock in the morning after a particularly late review of the case.

Years later Waddell, by then editor, faced the Press Council for a

Frederick Johnston was a well-respected figure in the newspaper world and was invited to become a founder member of the Press Council

second time when the Herald was accused by a Roman Catholic high school of being biased against Roman Catholics – a spurious allegation, but nevertheless one that had to be defended.

Under Frederick Johnston's direction the company experienced unprecedented growth – from just two titles to 24 Scottish weeklies – which is explored in detail in the next chapter.

Following his death in 1973 he was succeeded as managing director by his eldest son, Frederick Patrick Mair Johnston – known to everyone as Freddy – who also became chairman. And so the family dynasty was handed down to yet another generation and remained so until flotation in 1988.

Freddy, who had been working as company secretary, was fortunate in having a ready made right hand man – his father's general manager Tom McGowran, who by then had been plucked from the editorial floor and trained in management. Together they were to work tirelessly to develop Johnston Press.

The Falkirk Herald remains a key title in the much-enlarged Johnston portfolio and Falkirk itself was the divisional centre for the company's entire Scottish operation until 2006. Before the addition of titles from Score Press in 2005 the division had an annual turnover of £28.5 million from its 33 mainland newspapers. Twelve titles are published directly by Johnston (Falkirk).

As for the Herald, with a sale of around 32,000 copies it is not only the company's flagship weekly in Scotland, as it has always been, but also that country's largest selling weekly newspaper.

Fate almost decreed that it became an evening newspaper, for in 1969 Roy Thomson – Lord Thomson of Fleet, one of the biggest newspaper tycoons of the time – was rumoured to be interested in launching a new evening newspaper to serve the greater Falkirk area. He had already done so in England – with mixed success – in Reading and Hemel Hempstead.

It was a challenge the Herald could not afford to ignore. It rose to the occasion by installing a new, high-speed Goss Suburban web-offset press at its High Street offices so that it could, if necessary, produce its own evening paper at very short notice. The word was put around that if Thomson moved in Johnston's would be there first to greet them and beat them!

The threat never materialised, and in due course the climate for launching new evening titles changed, largely due to the salutary lessons learned from the Thomson ventures.

Around the same time publication day, which had changed

> The Falkirk Herald remains a key title in the much-enlarged Johnston portfolio

several times over the years, was switched from Saturday to Friday, but this was more a reflection of changing social habits and a changing market place than the Thomson threat. Gone were the days when the men poured out of the local ironworks on Saturday lunchtimes and went on to watch their local football team in action. Weekends of leisure were to become the norm and weekly newspaper purchase was not always a significant part of this.

A decade later the Herald registered its record circulation in less than auspicious circumstances. In 1979 the editorial staff of the paper responded to a national strike call for improved pay and conditions by the National Union of Journalists and for seven weeks editor Ken Waddell was left to bring out the paper alone.

"Unbelievably the paper achieved its highest sales of 40,000 during that period," recalls Waddell. "Public sympathy was with the paper and the sales soared."

Johnstons rewarded those who had worked on during the strike – advertising and newspaper sales staff, accounts people – with a slap up dinner at a local nightclub, hosted by managing director Harry Johnston.

Alcohol consumption was modest and restrained with small whiskies and halves of bitter keeping the bar bill well within budget. But when Johnston announced he was going home with two hours of the knees-up remaining he left Waddell to sign the tab – and must have been horrified at the result.

"Suddenly the drinks changed to exotic cocktails and doubles.

Princess Anne visiting the Falkirk Herald. She was presented with a bale of the newly-designed Falkirk tartan by then-editor Ken Waddell (right)

Modesty went out of the window and the cost rocketed in those last two hours," remembers Waddell.

That NUJ dispute served as a timely reminder of the newspaper's close bond with the community. "It's always been well respected," says Waddell proudly, looking back on his 21 years in the editor's chair.

The public rallied behind Waddell and the Herald again when the town's left-wing Provost proposed that historic Callender House should be knocked down. The stately home was famous for its Mary Queen of Scots connections and in Victorian days had been owned by the local laird, who was deeply unpopular in radical circles.

"The Provost said it was a relic of the master and servant days when the peasants touched the forelock to the lord of the manor. We fought him all the way – and won.

"Now it's firmly established on Scotland's tourist trail – they come from all over to see the restored house."

The Herald offices, in High Street, which by then had become unsuitable, were sold in 1982 and editorial, sales and administration departments transferred to new premises at Newmarket Street, over the Royal Bank of Scotland, while a new print centre was opened at Middlefield. While this was taking place the Herald was printed in Kirkcaldy.

However, the Middlefield move proved to be a short-lived operation, largely due to the increases in paginations and the press's limited capabilities to meet this demand. In 1991 printing was transferred to even larger premises at Camelon, on the outskirts of Falkirk, to linked factory units built by Johnston's bookbinding and library bookselling subsidiary Riley, Dunn and Wilson (which has since been sold although the two companies continue to share the premises.) Additional units were installed on the press.

There the Goss Community web offset press prints many of the group's Scottish titles and a number of other publications on contract – close on half a million newspapers every week.

Falkirk is a much-changed community these days.

A rare painting from the 1820s shows a rural, one-street town nestling in the shadow of the Ochil Hills. In the distance a plume of smoke is rising from the works of the Carron company, the iron foundry which was to become central to the future prosperity of the area.

From a population of 8,000 in 1841 Falkirk doubled in size to

16,000 inhabitants by 1891 and doubled again within another ten years. Now the town is at the centre of a population of more than 145,000.

Services, the public sector, hotels and catering, and retailing account for more than 11,000 jobs with only around 9,000 people employed in manufacturing industry – a statistic that poignantly reflects the story that has unfolded through the columns of the Falkirk Herald during the last 160 years.

The Carron ironworks – where the guns for Nelson's navy were cast – became the biggest in the world and another thirty or so foundries ensured Falkirk's place as the country's principal centre for light castings and domestic ironware. Now all are gone.

For a time British Aluminium filled the vacuum and at nearby Grangemouth the petro-chemical industry led by BP has provided a major source of employment. High-tech companies have moved on to business parks where the old ironworks once stood and others have been turned over to new housing.

"The town has a largely dormitory population supplying labour to Grangemouth. This is a place to shop, to eat, to socialise, to come for entertainment. It's not so much a place to come and work in any more," says local historian Ian Scott, who has charted the rise and fall of the old Falkirk and the rebirth of the new.

The decline of manufacturing industry and the renewal of communities during the second half of the 20th century is an experience shared by many Johnston Press publishing centres. (For Falkirk, read Sheffield, or Halifax, or Wakefield, or Sunderland, or Northampton...)

But in another way Falkirk is unique, as the birthplace of Johnston Press and the home of the one newspaper above all others that has come to typify the company philosophy that Life is Local.

It was Falkirk, too, that provided the springboard for growth within Scotland and far beyond the borders into England – moves that began in the Swinging Sixties. As the nation's attention was focused on flower power and The Beatles the company that until then had been content to publish its two old-established titles decided that the time had come to expand.

Chapter Two

Expansion in Scotland

By the early Sixties the climate was right for change. In Scotland the long-established order of independent, small-town publishers was about to be broken. New technology on the horizon would revolutionise the way newspapers were produced. And at F. Johnston and Co a new team was in place that would oversee the company's growth from just two titles to more than a dozen in the space of a few years.

The weekly newspaper scene after the war had resembled a landscape of medieval fiefdoms – minor press barons, each with their ruling family and each existing in relative harmony within their own well-defined boundaries. In the main they were content to return modest profits and showed no territorial ambitions over their neighbours.

But to the west there was a slumbering giant, the Glasgow Herald, and it was about to wake up. In a series of expansionist moves the Herald's owners, George Outram and Company, had bought the newspaper interests in Kilmarnock, Ayr, Perth, Dumfries and Hamilton. Soon Airdrie and Bathgate were added to the portfolio.

In Falkirk the Johnston management watched the developments with growing concern and unease. Chairman Frederick Johnston, cautious but shrewd, did not see himself in the role of empire builder but as a steward whose duty was to hand on to his sons a sound and prosperous family business.

Yet under the pressure of external events it became obvious that the company must either expand or be swallowed up itself.

However, it was not until the arrival in Falkirk in 1962 of his eldest son Freddy that the idea of growth began to be taken seriously. The human chemistry was also right – the ageing Johnston Snr a steadying influence at the helm, with the young and ambitious Freddy and general manager Tom McGowran, snapping at his heels and urging a more entrepreneurial policy.

"We hit it off immediately," says Freddy of McGowran. "He was a wonderful man."

Freddy Johnston might have been born with newspaper ink in his blood, but it was never taken for granted that he would eventually succeed his father as principal of the family firm – indeed, his ambition had always been to work on a national newspaper.

His upbringing and education followed a well-established pattern for the son of an aspiring businessman – Morrison's Academy, Crieff; Lancing College, Sussex; and New College, Oxford, where he gained an MA degree in modern history.

National Service for two years, 1954-56, saw him commissioned in the Royal Scots Fusiliers as a 2nd lieutenant and an attachment to the 4th King's African Rifles in East Africa – a period abroad that fuelled a lifelong interest in Commonwealth affairs.

Now it was time to find a job and Freddy opted for journalism, as an editorial trainee with the Liverpool Post and Echo. It was a tough, hard-edged stamping ground but an ideal place in which to learn the reporter's skills.

After an initial training period at the Echo he was transferred to the city's morning paper, the Liverpool Post, and joined the features sub-editing team. He must have impressed, for when the regular leader writer was taken ill he was asked to stand in and did so with considerable enthusiasm and ability.

Starting work at four in the afternoon, Freddy read the national and regional papers during the day and on the bus journey to the office, and by the time he arrived was well prepared to comment on major events.

In 1960 one particular story grabbed his attention. Prime Minister Harold Macmillan had made his famous "Wind of Change" speech to the South African parliament in Cape Town in which he spoke out against the country's apartheid system and of the mood for independence among black people that was growing in Commonwealth countries on the continent.

"I thought this was very important and wrote my main leader about this. In my view Macmillan had made a splendid speech, especially as a Conservative Prime Minister. The choice was mine – the editor at the time was always harassed and his first priority was not what went into the leader column but to see his paper come out on time."

But the Post's managing director Alick Jeans, later Sir Alick, had other ideas about the content of the comment column and rang Freddy as the paper's print run of the Welsh edition, its largest, was well under way. The leader, he said, was quite well written but injudicious – and the speech, too, was injudicious as it would probably inflame the natives.

"Take it out and writer another leader for the Merseyside edition," instructed Jeans. "There's a lot of congestion in the Mersey Tunnel caused by current roadworks – I would like us to comment editorially about that."

Freddy complied, reluctantly. "I immediately thought that if I am not allowed to write leaders about events that would change the course of world history I had better try and get into newspaper management."

Shortly afterwards he did just that, as assistant secretary of The Times Publishing Company, a two-year experience that indirectly was to shape the rest of his newspaper career.

Life in London was good for the now married Johnston – the excitement of Fleet Street, a rented flat in Raynes Park and a teaching post in Streatham for Freddy's new wife Ann. But they found it harder to manage after the birth of their first son, Michael, and reliance on only one income from The Times – "at that time bigger on prestige than remuneration."

Once Freddy's father became aware of their predicament he offered help – a return to Scotland and a job as company secretary. And for good measure there was a company house, a small property previously occupied by the recently deceased retired works manager, which would be redecorated and fitted with a new kitchen, and a company car, a Vauxhall Victor.

It was too tempting an offer to refuse, even if it did mean a drop in annual salary from £1,500 to £1,260. But the assessed rental for the house – the outdated Scottish way of calculating rent at the time – of £54 a year compared with a weekly rent of £6 in London more than compensated for this.

"I didn't particularly relish the thought of going to Scotland," recalled Freddy. "After working in London on a prestigious newspaper Falkirk didn't seem all that appealing.

"I considered myself at that stage to be starved into it."

The other Johnston brothers, meanwhile, were carving out their own careers in the newspaper industry. Jim spent most of his working life as a journalist on The Scotsman and never took an active role in the management of the family firm, although he was a substantial shareholder. For a number of years before the flotation of Johnston Press in 1988 he was a non-executive director, resigning when the board was restructured.

Harry Johnston's first job in newspapers was in the work study department of Westminster Press. He joined his father in Falkirk in

> I thought that if I am not allowed to write leaders about events that would change the course of world history I had better try and get into newspaper management

Freddy Johnston

the early Seventies and after a spell in management moved over to a non-executive role. He remained a member of the Johnston board after flotation with the largest individual shareholding in the company.

TOM McGOWRAN was a very different character from the tall and academic Freddy Johnston. A small, tough, wiry individual bursting with pent up energy he was affectionately known as "The Wee Man" on account of his size.

But what he lacked in stature – all 5ft 3in of him – McGowran more than made up for in personality and charisma.

His influence on the development of the Johnston business was considerable, especially the way in which he embraced new technology and harnessed its potential at the company's sites. He could lay claim to be one of the first men to install a web-offset press in Scotland, at Ardrossan, and for years visited the United States to study at first hand equipment that would eventually become available in Britain.

McGowran came into newspapers in the mid-1930s as a journalist, by the time-honoured route as a copy boy on The Scotsman, in Edinburgh. Delivering messages and typewritten scripts for senior writers and sub editors provided a valuable insight into the workings of a newsroom and eventually McGowran was offered the chance to train as a junior reporter.

And that in turn led to a move to the Falkirk Herald in 1939, where he was eventually given the job of covering the nearby town of Grangemouth. Fred Johnston Snr quickly recognised his ability – as he so often did with promising young people – not only as the best reporter on his staff but also as someone with management potential.

But his career was put on hold with the outbreak of war, and the years that followed were to impact on the rest of McGowran's life. He was serving with the Royal Army Ordnance Corps in Singapore when it was overrun by the Japanese in 1942.

He was among the lucky ones – he survived. But internment in the infamous Changi Gaol, followed by torture, malnutrition and unspeakable horrors on the Thai-Burma Railway, left him a six and a half-stone skeleton when he returned home to Scotland in 1946. By then The Scotsman had already published his obituary – "He was always smiling," it said – after no news had been heard of him for years and he was presumed dead.

But it was typical of the impatient, dynamic McGowran that within weeks, and against medical advice, he was back at work and keen to get on with life.

Despite the inhumane treatment he had received he remained remarkably tolerant of the Japanese. Years later when he and Freddy Johnston were at a printing exhibition in Dusseldorf he noticed a group of Japanese visitors, who were obviously lost, and offered to help.

How, they asked, did he come to speak their language so fluently, and where did he learn it? "Oh, I just sort of picked it up," was the nonchalant reply.

A whirlwind romance with Iris Brown, daughter of Arthur W. Brown, editor of the Linlithgow Gazette, saw the pair married before the end of 1946 and living in a flat above the Grangemouth office.

Then came the chance to move back to Falkirk as manager – but with strings attached. Fred Johnston Snr insisted that they find a home within two minutes of the office. This was a condition clearly designed to compensate for his own nocturnal lifestyle which regularly saw him arriving for work at three o'clock in the afternoon and staying behind his desk until the small hours of the following day.

Such unorthodox timekeeping on a weekly paper was a throwback to his days at The Scotsman when a regular late evening shift proved to be a habit-forming experience. Guests invited to lunch at the Johnston home became used to finding Fred still eating his breakfast when they arrived, with lunch delayed well into the afternoon.

On one occasion McGowran was called back from a family caravanning holiday in France when Fred Johnston was injured after falling through a hole in the office floor during the night. The accident happened while he was inspecting construction work under way at Falkirk.

Although a press crew was on duty his cries for help went unheard, and it was not until a blood-soaked Johnston staggered from the darkness that his predicament became apparent.

Freddy Johnston might have been the boss's son, but he still had a lot to learn when he joined the firm at Falkirk in 1962, and McGowran quickly educated him in the ways of business.

"He was an expansionist," recalls Johnston. "As soon as I arrived he told me that business was like riding a bicycle – if you don't keep pedalling you fall off. I have always firmly believed that myself, but it was Tom who first put the idea into my head."

It was McGowran, too, who favoured the straightforward, head-on approach to running a company and the Kirkintilloch Herald purchase, which was to come later, was typical of this.

"When a business became available we just went for it without a great deal of agonising," reflected Johnston. "Tom was not overwhelmed with life's complexities – he was always able to see direct to the heart of a problem. He came to some great conclusions just by making quick calculations on the back of an envelope."

McGowran retired in 1980 and the following year received the O.B.E. from the Queen for his services to newspapers – and never has an honour been more richly deserved. By then Johnstons were a force in Scotland and firmly established in England and he had been involved in all the major decisions during this period of expansion. He died in 2001 at the age of 82.

BY THE time the Johnston-Johnston-McGowran team was established in 1962 the company had already expanded from its two-paper base a year earlier by buying the Grangemouth Advertiser, which had been established in 1900 to serve the industrial town a few miles from Falkirk.

It was owned by a local doctor, who had seen the newspaper as an investment opportunity, but who was now struggling to keep it afloat. For the Falkirk Herald to mop up this minor competitor was a simple operation – by then the Herald was already selling more copies in Grangemouth than the Advertiser.

In the years that followed sales of the Advertiser – affectionately known as "The 'Tiser" – continued to decline and in 1976 it was converted into the company's first free distribution newspaper, with separate editions for Falkirk and Grangemouth. This also had the effect of strengthening the Johnston market place by improving the service the company could offer. Distribution of the combined editions is now 56,500 weekly.

Shortly before the arrival on the scene of Freddy Johnston, his father and McGowran had taken the bold step of launching a completely new weekly paper in Cumbernauld, six miles to the west, to serve the new town that had been created to accommodate the overspill population from Glasgow.

There were both defensive and offensive motives behind the decision. Cumbernauld was already within the circulation area of the Falkirk Herald, and Johnstons certainly didn't want a rival company setting up business there.

Rumours were rife that the Airdrie Advertiser was planning to start its own newspaper and it duly did so, a week after the Johnston launch, in the form of the short-lived Cumbernauld Courier. But equally important was the opportunity presented by a new town with a rapidly expanding population.

The proximity of the Falkirk print works, with its production facilities and expertise, meant that supporting the Cumbernauld News was a relatively simple affair and within a year the newspaper became profitable, further justifying its creation. But its launch was anything but simple.

Tom McGowran had been attending the annual conference of the Scottish Newspaper Proprietors' Association when he overheard the managing director from Airdrie, Jack Creighton, boasting about the new newspaper that they were about to start in Cumbernauld.

Within 48 hours he had alerted Fred Johnston Snr to the threat, persuaded the printers to take on an additional publication at such short notice, and put out the first four-page edition of the Cumbernauld News.

The next requirement was an office, and premises were found in the old village of Cumbernauld, on the fringe of where the new town was being developed. The accommodation had an added attraction – they came rent-free on condition that Johnstons agreed to display a religious poster in the window.

Later when a new office girl was being recruited, McGowran was given the task of conducting the interviewing.

"Of course," he told her. "The place is owned by some kind of religious nut."

"Yes, I know. That's my father."

A chastened Tom gave her the job.

The person chosen to spearhead the editorial effort was Peter Holt, a former sub editor on women's magazines with D.C. Thomson, in Dundee, and a reporter with the Falkirk Herald since 1961.

Holt and the more experienced Dick Hayes, from the Denny office, reported on the meetings of the New Town Development Corporation, the County Council and the courts, but human interest stories, stories about real people, were at the core of the efforts to build circulation and develop a loyal readership.

Immediately Holt was taken aback by the intensity of the religious divide among the Glaswegians flooding into the new town. When he ran a front page story and picture about the first Communion service celebrated in Cumbernauld by the Roman Catholic Archbishop of Glasgow he was accused by a Protestant of turning the paper into an edition of the Catholic Herald.

On another occasion, when reporting on a brains trust, the panel was asked how they would react if their son or daughter entered into a mixed marriage. Pen poised, and expecting to hear of the problems faced by interracial couples, Holt was amazed to find that all the talk was about mixing Roman Catholics with Protestants.

Clearly tact and caution were required when ferreting out the human-interest stories.

When Holt left the company in 1964 he had succeeded in striking up a warm and trusting relationship with many of his readers, a bond that was demonstrated by the round of farewell parties in his honour.

"It was their generosity and goodwill that made it possible to create an off-diary, human-interest paper," he recalled later. "The secret was to live and participate in the area's life – the launch reporters from the rival Courier did not live in the town and had no office there until it was too late."

Holt went on to take a doctorate at Stirling University and later became editor in chief of a group of international magazines based in Switzerland.

The Cumbernauld News went from strength to strength and now sells around 13,000 copies in the combined towns of Cumbernauld, Kilsyth and Bonnybridge. It serves a population of 100,000, many of whom work for the high-tech companies based in the area or commute to Glasgow for employment.

Locally the newspaper has the affectionate nickname of the Noddy News – nothing to do with Enid Blyton's children's character but derived from the Scottish pronunciation of the town's name as "Cumernod."

With the threat from the Glasgow Herald still very real and with Freddy Johnston and McGowran urging him to adopt a more expansionist outlook, Fred Johnston Snr agreed that the time had come to look around for potential acquisitions, although he had long since come to the same conclusion himself.

He had already made several earlier forays into the takeover market without success and seemingly without any real structure – the Retford Advertiser, in Nottinghamshire, the Grantham Journal (both subsequently acquired by Johnston Press), and the Ilford Recorder, Essex, and the Walthamstow Guardian were all targets at one time or another.

In about 1952 Fred Johnston reached an agreement to purchase the Walthamstow Guardian but the deal fell through when the company's bank at the time refused to provide top-up facilities. Johnston was furious after being turned down by the pompous manager, who had given him a lecture on the evils of usuary!

But the consensus of opinion among the Johnston directors was that they could not afford to stand still – they must either get on or get out. They were conscious, too, that it is a feature of the newspaper industry that established newspapers, unless they are very bad, are difficult to dislodge. The best way to expand, therefore, was to buy existing titles that offered scope for development.

In the fragmented situation that existed in Scotland at the time that was not always easy and there was a general reluctance to do meaningful business between close neighbours. A Johnston approach for the West Lothian Courier, at Bathgate, was repelled and some years later an overture to the owners of the Stirling Observer met with a similar response.

The company's first acquisition beyond Falkirk occurred under the most bizarre circumstances in 1963 – a combination of good fortune and what almost amounted to a piece of fun by Freddy Johnston and McGowran. It ended with the purchase of the assets of D. MacLeod Ltd, publishers of the Kirkintilloch Herald and the Milngavie and Bearsden Herald.

The intrepid pair found themselves in Riddrie, an eastern suburb of Glasgow, with the intention of persuading the manager of the ABC cinema to advertise regularly in the Cumbernauld News, only to find that he had decided to advertise with their rival publication.

Johnston and McGowran were disconsolate. The business was worth only nine shillings a week but was also editorially very significant, as it would have enabled the paper to publish reviews of films being shown at the cinema. It could have done so in any case, but in those days free publicity was almost unheard of.

The cinema advertisment on a long-term contract was also considered strategically important. Cumbernauld in those days did not have a cinema of its own and film fans travelled the few miles to Riddrie to watch the latest releases. Sadly, it was to be the Airdrie-based opposition that was now able to provide the all-important listings, and with them a potential boost to circulation.

As they sat in their car wondering what to do next McGowran broke the silence with a laugh and a smile. "Let's try and buy the Kirkintiloch Herald!" he exclaimed.

Despite the fact that it was published only 15 miles away from Falkirk the two men knew nothing about the paper, how many copies it sold or even who owned it. Unabashed they found the newspaper's offices and asked to see the manager, Eddie Pollock.

"Would your principals consider selling?" asked McGowran.

"I think they might," came back the reply.

And they did – for £20,000. And with assets of £6,000 in the bank it meant that this tidy piece of business had been concluded at a net cost of only £14,000, a sum that has been repaid handsomely ever since.

The tumbledown premises were repaired and a decrepit press retired, and in the space of a few years the Kirkintilloch centre became a key part of the Scottish operation, more so when the unprofitable Rod and Line fishing magazine, also published from there, was sold for £1.

The deal, like so many others taking place in Scotland around this time, was small and Johnstons comfortably accommodated it without resort to borrowing. Finance was raised from accumulated reserves and an annual profit of around £26,000.

Established in 1883, the Kirkintilloch Herald now has weekly circulation of about 12,000 copies in the towns of Kirkintilloch, Bishopbriggs, Robroyston, Stepps, Lennoxtown, Chryston and Springburn with a combined population of about 80,000.

Its sister paper, the Milngavie and Bearsden Herald, was established in 1901 and had a circulation of only 2,000 at the time it was acquired. It now sells 7,200 copies weekly in the wealthy Milngavie, Bearsden and Strathblane suburbs of Glasgow – a circulation area that boasts more than 100 millionaires among its 39,500 residents.

A few years later the Johnstons tried the upfront approach again when father and son boldly walked into the Dumbarton offices of Bennett and Thomson Ltd., publishers of the Lennox Herald, to make an offer for the business

"Can we speak with Mr Bennett?" asked Fred Johnston Snr., since his name came first in the alphabet. "Bennett's long dead. I'm Thomson," came back the reply. Thomson was in no mood to do business with two singularly uninformed strangers who had walked in off the street and eventually sold out to Outrams.

WITHIN WEEKS of the MacLeod deal at Kirkintilloch another opportunity for expansion arose when the Johnston directors heard on the Scottish newspapers grapevine that the Ardrossan and Saltcoats Herald, published by Arthur Guthrie and Sons in Ayrshire, was for sale. The proprietor, George Guthrie, a descendant of the founder, had died and his family had decided to dispose of his business interests.

McGowran was instructed to make an immediate appointment to see lawyers acting for the family, even though the next day was a Saturday, and he and Fred Johnston Snr drove independently to Ardrossan to open negotiations – both of them receiving a speeding ticket on the way.

Because of the level of interest shown by several prospective buyers it had been decided that the fairest way of concluding a sale was to invite offers in sealed envelopes.

But for how much? Fred Johnston and his team reckoned that the business was worth around £45,000 but for good measure submitted a bid of £45,750. Much to the chagrin of the rival Outrams, who had offered a straight £45,000, their smaller opponents from Falkirk had won the day.

A week later Outrams rang Johnston to offer a considerably enhanced price for the group, which would have fitted in well with their west coast interests, but were quickly rebuffed.

The purchase was significant for Johnstons, but also reflected the changing pattern of newspaper ownership in Scotland. It was one of the first substantial takeovers by a weekly newspaper of another weekly paper outside its own circulation area.

There was an uphill task ahead, however, for it soon became apparent that Guthrie's had been poorly managed and that considerable reorganisation and change would be needed to repay the Johnston investment.

However, when chairman Fred Johnston presented his annual report and accounts for 1963 he was optimistic. "The company's acquisitions in Ayrshire (and at Kirkintilloch) are beginning to respond to the new ownership, but much still remains to be done."

High on the list of priorities was a new press at Ardrossan to replace the antiquated Swiss Duplex machine, which had a top speed of around 3,000 copies per hour and, recalled Freddy Johnston, "looked like the engines of a Clyde paddle steamer."

> Tom McGowran and Fred Johnston Snr drove independently to Ardrossan to open negotiations – both of them receiving a speeding ticket on the way

It had been used to print the Ardorssan titles and other newspapers in the Guthrie portfolio, the Irvine Times and the Troon and Prestwick Times.

Eventually this was pensioned off in 1967 in favour of a Goss Suburban web offset press, at a time when this form of printing was relatively new in Britain. Thanks to the valuable experience this provided a similar press, but with greater capacity, was duly bought and installed at Falkirk.

Subsequently the company used its new press to print other Ayrshire acquisitions – the Ayr Advertiser, Largs and Millport Weekly News and the Cumnock Chronicle, all bought during the Sixties.

Distribution of the original Guthrie titles was as antiquated as the press on which they were printed, the whole operation being conducted by train. Newsagents were expected to go to the nearest railway station to collect their supplies – a method that was doomed once Dr Beeching began wielding his axe over rural services and unprofitable branch lines.

Freddy Johnston was despatched to buy a van and set up a new delivery system, direct to the newsagents' shops. Improved availability was matched by an almost immediate increase in newspaper sales, putting further pressure on the tediously slow Swiss Duplex press.

The entire Ayrshire operation, though profitable, was sold in 1984 for £1,200,000, partly to finance expansion in England but also to concentrate on less problematic areas. "We just felt we could use our energies and our cash better elsewhere," explained Johnston. "It was quite clear our titles were never going to be regional market leaders. We didn't have the principal titles in the main towns, especially Kilmarnock and even Ayr, and we were hemmed in by the sea.

"What's more, it was clear that greater development opportunities lay south of the border in England."

Despite the company's best efforts over 20 years, during which time profits had continued to increase, it had failed to gain dominance in the county over Outram's heavyweight titles, the Kilmarnock Standard and the Ayrshire Post.

On top of that, increasing union militancy, which was a feature of much of that period as the newspaper industry embraced new technology and new working practices, had led to an unacceptable level of unrest among the Ardrossan printers.

This culminated in a bitter strike during the summer of 1981, which engulfed the whole company in Scotland and meant that for six weeks its titles north of the border were suspended. Johnstons stood firm against what it considered to be unreasonable pay demands and the printers eventually returned to work for only 50p more than they had been offered originally.

Group managing director Iain Bell, who by then was looking after all the company's interests from a base in Chesterfield, was given the task of dealing with the most serious industrial relations problem in the company's history. What he found was a situation that had been slowly simmering for a number of years.

As a result of acquisitions since the early Sixties there were widely differing rates of pay at the Johnston centres and numerous deals within deals, concessions that had been granted to individual employees in return for past favours.

The anomalies were seized upon by the Scottish Graphical branch of the Sogat (Society of Graphical and Allied Trades) union, who formed a federated chapel to fight for uniform rates across the company. Their claim for a 42 per cent pay rise left the Johnston management reeling.

It brought the unrelenting Bell into direct conflict with the powerful Sogat leader in Scotland, Alan Watson, a man he dubbed as "King Kong." Yet despite their apparent enmity the two developed an enormous respect for each other and years later Watson was among the guests at Bell's retirement party.

But for now it was open warfare. Protracted negotiations were getting nowhere and the unions were becoming impatient. They targeted the most sensitive part of Johnstons, the Falkirk Herald, and their members walked out, as the weekly edition was about to start its press run.

The company issued an ultimatum: if another paper missed publication they would close all the titles. The trade unions reacted by ordering all the print centres to come out on strike, and the following week the group's presses remained still and silent. Union members were never ballotted to ascertain their views and many were known to be unhappy with such precipitous action.

Alarmed Johnston directors realised that this had become an issue of who was running the business, them or the trade unions, and their mood was not helped when Bell rightly predicted that the strike would last six weeks.

But they supported his tough stand and as a signal of their solidarity allowed Bell to take his family on holiday to the South of

France, although he kept in daily telephone contact. This display of gamesmanship did nothing to raise the morale of the strikers.

Five weeks elapsed before the dispute showed any sign of weakening, five weeks in which all the remaining Johnston employees had been paid in full, five weeks in which not a penny in revenue had been received by the company from its Scottish titles, except the Oban Times, which was organised by a different union. By now it was starting to hurt.

Then came the breakthrough. After a meeting at Leith town hall, Sogat leader Watson and a delegation arrived at Johnston's Manor Place headquarters in Edinburgh to see Bell.

Still uncompromising, he refused to meet them, preferring instead to talk to Watson face to face. In a private room the two men thrashed out an agreement for a 15 per cent increase and the following week the printers returned to work – but still bitter and resentful.

There was an even higher price to pay – about 50 jobs were cut across the Scottish titles as the company looked to rebuild its depleted financial resources. Throughout the strike the main revenue stream had been from the Chesterfield-based Derbyshire Times, where printers were members of the National Graphic Association and were unaffected by the dispute.

It had been a high-risk strategy, but for Johnstons it marked the end of union militancy. Bruised as the company was by the episode it has continued to negotiate with the trade unions ever since. When de-recognition became the fashion during the Thatcher years it declined to follow the flow, confident that the management's right to manage was clearly understood and respected by the union membership.

In 1984 when the decision to sell the Ayrshire titles was announced it left the workforce numb with shock and surprise. Despite the industrial unrest Johnstons had not been regarded as poor employers and the staff could not understand why the company was abandoning them now.

AFTER THE purchase of Guthries and the smaller Ayrshire titles it was 1970 before Johnstons made the next acquisition to further strengthen the group's position in Scotland. This time it looked across the waters of the Firth of Forth to the old-established business of Strachan and Livingston, in Kirkcaldy, Fife.

At the time it was being run by the Livingston family, with

Founders of the
Fife Free Press
William Greig
Livingston (far
left) and James
Strachan

brothers Harold and Bill as the working proprietors, and as part of the arrangement Harold Livingston, the younger of the two men, stayed on with the company as managing director in Fife. He later became the deputy chairman of Johnston Press and played an important role in the further development of the business.

A long-standing friendship between chairman Bill Livingston and Fred Johnston Snr was instrumental in ensuring that when the time came to sell, as the male line of succession petered out, the Falkirk family was in pole position to take over the reins.

The acquisition of the Fife titles substantially increased the company's presence in Scotland and its position in the county has been strengthened since with further acquisitions and the launch of new free distribution newspapers.

Among the Strachan and Livingston assets was the flagship paper, the Fife Free Press, which had been serving Kirkcaldy, Kinghorn, Burntisland and surrounding towns since 1871. In 2005 it held a pre-eminent position in the county with a weekly sale of 20,400 copies.

By the time of its centenary in January, 1971, the Free Press was able to claim 90 per cent household penetration, a fact that was not lost on Fred Johnston when he took over as chairman of Strachan and Livingston at the time of the anniversary.

By then he had been at the Johnston helm for 35 years and his own longevity was matched by the man he succeeded – William Livingston, grandson of one of the co-founders of the company, connected with it for 42 years and chairman for 13 years.

The Fife Free Press was the brainchild of James Strachan and William Greig Livingston, who had worked for the Fifeshire Advertiser in Kirkcaldy as a journalist and overseer respectively. Both shared the vision of a penny newspaper for the coastal town – known as the "Lang Toun" because of its ribbon development.

They set out their aims and objectives in the leading article in the first issue of their fledgling newspaper by turning to verse to get their message across – a highly unorthodox, if not unique, way of doing so. Entitled "The Ship" it read:

This morn glad voices filling all the air,
With hearty Godspeeds our good ship will sail
O'er the sea – the skies serene and fair,
And sighing mid the cords a prosperous gale.

The sea is wide, the winds are free to all,
And manned by loving hearts, we have no fear,
But trust to plough the waves for many a year
Welcomed at every port where'er we call.

We make no promises, but when we come
Our cargo, like a merchantman's, will bring
Something for all; o'er every happy home
Some gleams of sunshine will strive to fling.

And if you like us, open wide your door,
And greet the "Free Press" with a loving smile,
And wish us Godspeed; we will ask no more –
Ours be the task to cheer you mid your toil.

By the time Strachan and Livingston joined the Johnston group it had progressed from one "ship" to a "fleet" of newspapers – the Glenrothes Gazette, established in 1962 to serve the new town and surrounding areas; and the East Fife Mail, which had editorial and advertising offices in Leven and was acquired in 1966 when the rival Fifeshire Advertiser closed down.

Today the subsidiary company publishes seven titles, including the Fife Free Press, from its offices at Kirk Wynd, Kirkcaldy, a veritable "navy" of newspapers, to continue the nautical analogy.

The Fife Herald, with a circulation of 6,625 in North East Fife, was established in 1822 and is the oldest weekly newspaper in Fife and the fourth oldest in Scotland. It was acquired by Johnston Press in 1974.

The Fife Leader North, with a weekly free distribution of 26,300, was set up in 1986 to serve the towns of Levenmouth, Leven, Cupar and St Andrews. It covers a diverse area with a mixed economy

ranging from shipyards and mining to agriculture and learning.

The Fife Leader South covers the south of the county with a weekly free distribution of around 53,000 in the towns of Kirkcaldy, Kinghorn, Burntisland, Dalgety Bay, Aberdour and Glenrothes. It was in this area that the world-famous linoleum industry was developed.

The Glenrothes Gazette now has a weekly circulation of about 6,300 copies, based on the new town which was created in 1948. Many of the district's traditional industries have declined in recent years but papermaking and farming still survive along with electronic and high tech industries. The decision to launch the Gazette by Strachan and Livingston was a bold one as the new town was in the doldrums following the closure of the Rothes colliery and slow progress being made in attracting business to the area. But it had an upbeat story for its launch edition with the exclusive news that an American engineering company was about to set up base in Glenrothes with the prospect of 100 new jobs.

The St Andrew's Citizen was established in 1871 and joined the Johnston group exactly 110 years later. Today is sells 6,700 copies weekly in a population of around 21,000, although seasonally this is considerably increased by thousands of visitors to the home of golf, and students at the university.

Managing director of Strachan and Livingston, Harold Livingston, signs the deal to buy a new web offset press for the Fife Free Press group at Kirkcaldy. Looking on are group chairman Fred Johnston, his sons Freddy, and Harry, Tom McGowran and a representative from the Goss press company

The East Fife Mail was established in 1966 and was previously known as the Fife Mail. Its weekly circulation of 11,500 copies is mainly confined to the former mining and heavy industry town of Levenmouth and the East Neuk of Fife, an area of traditional fishing villages that now mainly relies on income from tourism – many visitors are attracted to the birthplace of the original Robinson Crusoe, Alexander Selkirk.

The purchase of Strachan and Livingston for £202,003, while resulting in a bank overdraft of £213,000 at the time, greatly enhanced the Johnston group's performance. In the first full year turnover increased from £621,665 to £973,314 and pre-tax profit rose from £50,805 to £147,088.

In practical terms, Johnstons now enjoyed the major position to the east of the kingdom of Fife, a position it has consolidated in the years since. Moreover, Strachan and Livingston had been run on similar lines, and with the same ethical values, to the Falkirk operation and slotted neatly into the business.

Almost immediately an order was placed for a new web-offset press at a cost of £170,000, and this became operational in April, 1973. Three years later the directors were seriously considering further capital investment of £80,000 to keep Kirkcaldy abreast of the latest technology.

The investment was made against a background of trade union militancy throughout the country, rising inflation and soaring newsprint prices, all of which posed serious threats to the group's profitability.

The closure of paper mills in Scotland and north east England during 1973, and the resultant shortfall in supply, saw prices rise from £92 per metric tonne to £160.50 per metric tonne – adding £175,000 to group costs. The chairman sent out a letter to shareholders warning of the dire consequences, although his worst fears were not realised.

But the twin dangers of inflation and expensive newsprint were to characterise much of the Seventies. In 1976, for example, turnover increased from £2.4 million to £3.14 million and pre-tax profits rose from £266,591 to a record £334,306, but the chairman was at pains to point out that profit on turnover was down from 11 per cent to 10.6 per cent – "A chastening reminder of the dangers of inflation."

In the same year newsprint reached £235 per tonne, adding a further £180,000 to the company's bill.

The presence of Harold Livingston was invaluable during these uncertain times – vastly experienced, mature and astute, he proved to be a steadying influence as the directors guided the company through troubled waters.

"As deputy chairman he became a kind of father figure and the constant source of shrewd advice," recalled Freddy Johnston, who was in his early forties at the time and happy to learn from a man more than 20 years his senior.

BY THE time of the company's next significant acquisition – the Oban Times, in 1976 – structural changes had taken place in the management of Johnstons that were to have a long-lasting effect.

Fred Johnston, a heavy smoker throughout his life, died of lung cancer in 1973, to be replaced as chairman and managing director by his eldest son, Freddy.

A rising star, in the shape of the hard-hitting, no-nonsense Iain Bell, was about to become part of the head office team, and the ebullient Marco Chiappelli had been recruited to take charge of the financial side of the business.

The death of Fred Johnston at the age of 70 marked the end of another era in the company's history. Universally respected and admired, for 37 years as chairman he had proudly upheld the family tradition of responsible newspaper publishers and sound, shrewd business people.

A note in the company's report and accounts said he was "recognised throughout the industry as one of the outstanding newspapermen of his generation."

Under his leadership the company had enjoyed remarkable stability during exceptionally difficult trading conditions and in his later years experienced a steady period of growth by acquisition.

With son Freddy and McGowran operating so successfully as a team, Johnston Snr had felt confident in handing over the day-to-day running of the business to them, but no major decisions were ever taken without his full knowledge and approval. His involvement had been crucial in the purchase of the newspapers at Ardrossan and Kirkintilloch, and even more so at Kirkcaldy.

Fred Johnston's business dealings were relatively simple and straightfoward – agree a fair price and conclude the deal, often signing there and then over a sixpenny stamp!

"He was prepared to trust people if he thought they were trustworthy, and he was never let down," recalled Freddy.

" Fred Johnston's business dealings were relatively simple and straightfoward – agree a fair price and conclude the deal, often signing there and then over a sixpenny stamp! "

"With that attitude and Tom McGowran's get-up-and-go it was a formidable combination. I was there as the young man in support and I wholly shared these objectives."

Fred Johnston had run the company like one big family and is best remembered for his humanity to all who came in contact with him. But when it came to remuneration he often went months without drawing a salary himself and even forgot to pay others on occasions. When that happened to McGowran his wife, Iris, left a note on Johnston's desk – "Twas a month after pay day and all through the house, every creature was starving, even the mouse!" The money duly arrived – plus a modest increase.

Brought up in an age of typewriters and Linotypes, Johnston took a very relaxed view of the new technology appearing on the horizon.

"What exactly is a computer?" he asked McGowran on one occasion. "Give me it in three words."

"Well, it's nothing but a lot of switches. It's an 'On or Off' machine, a 'Yes or No' machine."

"Well," said Johnston. "Let's make it a 'No' machine."

IAIN BELL'S long association with Johnstons began when the company purchased the Carluke Gazette and Lanark Gazette, in 1972, and his services were retained as part of the deal. It was a decision the company never regretted. Fred Johnston Snr had spotted Bell's management potential and carefully began grooming the younger man for a wider role within the organisation.

Bell responded with enthusiasm in the cutting, thrusting style that became his trademark for the next 20 years.

Both his grandfather, who founded the newspaper in Carluke in 1906, and father William were master printers and in due course Bell's brother, Morris, followed the family tradition to became editor of the two titles. Because of the ill health of their father in the mid-Sixties, Iain quit his job as a manager with J and P Coates, the well-known thread manufacturers, and returned home to help run the business – the two local newspapers, commercial printing works, and several newsagents and stationers' shops.

After the death of William Bell, in 1970, and the payment of crippling death duties, it became increasingly difficult for the Bell brothers to make a decent living out of the business. After serious consideration they decided to build up the newspaper side of the operation with a view to selling it on.

Enter Freddy Johnston, who in late 1971 made a speculative inquiry. This in turn led to discussions in Falkirk between the Bell brothers and Fred Johnston, his sons Freddy and Harry and Tom McGowran.

It was the first time Iain Bell had met the Johnston team, and it almost turned out to be the last. In typically forthright style he rejected the Johnston offer for his newspapers as derisory, and after further fruitless negotiation both Fred Johnston Snr and Bell walked out of the room, exchanging insults and accusations of wasting each other's time.

In the corridor outside Johnston stopped in his tracks and looked the younger man straight in the eye. "Don't be so bloody silly," he said. "Get back in there, you'll get what you want."

In August, 1972, the Bell family newspaper interests were transferred to the Johnston group for the modest sum of £15,000 – an investment that provided a vital platform for development in Lanarkshire.

Johnston's took on their old adversary Outrams, who were well established in the county, and focused attention on the historic town of Lanark. Over the years circulation expanded from 3,000 to more than 12,000 today, having also displaced the Hamilton Advertiser as the principal paper in South Lanarkshire.

Iain Bell, meanwhile, agreed to stay on as manager of the newspapers for six months, fully intending to leave at the end of that time. But he had reckoned without Fred Johnston and his powers of persuasion.

While on a visit to Falkirk, Bell was taken to one side by Tom McGowran. "The old man wants to see you. He wants you to stay – what will it take?"

"A damned good offer. But I'm always prepared to listen."

Face to face, Johnston and Bell viewed each other with mutual respect.

"There goes No 1 son, the eldest," said Johnston, turning his eyes towards the door as Freddy walked past the office. "He has great drive and great ambition. He will go places and take this business forward. And he needs someone like you to help."

Bell's own business plans flashed through his mind, an ambition to run his own company maybe, but Johnston was not in the mood to take no for an answer. Terms were agreed and Bell was given the task of securing and developing Lanarkshire as a key centre for the Johnston company.

> After fruitless negotiation both Fred Johnston and Bell walked out of the room, exchanging insults and accusations of wasting each other's time

The papers were changed from tabloid to broadsheet, printed web offset instead of letterpress and given the resources to mount a determined drive in the south of the county.

Johnston policy at that time was to have a newspaper in every new town that was created as part of the post-war regeneration in Scotland, and when the area around Stonehouse, in South Lanarkshire, was selected as a development site the company decided it should have a presence.

It was almost a re-run of the Cumbernauld operation some years earlier, especially when gossip on the grapevine indicated that Outrams, too, was about to launch its own weekly newspaper.

Iain Bell was given the task of meeting the challenge – to get a new paper, the Stonehouse, Strathaven and Larkhall News, on the streets within 48 hours. Aided by Tom McGowran's earlier experience, the launch went like clockwork but the title was a short-lived affair after the Government abandoned the new town project.

Johnston shareholders were told in the 1977 annual report and accounts that the paper had been closed "with no prospect of developing sufficient circulation to ensure long-term viability."

Bell had already taken on added responsibility, running the newly-acquired Ayr Advertiser and buying the Girvan-based Carrick Advertiser with a view to integrating them into the Guthrie operation. In his first week at Ayr he redesigned the paper and increased pagination by 50 per cent. The staff were left in no doubt that their new managing director was a man who knew what he wanted and liked to get his own way.

"When a paper changes hands you need to show your readership that things are happening," says Bell. "Even if what you do is wrong, as it is sometimes, you must do something.

"That's the first rule, and the best time to do anything when you've bought a business is in the first six months. After that it can take years to achieve change."

The daily 45-mile drive from Lanark to Ayr gave Bell plenty of time to contemplate. And on one such journey it struck him that the only newspaper Johnstons did not own on his route was the tiny Muirkirk and Douglasdale Advertiser – usually four pages, six on a good week, with a circulation of 1,500.

With Freddy Johnston's approval, Bell was authorised to make an offer and tracked down the proprietor at the village bowling green. In the calm of the clubhouse the pair shook hands on a deal – at £1,000 the cheapest Johnston acquisition on record.

Having eliminated the "opposition", the Advertiser was subsequently merged with another group title, the Cumnock Chronicle, only a few miles away, giving greatly improved coverage to the Muirkirk area.

Bell's next promotion was to become managing director of D. MacLeod Ltd, at Kirkintilloch, and to oversee the £100,000 move to new offices at Lurggiebank House, an imposing property set in five acres of land.

Before long he was to become a key player in the Johnston management team, eventually becoming group managing director in 1979 and retiring in 1994 at the age of 55. This was a goal he had set himself years before and which he stuck to, despite determined attempts from his fellow directors to change his mind.

Nicknamed The Rottweiler, he once famously said, "you don't go into management to be liked," and in some people's eyes went on to prove it. Bell was a hard taskmaster, intolerant of people who he perceived were not pulling their weight, but skilled at recognising those with ability, promoting from within and supporting those who matched his own tough standards.

Freddy Johnston was equally skilled at recognising ability and when, in 1974, he decided that the company needed a full time financial controller he knew instinctively where to look for the right person to fill this key role.

For a number of years a charismatic young accountant had audited the company's books in Glasgow. That person was Marco Chiappelli, and once he had been persuaded to join the Johnston team his uncanny skill with figures and entrepreneurial approach to business became a vital ingredient in the growth years to follow.

Fifty years before his father and grandfather and their families had moved from a small village in Tuscany to Glasgow, forsaking their peasant background in Italy – farming the land, growing grapes and producing wine – to seek a new life in the big city.

In time they opened a small café, working long hours but all the while retaining the closely-knit family unit that is a feature of the Italian way of life. Learning to live with prejudice was one of the more unpleasant aspects of growing up as Catholics in a city divided on religious lines and among people still harbouring strong feelings from the war.

Chiappelli's father was sure of one thing – his son could do better for himself than cooking fish and chips and serving pizzas, and it was he who first suggested accountancy as a career. Young Marco was interested.

By 1969 he had qualified with the Glasgow practice of Alexander Sloan and Co, the accountants responsible for looking after the affairs of F. Johnston and Company. One of the very first audits Chiappelli undertook as a rookie in 1963 was at D. MacLeod Ltd, publishers of the Kirkintilloch Herald.

Eventually, as an audit manager, he had the task of ensuring that the somewhat haphazard and chaotic Johnston books were turned into an acceptable final report that he could present to the chairman and the other directors.

In early 1974 the phone rang on Chiappelli's desk. At the other end of the line was Freddy Johnston requesting a meeting, and in due course this took place seated side by side in the front of Johnston's car – parked outside the Scottish Television studios, where he was about to give a live interview about newsprint shortages.

Chiappelli took the weekend to think over the offer he had received – a newly-created position of financial accountant and secretary, and an attractive salary to match.

"I knew by then that I was not going to make partnership material. I was more attracted to management than the professional side of chartered accountancy, so it wasn't a difficult decision to make," recalled Chiappelli.

"I jumped at the chance – I liked the people, I liked Freddy, I liked Tom, and I knew the accounts side needed a great deal of surgery. That attracted me – it was a major challenge but I knew I could cope with it."

He was immediately struck by the Johnston culture of getting the best out of people, motivating them, communicating at all levels and encouraging participation. "The managers were very shop floor people – they made a point of knowing everyone who worked for them."

He was struck, too, by the culture of honesty. "The company's integrity, its reputation, was very important."

The accountancy shambles that confronted Chiappelli on his arrival took two years to unravel – virtually no credit control; no accruals for costs, resulting in wildly erratic monthly profit and loss accounts; the tangled trading records of subsidiary companies; old fashioned accounting equipment.

His reorganisation transformed Johnstons into a more efficient and smoothly operated company following recognised accountancy practices, so important as its affairs became more complex and on a wider scale.

Freddy Johnston, who once described the Scots Italian as "an accountant with imagination", looked on admiringly as his protégé sought ways of increasing profits by scutinising every nook and cranny of the business. The better utilisation of press resources, for example, was part of the drive to keep costs down and improve efficiency.

Chiappelli's contribution was formally recognised in 1981 when he was appointed finance director, by which time his expertise was needed more than ever as the company hit the acquisition trail in England with a vengeance. From then on he was intimately involved in every purchase until his retirement in August, 2001.

FREDDY JOHNSTON was keen to make his mark in 1973 after taking over as principal of the family firm following the death of his father, and his attention turned to the Stirling Observer, another successful weekly newspaper published only a few miles north of Falkirk and with common circulation boundaries.

"In retrospect, I didn't stand a chance," he recalled later. "There had been a long history of bad blood between the proprietors of the Observer and my great uncle Fred. He had fallen out with the chairman, J.J. Munro, for several reasons and had manoeuvred him out of the chairmanship of the Scottish Newspaper Proprietors' Association, which he felt he had occupied for too long.

"Munro never forgave him for this, and there were other commercial rivalries that led to hostility."

It later emerged that Munro had given instructions that whatever happened to the business after him it must never be sold to the Johnstons of Falkirk.

By the time Johnston went knocking on the Observer's door it was owned by a charitable trust formed after the death of Munro – but the trustees were well aware of the old man's wishes and fully intended to honour them. To the fury of Johnston they sold the company to the Glasgow Herald for an amount substantially below his offer.

"I was devastated at the time," said Johnston. "But it set us on a different tack and I realised that we would have to look beyond Scotland if we were going to make really meaningful expansion. In retrospect, the rebuff from the Stirling Observer can be seen as a blessing in disguise."

Three years later, however, Johnston was on the acquisition trail again in his native country. The purchase of the Oban Times in 1976 took the company into new territory in Scotland, away from the industrialised Central Belt and north west to Argyll and the Highlands and Islands.

Imposing red sandstone premises, four storeys high, on The Esplanade came with the purchase – offices on the ground floor, printing works above, a flat on the third floor and the editor's home on the top floor, all with dramatic views looking towards the Sound of Mull.

There were fond memories of the Oban experience, not least the holidays that directors and senior managers and their families spent in the refurbished flat. The loss of the perk when the business was sold eight years later was universally unpopular.

For many years the resident proprietor at Oban had been the gentlemanly Alan Cameron, and when he decided to retire the business was offered to Johnstons. The acquisition, worth £194,400, was concluded in June, 1976, and almost immediately Hugh Graham was installed as director and general manager, a position he had previously occupied with MacLeod's in Kirkintilloch.

Graham, who retired to Derbyshire, had the right credentials – at one time advertisement manager at Falkirk, he displayed the managerial and commercial qualities that Johnstons admired.

Six months later the company added the Campbeltown Courier, on the remote Kintyre peninsular, to its Argyll operation and transferred the printing to Oban, partly as a means of better utilising the press, which stood idle when not printing the Times, its sister paper the Argyllshire Advertiser, and a free newspaper.

The Oban Times holds a special place in the hearts of Scottish people, more especially those who have migrated from the Highlands and Islands to find work in other parts of the country and around the world.

A large proportion of its sales, for example, were in Glasgow, to those who had moved to the city in search of work, and it is even possible to buy a copy on the news stands in Times Square, New York, alongside far more illustrious publications.

Throughout the Johnston ownership the Oban Times made a valuable contribution to group profits, but as time went by it became increasingly evident that there was little chance of advancing the business in a vast circulation area where sheep far outnumber humans.

But the opportunity to sell the Argyll operation came from a totally unexpected source in 1984, when Freddy Johnston was on a visit to New York with his wife and mother-in-law. Out of the blue a message was received at his Manhattan hotel that a man called Howard Bennett was anxious to see him.

Johnston agreed to meet the stranger who, quick research revealed, was the former managing director of a subsidiary company of George Outram, the Glasgow publishers.

"I can do something for you," said Bennett. "I can put you in touch with the proprietors of a good weekly newspaper in the north west of England who want to sell. It seems to me that you might be potential buyers."

"And what do you want in return?" responded a slightly bemused, but interested, Johnston.

"The Oban Times would be very suitable," said Bennett, who explained that he was anxious to return to Britain to buy and manage his own newspaper business.

Johnston flew home, persuaded his fellow directors that the deal – worth £540,000 – would make good sense and within weeks Bennett was the new owner of the Oban Times. Johnstons, meanwhile, concluded the other half of the arrangement and added the Bury Times, in Lancashire, to their growing portfolio of English titles.

AS THE troubled Seventies drew towards a close the directors of F. Johnston and Co took stock of their situation. In Scotland they controlled almost 30 per cent of the weekly newspaper market. The businesses in Fife, Falkirk and Kirkintilloch were doing well; Ardrossan, while profitable, had limited potential for further growth, hemmed in by stronger newspapers on one side and the sea on the other.

Freddy Johnston was proving to be an able and enthusiastic chairman, the veteran Tom McGowran continued to play an active role, Iain Bell was moving centre stage and Marco Chiappelli had already put the financial accounting on a professional basis.

"It is very plain that we need to look elsewhere – and that means South," Johnston told his team.

Targets for acquisition had to meet strict criteria – potentially profitable, well-run companies, capable of growth and development and, especially, leaders in their own local market place.

> The Oban Times made a valuable contribution to group profits, but it became increasingly evident that there was little chance of advancing the business in an area where sheep far outnumber humans

"The closer a paper was to its community the more interested we were," says Chiappelli.

Bell was given the task of doing the homework, analysing balance sheets, on occasions seven or eight at a time, and assessing potential. He relished in the unofficial role of special projects manager.

One of the first approaches was to the owners of the Andover Advertiser in Hampshire, but little progress was made and the attempt was abandoned.

On the same tour Johnston and Bell arranged to meet the proprietor of a Wessex weekly paper but were shocked when the manager casually opened the till, took out a handful of uncounted money and entertained them to lunch. "If he is doing that without any record how many others are doing the same thing," said a horrified Johnston.

The Hampshire Chronicle, in Winchester, also attracted attention. Johnstons were not the only interested buyers and several suitors were lining up to woo the charming owner, Monica Woodhouse.

"She was very polite and agreeable and always prepared to see me," recalls Johnston. "But that came to an end during one of my calls when we were in a lovely office overlooking the high street at Winchester.

"There was a scuffle at the door, which then burst open and a small, aggressive dog came in and bit me.

"After that there were no more serious discussions. Obviously the dog didn't like me and from then on I wasn't considered a suitable purchaser."

The next approach was to the Western Telegraph, in Haverfordwest, which had been singled out as a likely acquisition. Johnston visited the owners, the Thomas family, while on holiday in South Wales with his wife and family, but the approach floundered when they sold to someone else, having used the Johnston interest to inflate the price. It was just one of numerous newspapers that came under the spotlight and which were visited by Bell and his chairman, but still the breakthrough into England eluded them.

But in 1978 there was a dramatic change in the Johnston fortunes.

Bell had been despatched to the Irish Republic to look at possible acquisitions and excitedly rang Johnston to say that the managing director of a newspaper in Carlow was flying to Edinburgh and was prepared to meet him. But Johnston had an even more pressing engagement . . .

While attending a Newspaper Society conference in the Channel Islands his brother and fellow director Harry Johnston had engaged in discussion with Harry Windle, the group advertising manager of the Derbyshire Times, who said he was sure a move was afoot to sell the newspaper.

It was only a snippet of information but it was enough to galvanise the Falkirk team into action. Freddy Johnston quickly contacted the chairman of the operating company, Wilfred Edmunds Ltd., and the two men had a brief telephone conversation in which the real reason behind the call was never mentioned.

"It just so happens that I shall be passing your way. Can I pop in and maybe have some lunch with you?" inquired Johnston, unaware at that time of the bizarre circumstances surrounding the Windle tip-off.

Some months earlier the dapper ad-man with the trademark bow tie had found himself in Brighton at another of the annual round of advertising conferences. Over a drink a senior manager from the Thomson Organisation confided that his company had been negotiating to buy Edmunds but that the deal had fallen through. Windle reckoned that once word got out there would be other suitors beating a path to Chesterfield.

Not long after he was invited to be a guest speaker at the Newspaper Society advertising conference in Guernsey, to enlighten delegates on life at the sharp end on a leading weekly paper and one which had been among the founding members of the NS.

But Windle's pleasure was short lived when his joint managing director Gordon McEwan unexpectedly refused to foot the bill for travel and accommodation. Desperate measures were called for if he was to avoid bitter disappointment and embarrassment.

Back in his office, Windle became aware that the other joint managing director Buster Lumsden, who was standing out of sight behind the door, had followed him. Picking up the telephone he then began a fictitious telephone conversation as though with someone from the Newspaper Society.

"No, I'm sorry I can't make it . . .you'll have to find someone else to speak . . . the truth is the managing director says I can't come and that's final."

Lumsden retreated and minutes later the phone rang. It was McEwan – Windle's bluff had worked. This time he was giving permission for the trip.

Windle called in a favour and hitched a lift in the private plane belonging to the senior directors of W.J. Linney Ltd., publishers of the Mansfield Chad and the Worksop Guardian, both of which were printed at Chesterfield. He was even offered a room at the five star Duke of Richmond Hotel, in St Peter Port, when one of the Linney party backed out.

On the first night Windle decided a stiff drink was in order. Double whisky in hand he was propping up the hotel bar, running over in his mind the fine detail of his speech to the conference, when Falkirk Herald delegate Harry Johnston introduced himself.

Several drinks later the two men were still talking shop, comparing notes about the advertising markets in England and Scotland, when Johnston switched the converation.

"Harry," he inquired. "Can I ask you a pointed question – do you think the Derbyshire Times would sell?"

"Yes, I think they would."

Johnston left the bar, ostensibly to book a table for dinner for he and his wife and Windle. Back in his bedroom he telephoned brother Freddy in Scotland and the rest, as they say, is history.

And so on a warm late spring day Freddy Johnston set off by rail from Edinburgh to Chesterfield – a journey that entailed a change at Newcastle to catch the Bristol train. Frustratingly, signal failure at Durham resulted in delay and when Johnston arrived in Chesterfield he was already an hour late for his appointment at the Edmunds' offices in Station Road.

The thought crossed his mind that once again luck was not on his side. But this time it would be different, he told himself. This time he was determined that the quest for the company's first English newspaper would not end in disappointment again.

Chapter Three

A break for the border

Freddy Johnston concluded that it was a good day on which to do business.
When he eventually alighted from the train at Chesterfield the sun was shining, bright and warm, and the signs of approaching summer were all around, birds singing and chirping and trees already dressed to impress in their fresh green finery.

Despite being an hour late for his appointment he felt relaxed and mildly optimistic at the prospect of meeting the directors of Wilfred Edmunds Ltd. There was a sense of purpose in his step as he walked the short distance to their offices in Station Road, almost within the shadow of the famous crooked spire of St Mary and All Saints.

Chairman and joint managing director Gordon McEwan and his fellow director Wing Commander Dugald "Buster" Lumsden greeted Freddy with friendly smiles and firm handshakes. Their confidence was well founded, for both had grown to appreciate the rock solid family tradition it was their duty to uphold, McEwan through a substantial legacy of Edmunds shares from his grandfather Hawksley Edmunds, and Lumsden by marriage – his wife Mary, a wartime ferry pilot, was the daughter of Gerald Edmunds.

Once the polite preliminaries were over McEwan, well-built, taller and younger than his tubby colleague, suggested they should adjourn immediately for lunch at the nearby Station Hotel, an imposing red brick building with distinctive arched windows.

It was turned 1.30pm on Wednesday, May 17, when the trio began their meal of roast beef and Yorkshire pudding, washed down with a glass or two of red wine. There was no small talk and almost immediately Johnston made clear the purpose of his visit.

"I don't suppose you'll find it hard to guess why I'm here, but I've heard that you may be prepared to consider an approach to buy your company.

"If that is the case I would like to throw my hat in the ring."

McEwan, a veteran of the Korean War who was wounded in the conflict, was the first to respond.

"It is true that we are considering a possible sale, but you're too late. We have virtually completed a deal with United Newspapers."

Johnston tried hard not to show his disappointment, and in any case he was not ready to accept that his frustrating journey from Edinburgh had been a waste of time. He decided to call the bluff of his luncheon companions.

"I'm sorry to hear that. There's a train back to Edinburgh at three o'clock, but before I go I'll tell you what my offer would have been."

The figure of £1.4 million brought a silence to the table.

McEwan and Lumsden, a decorated World War Two pilot who had been shot down and taken prisoner while attacking the German battleship Tirpitz in a Norwegian fiord, exchanged glances. McEwan was the first to speak.

"On that basis we could have the makings of a deal."

Little more than half an hour had elapsed.

The three men did not waste time on puddings and coffee and returned to the Edmunds office to explore further the prospects of doing business together.

Once inside Johnston began to take stock. The buildings, he observed, were more substantial and grander than he had been used to in Scotland. Portraits of the Edmunds family lined one of the corridors in what amounted to a shrine to the dynasty, and, surprise surprise, the directors had their own exclusive toilet, a form of apartheid that had not been practised in Falkirk!

The Johnston offer had two distinct advantages – not only was it about £250,000 more than United Newspapers were prepared to pay, but because of Johnston's modest size as a company and remoteness from Derbyshire it was unlikely that the Monopolies and Mergers Commission would be required to give a ruling on the sale.

United, on the other hand, already had other newspaper interests in the region – the Morning Telegraph and the Star at Sheffield, and a Chesterfield edition of the latter.

Dugald "Buster" Lumsden, director at Wilfred Edmunds Ltd

Freddy Johnston reported developments by telephone to his fellow directors in Scotland and it was seven o'clock in the evening when he finally boarded a train for York to stay the night at the Royal Station Hotel, for by then the last train to Edinburgh had long since departed.

Reception staff viewed the late arrival with some suspicion and demanded cash up front for his stay. It wasn't the first time they had come across a "businessman" with no luggage booking a room for the night.

Unshaven, slightly unkempt but inwardly excited, Johnston took the first express to Edinburgh the next day, arriving in Falkirk in time to brief his colleagues over lunch. After relating the situation in Chesterfield and answering a barrage of questions a formal board meeting of F. Johnston and Co. was called for Friday, May 20.

Those present were Johnston, as chairman, Tom McGowran, Harry Johnston, Harold Livingston, Marco Chiappelli and, by invitation, Iain Bell, then the managing director of D. MacLeod Ltd.

Wilfred Edmunds Ltd., they were told, had recorded poor trading performances in 1975 and 1976, sustaining losses in both years, but had improved in 1977. Its main publication, the Derbyshire Times, had a circulation in excess of 53,000 copies a week.

There was unanimous agreement that serious negotiations should proceed and that an offer in writing should be made immediately to follow up the gentlemen's handshake that had concluded the Chesterfield meeting.

The directors sensed a great opportunity. This was just what they had been waiting for after Freddy had devoted his working life for years to making contacts within the industry, visiting other newspaper proprietors and looking for the elusive first purchase south of the border.

But, for now, there was still a major obstacle to overcome – money!

Johnstons knew they would need to borrow heavily to finance the acquisition and Chiappelli was soon ringing his contacts at the Royal Bank of Scotland. In a highly unusual concession the bank agreed to a meeting on the following Monday – a national holiday.

Regional director Andrew Buchan even delayed his planned round of golf and opened up his office at the bank's St Andrew's Square headquarters in Edinburgh to discuss the application to borrow more than £1 million.

The local branch manager from Falkirk joined Freddy and Chiappelli and in less than half an hour Buchan agreed to support the proposal.

The Johnston directors had had only a short space of time to put together a presentation that was sufficiently detailed, including the latest balance sheets and trading figures for their own company and Edmunds, but it was sufficient to convince the banker that the necessary finance should be made available.

Nevertheless, there was a considerable element of risk and in today's banking climate it is unlikely that such substantial borrowing would be dealt with so simply.

"Here we were buying a company that wasn't making much money, outside our own geographical area and we didn't really know the people themselves. We also knew that a further big investment would be needed in the future," recalled Chiappelli later.

Within a week the Royal Bank's senior executives had rubber-stamped the arrangement. Freddy Johnston was impressed and privately reflected how banking attitudes had changed since his father was admonished by his bank manager when seeking a loan to buy the Walthamstow Guardian years before.

From then on negotiations with Edmunds proceeded quickly and without hitch, thanks in part to the expertise of Glasgow lawyers MacRoberts, who were hired to represent Johnstons and have continued in that role ever since. The junior solicitor detailed to handle the case was Ian Dickson, who in due course became a non-executive director of Johnstons.

Edmunds shareholders were recommended to accept the detailed cash offer of £1,422,149 in a letter from their chairman dated June 29 in which he described the deal as "extremely good."

Johnstons were prepared to pay handsomely for the company, and in the same letter shareholders were told that the offer included £6 in cash for the preferred shares, which valued them at £257,052 – six times the par value and "well in excess of the most recent valuation." In January, 1977, the preferred shares had been valued for capital transfer tax purposes at £1.26 each.

The letter also set out the rationale for sale. After losses in 1975 and 1976 the company had returned to profit in 1977 following an intensive reorganisation to reduce overheads. "However, it is clear to the board that further substantial investments in new technology are necessary if profitability is to be maintained. Your board has had doubts about the ability of a relatively small family business to continue financing further developments on the required scale.

"Last year your directors were already moving towards the view that the future of Wilfred Edmunds Ltd, shareholders and employees, would be best secured if Edmunds became part of a larger organisation with greater financial and technical resources."

The experience gained by the Johnston directors in concluding the acquisition proved invaluable in future negotiations for other businesses. Chiappelli, for example, found himself on a learning curve that involved detailed discussions with senior bankers and experts in company law as well as the complicated diligence process that the purchase required.

The assets of Wilfred Edmunds, and more especially the prestigious Derbyshire Times, were transferred to Johnstons on July 21,
1978 – at long last a toe-hold in England. The acquisition also
included two smaller weekly papers, the Buxton Advertiser and the
Hucknall and Bullwell Dispatch.

That year the Johnston group made a pre-tax profit of £812,359
with a small contribution from Edmunds. Chairman Freddy
Johnston warned shareholders to be patient and remarked that it
would be "some considerable time before results reflect the full
potential of the Derbyshire operation." His report also spoke of a
"fairly substantial" financial commitment ahead to convert the
typesetting operation to photo composition. It was recorded that
the total number of employees in the group now stood at 702.

"When news of the purchase came it was well received, both in
the town and among the workforce," recalled Johnston. "They
knew that we were not going to have a mad orgy of redundancies.
They knew that we were serious newspaper people – we would
maintain the paper and try to develop it, which we did."

But while there was only one topic of conversation – and speculation – among the Edmunds employees the sale was not considered
the most important item of local news that week. It was announced
on the front page in a double column box with a black border
above the right hand solus advert. The lead story told of plans for a
new shopping centre in Chesterfield and other eye-catching
headlines included "Tragedy strikes as husband dies on holiday"
and "Three die in car crash in Spain."

Elsewhere in England, and in the Midlands in particular, there
was a decidedly mixed reaction to the Johnston acquisition among
newspaper proprietors. The Scottish "invaders" were taken
seriously by some and viewed with deep suspicion by others.

The deal had been kept such a closely guarded secret that there
was an air of disbelief when it was announced, and especially the
way in which the prize had been snatched from under the nose of
United Newspapers. The stature of Freddy Johnston within
Newspaper Society circles was enhanced enormously.

A tongue in cheek warning shot came from Ken Morgan, former
general secretary of the National Union of Journalists and soon to
become Director of the Press Council, who reminded Freddy that
Bonny Prince Charlie had never got further south than Derby!

The gentlemanly and well-respected Sir William (later Lord) Barnetson, chief executive of United Newspapers, was more sanguine.

> " Elsewhere in
> England, there
> was a decidedly
> mixed reaction
> to the Johnston
> acquisition.
> The Scottish
> "invaders" were
> taken seriously
> by some and
> viewed with
> deep suspicion
> by others

A Scot himself, Barneston was familiar with Johnstons and while an executive with the Edinburgh Evening News had even made an attempt to buy the Falkirk company. "In 1946 and still wearing his military uniform he called to see my father and suggested we might sell him the Falkirk Herald.

"He was politely but firmly shown the door but we still laughed about that until the day he died," said Freddy.

Barnetson and United were magnanimous in defeat. Sir William, while letting it be known that he thought Johnstons had paid too much for their new business, sent a letter of congratulations and offered to make available the detailed work his company had carried out in readiness for their own bid.

Johnstons were in no doubt that they had acquired one of the finest weekly newspapers in England, even if annual profits of around £80,000 were not as sprightly as they might have been. "The more we saw the more encouraged we became. The heart of the business had disappeared but there was a clear route to recovery," said Chiappelli.

They discovered, too, that the equipment and machinery at Chesterfield was somewhat inadequate, especially the letterpress rotary press – the result of a questionable management decision not to go for litho printing. The press was possibly the last installation of its type in Britain and had been bought in 1973, at a time when other newspaper publishers were converting to web offset production.

Within a couple of years Johnstons sold the letterpress equipment to News International, who used it as a temporary measure while they were re-equipping at Wapping, and replaced it with a new French web offset press.

The man charged with this and many other key decisions at Chesterfield was the redoubtable Iain Bell.

"At that time I had no idea where Chesterfield was – I always thought it was a packet of cigarettes," he joked later.

"There wasn't much discussion about my moving down there – Freddy seemed to expect it and told me to find a house."

AFTER A short period working alongside Gordon McEwan, as deputy managing director, he took sole charge and promptly set about integrating Wilfred Edmunds and Co into the Johnston method of running a business.

Bell moved his wife, son and daughter to live in Derbyshire and

remained there for several years, even when he took on the wider responsibility as group managing director.

He was actively involved in the purchase of other newspaper interests in Derbyshire and Nottinghamshire that followed within five years, but of greatest significance was his success at Chesterfield. This in turn put out all the right signals about the credentials of F. Johnston and Co and convinced the company's bankers that they were worth supporting on subsequent occasions.

Bell's commitment was total, living and breathing the business and even sleeping there when the need arose. On many occasions he rolled up his sleeves to help when the press broke down and went out for fish and chip suppers to lift the spirits of the crew.

"He gave us the impetus. He was the major influence without a doubt," recalled Chiappelli. "He earned the respect of every single individual."

This is a sentiment echoed by the majority of now-retired employees at Chesterfield from the Bell era who when they meet in the street remember the forthright Scot. "Bloody good fella weren't he?"

On his return visits to Scotland Bell often stopped with Chiappelli and his wife Jane at their house in Balerno, near

Edinburgh, preferring their home comforts to a lonely hotel room. But on one occasion his plans were thwarted when the Presbyterian Bell was told that the parish priest was blessing the house, and celebrating mass for the Chiappellis and other Catholic neighbours. That night he decided the hotel was more to his liking.

AT THE Derbyshire Times Bell quickly discovered that here was a newspaper that was very much a part of the fabric of the county it served, its numerous editions reaching into every corner, an institution that commanded great respect among its readers.

This was never more evident than when the paper celebrated its centenary in 1954. The messages of congratulation flooded in from far and wide.

The Duke of Rutland remarked that the "standard of journalism has always been of the highest order" while the Duke of Portland described the newspaper as "one of the highest class publications in the country."

And Lily Sharplin, a newsagent in Ironville who had delivered the Derbyshire Times as a child, added her own tribute. "Personally I consider it a good paper," she wrote. "It has all the qualities, style, set up and good reports of local events."

Yet more tributes were received when the paper celebrated its 150th anniversary with the publication of a special souvenir edition. The Duke of Devonshire, writing from his stately home, Chatsworth House, said the Derbyshire Times was "compulsive reading" for himself and the duchess. "Without it we would be infinitely less well informed of what is going on within the county's boundaries." For many years the Duke had enjoyed a complimentary copy of the paper each week – the Peak edition, delivered hot off the press to his magnificent residence.

The first edition of the Times was published on January 7, 1854, and the newspaper has occupied the same site in Station Road, Chesterfield, for most of that time.

Wilfred Edmunds, who eventually became the proprietor and gave his name to the operating company, joined the paper in 1866. He and his descendants published it for 112 years, a line of succession that only came to an end with the acquisition by Johnstons.

For more than 50 years Edmunds' eldest son, W. Hawksley Edmunds, was editor of the paper, having also been twice Mayor of Chesterfield and chairman of Derbyshire County Council. In true family tradition he was succeeded by his son Morton Edmunds.

While the Derbyshire Times had been blissfully unaware of the technological change taking place all around when buying a new press, it claimed the distinction of setting an industry trend in 1893.

In that year in became the first weekly newspaper in England to introduce the Linotype typesetting machine, which was to revolutionise composing rooms everywhere.

BY THE time of the company's sale Wilfred Edmunds employed 208 staff at Chesterfield and on the Buxton Advertiser, which was established in 1842 to serve the mid and southern High Peak areas of the county, and the Hucknall Dispatch, acquired in 1947. It was also printing a number of newspapers on contract including the Mansfield Chronicle and Worksop Guardian, both later to become Johnston titles.

Under the new owners the number of titles published by the Edmunds subsidiary rose to 20 by 2005, with a total weekly sale and free distribution of around 350,000 copies.

The Wilfred Edmunds portfolio

- The Derbyshire Times
- Chesterfield Gazette
- Chesterfield Express
- Buxton Advertiser/Times
- High Peak Courier
- Alfreton Echo
- Chesterfield Advertiser
- Dronfield Advertiser
- Bolsover Advertiser
- Ripley and Heanor News
- Eastwood and Kimberley Advertiser
- Eastwood and Hucknall Shopper
- Matlock Mercury
- Peak Times
- Belper News
- Ilkeston Advertiser and Ilkeston Shopper
- Eckington Leader
- Erewash Valley Weekly News
- Elite *(a glossy coffee table magazine)*

A meeting at Chesterfield attended by the directors of Johnstons and Edmunds and their lawyers completed the transfer of the business.

Late in the afternoon when the formalities were over Bell waved off his colleagues at the station, walked back to his hotel and decided to make his first official visit to the Derbyshire Times offices the following morning, a Saturday. Until then no one from

Johnstons had had chance to look round every nook and cranny of the premises and Bell wondered what he could expect to find.

His first encounter was with the caretaker who blocked his way into the building.

"There's no right of way through here. I'm sorry you can't come in."

"I can and I am," said Bell. "I'm your new managing director."

Bell's eye immediately fell on the brass plates inscribed with the names of the directors that were fixed to the wall of the car park. There were similar brass plaques, buffed regularly by diligent cleaners, inside the building on the door to the management toilets and washrooms.

"Make sure they're all screwed off by the time I return on Monday, " he told the caretaker.

"Yes, sir"

"And by the way, don't ever call me sir again."

The jungle drums were busy that weekend as news about their new boss spread among the workforce. The buzz that change was on the way was the talk of the office.

Apart from the symbolic removal of the brass signs, the need for more fundamental change at the Edmunds operation quickly became apparent. Much of the plant was out-dated and the premises were not being used to full advantage, among them a brand new extension whose sole purpose was as a canteen and recreation area. It was rapidly converted into a new typesetting department, the added efficiency contributing to company profits.

The newspaper's circulation area and, worryingly, its declining sale also attracted critical attention. Although its core sale was centered on Chesterfield the Derbyshire Times was available over a vast area, right up to the borders with Manchester.

Statistics prepared at the time of the takeover showed the extent of the downward spiral, further exacerbated by a 6p cover price increase that had been deemed necessary as an emergency measure to boost revenue.

The audited sale of the Derbyshire Times for the six months to December 31, 1972, was 74,519 copies per week. Within 12 months this had fallen to 73,654.

The corresponding period of 1974 registered a sale of 68,990, and by December, 1975, the ABC figure was 66,667. Eighteen months later in June, 1977, the six-monthly sale was recorded at 58,230.

The need for change at the Edmunds operation quickly became apparent. Much of the plant was out-dated and the premises were not being used to full advantage

In comparison the circulation of the other titles published by Edmunds had done well. Between 1972 and 1977 the sale of the Hucknall Dispatch had gone up from 7,333 to 7,549, while the Buxton Advertiser had increased its sale from 13,412 to 14,633 in the same period.

"The sales outlets of the Derbyshire Times in some areas were not economically viable and were there just because they happened to be in Derbyshire," recalled Freddy Johnston. "In reality they had very little in common with the rest of the county and especially the commercially-influenced region around Chesterfield.

"It was a circulation that was not backed up with advertising revenue from many of the places in which they were selling.

"They clearly had problems knowing exactly what their circulation area should be. They had also raised the cover price substantially and that had led to a fall in sales.

"We concluded that there had been very little cost control and to some extent a failure to appreciate what the business was all about."

Turning the tide and putting the Derbyshire Times back into sustained profitability was Bell's top priority. Mischievously, he remarked that most of the company's £80,000 annual profit was derived from rents on various properties it owned rather than its newspaper activities.

A starting point was to trim the number of geographical editions – nine of them, some for just a few thousand copies but involving numerous plate changes and all the attendant risks of stopping and starting the press. Off they went to the four corners of the county . . . First Peak, Matlock, Second Peak, Belper, Alfreton, North Derbyshire, Northeast Derbyshire, Clay Cross, Chesterfield.

Bell gathered his managers together and spelt out the new ground rules, the first of which was that under no circumstances would an edition ever be missed. "It never happens in Scotland and come hell or high water it won't happen here," he declared.

Another innovation was the responsibility given to group advertising manager Harry Windle to decide the pagination of each week's paper based on the amount of paid-for advertising. Until then this had been a production decision and often the size of the paper was based on a whim of the composing room overseer.

Edmunds had not been alone in their reticence to embrace the latest technology. Like many other companies at the time they were happy to let someone else act as guinea pigs while the bugs were

> " Bell gathered his managers together and spelt out the new ground rules, the first of which was that under no circumstances would an edition ever be missed "

ironed out and prices started to fall. The production process at Chesterfield was evidence of this cautious approach – an old Crabtree press and alongside it the Goss Headliner bought five years previously, both of them letterpress, and typesetting based on Linotype, Intertype and Ludlow machinery.

Trade unions were strongly represented at all stages, for this was before the Thatcher years and the bitter power struggle that led to the demise of union domination. NGA, Slade, SOGAT, Natsopa, NUJ all had their well-defined lines of demarcation and individual national and house agreements.

Fixed manning levels among the printers, for example, meant that if a man took a day off sick or holiday he was not only paid for this but his wage was also shared among the colleagues who covered for his absence.

Paging bonuses were an additional lucrative source of income, especially for the NUJ sub editors handling between 60 and 70 page changes for the numerous separate editions.

Johnstons set a loose target of 12 months to begin the conversion from hot metal to photo-composition and the introduction of web offset printing, or at least a half-way stage through the use of polymer plates. Working practices would take much longer to change – this would have to wait for an industry-wide reappraisal – but the renegotiation of local agreements wherever possible was high on Iain Bell's agenda at the time.

Within a year of new ownership The Derbyshire Times faced a stern test when its journalists, all of whom were members of the National Union of Journalists, joined a seven-week provincial strike in support of a new pay and conditions claim.

As the reporters, subs and photographers walked out the editor, Jack Sanderson, prepared to bring out his paper alone with the help of managers and any non-union staff as he could muster.

The dilemma facing Bell was how to maintain publication of the Chesterfield titles and continue to pay the rest of the workforce who were unaffected. Even though the Derbyshire Times was reduced to two editions for the duration of the dispute and news items flooded in from supportive readers, finding sufficient pictures was a problem.

Bell had the answer: He would turn himself into a photographer! A self-confessed duffer at taking pictures he called on a friend in Scotland, met him at a hotel off the M1 and received a crash course in how to use a camera.

"On my way to the meeting I passed a really bad accident, "he recalled later. "Here I was with a car full of cameras and I hadn't a clue how to use them."

When at last the national dispute was settled the Derbyshire journalists indicated their willingness to return to work, but a determined Johnston management had already warned that the current house agreement would no longer be recognised. Bell, who had lived at the office in an improvised bedroom for the previous seven weeks, found himself camping out again as the dispute rumbled on for several more days until the NUJ agreed to renegotiate local working arrangements.

Now attention could be turned to photo composition and all that that implied for print workers brought up in the traditional ways of handling type and making up pages. A difficult transition was made all the more complicated because of the decision by the Newspaper Society that none of its member companies should enter into individual house agreements with the NGA and Slade trade unions, insisting instead on a binding national agreement.

The stance had all the signs of a strike in the making – the last thing that the Johnston directors wanted at Chesterfield. They took the brave decision to break ranks with the Newspaper Society and authorised Bell to talk to local union officials, a move that cost Freddy Johnston his place on the Society's industrial relations committee.

This was followed by an emergency meeting of the North Midlands Newspaper Association, to which Bell was summonsed, with the clear intention of persuading Johnstons to toe the official line. When it was the belligerent Scot's turn to speak he did so with a broadside that left those present in no doubt where he and his company stood on the issue.

"This is a major policy decision for Johnston affecting its first acquisition in England," he told them. "We have already gone through a very difficult NUJ dispute and now we believe that changes, rapid changes, are needed elsewhere.

"What the Newspaper Society is proposing is wrong and does not take account of today's industrial climate. I am quite sure that many of you here would agree with me but unfortunately you are not allowed to say so – but I'm lucky because I work for the right company and the right chairman.

"There is no way in which we shall be entering into a national agreement. We may not have a company left if we do not go $\Longrightarrow$

Johnston Press in pictures...

James Johnston (above), whose playboy lifestyle meant a short tenure at the helm of the company; Iain Bell; Freddy Johnston

Tom McGowran relaxing with a copy of the
Falkirk Herald, and (left) with Fred Johnston Snr
in July, 1970, examining the first edition of the
Falkirk Herald to feature front page news

The Falkirk composing room of 100 years ago, and (below) members of the Falkirk Herald team at Camelon in 2005

The Falkirk office (below), decorated for the visit of King George V in 1914

In the Falkirk press room in 2005 (above, from left): Tom O'Hare, production manager, Falkirk; Colin Hume, editor, Falkirk Herald; Stuart McPherson, divisional managing director, Johnston Newspapers (Scotland), and managing director Johnston (Falkirk) Ltd; David Caskie, divisional finance director, Johnston Newspapers (Scotland) and finance director, Johnston (Falkirk) Ltd; Keith McIntyre, newspaper sales director, Falkirk

69

The Falkirk Herald,
AND
Stirlingshire Monthly Advertiser.

No. I.

FALKIRK, 14TH AUGUST, 1845.

Price 2d.

Selby Times

Thursday June 30 2005

STAB HORROR

Needle nightmare as toddler pricked by dirty drug syringe

Cells campaign hope

Controversial 'fuel from hell' trial burn starts

YORKSHIRE POST

SUPER-HERO SEB

Dream that began in Yorkshire 37 years ago: Page 11
The London vision: Pages 2-4
Brendan Foster and Steve Cram: Page 13

Nation celebrates as 2012 Olympic Games handed to UK after 'awesome' bid team dash French dreams

London scoops sport's richest prize

This is one of British sport's proudest days

Running battles as world leaders gather

Evening Post

TERROR COPS SWOOP IN LEEDS

5 homes raided in hunt for London bombers

The Fife Free Press

No. 9101 · FRIDAY, JUNE 10, 2005 · PRICE 42p

Win a fantastic MP3 player

Take your family to the circus FREE

It's your only chance to save your club

Fans united to buy Raith Rovers

Stand up and be counted

Pubwatch plan to call time on the troublemakers

The News

www.portsmouth.co.uk · Wednesday, June 28, 2005 · 35p

SEA OF FIRE

SOUVENIR EDITION: 8-PAGE SPECIAL PLUS PAGES

The Horsham premises
of the West Sussex
County Times (above
opposite), the County
Times team in 2005
(left) with managing
director Mike Pakes,
front; staff from the
Wakefield Express
with managing
director Helen
Oldham (centre)

73

Kettering Evening Telegraph deputy production editor Phil Balding and sub editor Andy Wyman, discuss an edition of the paper; the Peterborough Evening Telegraph headquarters; Falkirk production manager Tom O'Hare (left), and Arbroath editor Craig Nisbet with the first copy of the Arbroath Herald to carry front page news in 2004

Editor Mark Edwards of the Northampton Chronicle and Echo (right) and Steve Scoles, editor of Northants on Sunday

The Northampton Chronicle and Echo offices, opened in 1978

Celebrating in style: Guests gather for a champagne reception at the Derbyshire Times 150th anniversary celebrations at Chatsworth House in 2004 (top), and (above left) Derbyshire Times managing director Mark Rogers and finance director Angela Bramall; Freddy Johnston celebrates the Whitby Gazette's 150th anniversary with editor Damian Holmes in 2004 (above)

The Market Harborough Mail team (opposite) get into the carnival spirit to celebrate the paper's 150th anniversary in 2004

Special guests: The Duchess of Kent with managing director Edward Wood on a visit to the Isle of Man (below) to open the new offices of the Isle of Man Courier in 1993, and (below right) and Prime Minister Margaret Thatcher is shown around the offices of the Halifax Evening Courier in 1983

Lynn News editor Malcolm Powell greets The Queen at the opening ceremony of a Macmillan cancer care centre in 2002, and (far right) Neil Hodgkinson, former editor of the Yorkshire Evening Post, plays host to the Prime Minister Tony Blair in 2005

forward and keep the momentum going.

"So gentlemen, you can do what you want, but count me out"

Bell turned on his heels and left the meeting. Back at Chesterfield his stance was greeted with approval when news of it leaked out and in due course the printers there took no part in the NGA action that followed.

Two years later the North Midlands Newspaper Association invited Bell to be its chairman.

Photo composition was duly introduced after a massive retraining exercise, redeployment of staff and early retirements. Linotype operators were sent in small groups to Manchester for special training courses, but there was a surprise in store for the first batch when they returned. Bell had used their absence to strip out the old Linos and install the new computerised typesetters. But after the initial shock there were few complaints and most men were happy to say goodbye to the noisy, smelly, dirty days of hot metal.

This was followed by the installation of an eight-unit Cruesot Loire web offset press, which was eventually joined by a larger and more efficient seven-unit Goss Urbanite press. The French press formed the bulk of capital expenditure of £400,000 by the group in 1980.

WITHIN 12 months of gaining a foothold in England, Johnstons set about consolidating its position in the North Midlands by further acquisitions, the first of which were the company and newspaper interests of G.C. Brittain and Sons, of Ripley, a town made famous as the birthplace of "Dambuster" Barnes Wallis, inventor of the wartime bouncing bomb.

Freddy Johnston and Bell quickly tied up the purchase after amicable negotiations with the charming owner of the family business, Mrs Winifred Stoakes.

The deal added the Ripley and Heanor News, established in 1889, and the Eastwood and Kimberley Advertiser, established in 1895, to the English portfolio. The new titles also meant more work for the under-utilised Chesterfield press.

By the end of 1979 the new acquisitions were making their mark on group profits, which rose to £996,504. This included a six-month contribution from Brittain's, which had joined the group on July 1.

In 1980 the Johnston presence in England was further extended with the purchase of Local Network Publications from the company's founder, Ron Gusterson, who had successfully created two free distribution newspapers in Doncaster and Chesterfield.

Gusterson was a local accountant and entrepreneur who had spotted the new markets opening elsewhere in the country and stepped in with his own niche publications ahead of the disinterested Derbyshire Times. By the time of the Johnston takeover his Chesterfield Advertiser was providing serious competition for the paid-for title and making inroads into its lucrative local advertising revenue.

Bell was given the task of dealing with the situation and in a series of tough meetings with the likeable Gusterson negotiated the purchase of both of his Advertiser titles, the deal being concluded in November.

IN 1983 Johnstons turned their attention to the attractive Peakland town of Matlock and the small circulation weekly, the Matlock Mercury, published there by the Uprichard family.

Johnstons concluded that while the Mercury was probably too small to prosper as a stand-alone business in changing economic conditions, it did have a bright future with the increased support and resources that could be provided from Chesterfield – a judgement that has been fully justified since.

It was eventually purchased for £217,000 after difficult and at times acrimonious negotiations with the Uprichards. They had been upset by the manner in which the Derbyshire Times had vigorously encroached on their restricted and vulnerable circulation area following the Johnston takeover. It took a forthright telephone call to the Matlock lawyers involved to bring the discussions to a conclusion.

The Matlock purchase was a clever strategic move. Not only did it expand the business and fill another print slot at Chesterfield, but it also completed a ring of successful, yet still separate and individual, paid-for titles around the heartland of the main county newspaper.

"By then we had got the taste for business in England and were actively looking elsewhere," recalled Freddy Johnston, who was beginning to enjoy the rewards after all those years of knocking on doors and enduring a succession of rebuffs.

Not a lot happens in the stunningly beautiful Peak District to attract national attention but events that occurred in 1973 were subsequently to place the Matlock Mercury and its editor Don Hale

Stephen Downing
visits the offices of
the Matlock Mercury
to read the story
about his release
from prison

in the full media glare.

It that year the normally sedate and virtually crime-free small town of Bakewell, best known for its proximity to one of England's finest stately homes, Chatsworth House, was shaken to its core by an horrendous crime that was committed in the local cemetery.

It was there, in broad daylight, that typist Wendy Sewell was brutally attacked with a pickaxe handle and sexually assaulted. Several days later she died from her injuries. A 17-year-old council worker, Stephen Downing, was convicted of her murder and sentenced to life imprisonment in 1974.

His refusal to admit his crime meant that he was classified as IDOM (in denial of murder) and ineligible for parole. To all intents Downing faced the rest of his life in prison and the more he protested his innocence the less likely he was to be released.

But editor Hale took a different view after being approached by Downing's parents, who were concerned about their son's open-ended incarceration that had begun some 20 years before.

Hale was convinced there had been a serious miscarriage of justice and for the next six years campaigned for Downing's release, filling thousands of column inches in the Matlock Mercury in the process. When the conviction was overturned on a technicality in 2002 Hale and the Mercury were feted as the story attracted widespread attention at home and abroad.

However, the euphoria of the campaign's success was short lived. One year on, Derbyshire police announced that following an exhaustive reinvestigation of the murder they were not looking for any other suspect.

Nevertheless public interest in the case continued and in 2004 the BBC brought it sharply back into the spotlight with a two-part drama-documentary which, of course, prominently featured the Matlock Mercury.

By then Hale had left the newspaper, where he was replaced as editor by Amanda Hatfield, the first woman to hold the position since the Mercury was established in the 1950s.

THE CHANGING nature of Johnston Press, especially its geographical spread, had been acknowledged with the leasing in 1980 of premises at 53, Manor Place, Edinburgh, for the creation of new corporate headquarters.

Several factors prompted the decision to leave the ancestral home of the company in Falkirk, not least of them overcrowding. But there were clearly advantages in being based in Scotland's capital city and financial centre, including the credibility that came with a city address.

Visitors are surprised at the scale of the Manor Place operation – tucked away in an elegant Victorian terrace, it is tiny compared with the head offices of many public companies. But the pyramid structure of Johnston Press, with control passed down through divisional offices to individual centres, has avoided the need for large and expensive premises. At the time of the move head office staff totalled eight out of a payroll of about 700 and directors pledged to maintain that proportion. The premises have since been purchased outright.

By 1983 the Derbyshire operation was ticking over smoothly, the addition of the Matlock Mercury helping to strengthen the company's trading performance. Even Iain Bell found more time to relax, and usually that meant indulging his twin passions of golf and horse racing.

His annual England v Scotland golf matches were eagerly anticipated by those fortunate enough to be invited to join his English team while Chiappelli scoured Johnston centres north of the border for golfing talent to make up the Scottish contingent.

The meetings were about far more than national pride. The jolly banter and ninthteenth hole socialising were seen as important in helping to unify the two halves of the group, but once Bell had been recalled to Edinburgh the golf days were allowed to lapse.

THE NEXT development came completely out of the blue – the deal which saw the Oban Times being sold to Howard Bennett and the introductions he made to the owners of the Bury Times, the bi-weekly tabloid newspaper serving the Lancashire cotton town.

Freddy Johnston saw a good business opportunity, even if Bury did appear somewhat out on a limb, separated physically and psychologically by the Pennines from the company's other English interests.

Following up Bennett's lead, Johnston met with the two proprietors, Harold Tomlinson and Wilf Ainscow, and eventually a sale price of £1,600,000 was finalised in June, 1983.

Although the negotiations had been amicable Johnston still ended up with cuts and bruises for his efforts . . .

During one of their meetings Ainscow, who though in his sixties had only recently learned to drive, suggested lunch together at his local golf club. A relaxed Freddy fastened his front seatbelt as Ainscow began to ease gently out of the company garage.

Suddenly his foot slipped, the car shot across the road and collided broadside with a Manchester Corporation double-deck bus. Johnston was thrown forward and received considerable bruising to his face and body.

"My wife had seen me off in the morning to fly down to Manchester and when she met me at the airport again I was in a wheelchair," he recalled later. "I even had to miss a Scottish rugby international because of the accident.

"I was prepared to do a lot for the company, but not putting my life on the line."

Ainscow, a former editor of the Bury Times, and Tomlinson, at one time the production manager, had been running the company for several years after buying out the interests of the controlling family.

Although both men had family of their own – Ainscow a son who worked for the newspaper, and Tomlinson two daughters – none of their children was interested in taking charge of the business. As they grew older the two partners decided that they had no option but to sell the company.

And so Johnstons took over a profitable business, which also included a commercial print works and a good deal of contract printing. But it transpired all too soon, that the company had not been particularly well managed. A lack of firm leadership had created an atmosphere in which trade union militancy had been allowed to flourish – of one union official it was said, "he made Trotsky look like a Tory!"

Bury had been the birthplace of Eddie Shah's Messenger Group of free newspapers in the early Eighties that in due course were at the centre of some of the most ugly scenes of industrial unrest ever seen in the British newspaper industry..

Eddie Shah sprang into public consciousness in 1983 as a result of a dispute at his Messenger Newspapers group plant at Warrington. Shah intended to launch a brand new concept in newspapers – Today, the first-ever national daily newspaper to be printed in colour. Hitherto, he had been a relatively obscure publisher based in Manchester.

This new concept required a revolutionary approach, which the print industry, hide-bound with old traditions, was loathe to accommodate. Shah decided to print without the unions and employed unqualified printers, prompting violent "strike busting" protests and street fighting. His own house was fire-bombed on several occasions.

As the protests grew the militant Bury printers lent their support on the picket lines. Back at the Bury Times morale was at an all-time low.

Imagine the surprise when, in 1984, Johnstons bought the two-edition Bury Messenger from Shah, took on several of his printers as part of the deal, and brought production of the title into the unionised Times offices. The £300,000 deal for a barely profitable newspaper had strategic value and a heavy touch of irony as far as industrial relations were concerned.

The initiative for the purchase had come from Iain Bell who had realised the importance of taking over the opposition free newspaper as a way of bolstering the position of the Bury Times.

Shah proved an elusive person to contact, but eventually he was persuaded to fly to Edinburgh in his private plane to discuss the sale with Freddy Johnston, Chiappelli and Bell.

By late evening an agreement had almost been reached and Shah and his team adjourned to a private office at Manor Place to consider the final details. It was then that one of his lawyers pointed out a clause that had been inserted by Bell: that purchase would be subject to trade union agreement – a vital condition in view of the volatile history of the Messenger group.

Shah, the man who had done so much to smash union influence, was enraged.

The doors of the board room burst open and in stormed the powerfully built man brandishing the papers relating to the deal, a

Picture courtesy EMPICS

Eddie Shah, owner of the Messenger Group, who set out to curb trade union influence in the 1980s

dossier as thick as a BT telephone directory. There he launched into a fearful tirade in which Freddy Johnston was accused of despicable tactics and of bringing him to Edinburgh under false pretences.

In a mood of cold fury Shah threw his papers down on the table, and walked out of the building. A stunned silence descended on the room.

The following morning the telephone jangled on Johnston's desk. On the other end of the line one of Shah's advisors set about building bridges – "Eddie was over-wrought," he explained. "He realises now that he might have acted rather hastily."

Bell was given the task of trying to stitch the deal together again. "We're not interested in buying a title that the Bury Times can't handle because the NGA has put a black on it," he told Shah's emissary. "It's as simple as that."

Finally Shah agreed to the sale, but for the Johnston management there was still the tricky task of persuading the Bury printers, who were all members of the National Graphical Association, of the wisdom of the purchase.

Bell started by winning over the NGA's branch president and secretary, neither of them Bury Times employees, who were flown to Edinburgh to be told the news. Together they then received the approval of NGA general secretary Tony Dubbins, who was quick to appreciate the political significance of the Messenger being produced in a union house. He in turn then convinced the sceptical Bury chapel that the additional work was in their own best interests.

Johnstons soon realised they had taken on an unprofitable publication and at the board meeting in September, 1985, directors were told that action was necessary to stem the losses, including closing the paper's offices, making staff redundant and reducing the print run to 48,000 copies per week. But group managing director Bell stressed that the Messenger "must be kept going under any circumstances" given its importance in the Bury marketplace.

The Bury operation was further extended in 1985 with the purchase, at a cost of £40,000, of two Manchester-based specialist titles, Our Dogs, a weekly tabloid, and Our Cats, a colourful A4 magazine, both of which were already printed on contract.

Our Dogs, one of two competing national titles at the time and heavily involved in the annual Crufts show, was a valuable source of revenue at Bury. When the owners ran into difficulties Johnston came to the rescue by agreeing to take over both titles as a means of protecting this income. Several years later Johnstons sold both niche publications having failed to turn either of them into profit making enterprises.

And there was a surprise sequel to the Eddie Shah link when the entrepreneur visited Edinburgh again to ask Johnstons if they would consider selling the Bury Times to him. His inquiry was politely rejected.

Poor industrial relations continued to plague the Bury operation for some time after the Johnston acquisition, although these had been largely overcome when the Bury Times was exchanged for the Doncaster Free Press in an arrangement with the Reed group in 1996, by which time the press had been closed and pre-press operations slimmed down.

At the time Johnstons concluded that there were few opportunities for expansion and growth in Lancashire as most of the neighbouring newspapers of any size and quality were themselves owned by large companies.

"It was very much like the Ardrossan situation ten years before," recalled Freddy Johnston. "A very good business but with limited potential for us."

Despite its name the Doncaster Free Press has always been a paid-for weekly title since it was established in 1925 to serve the thriving south Yorkshire town that became famous as a mining and railway centre and has been the home of the St Ledger since 1776.

But by the mid-Nineties Reed found themselves in a similar situation to Johnstons in Bury, with a profitable newspaper that had been acquired some 20 years earlier but that was now somewhat isolated beyond their normal sphere of operations.

"We both realised we could operate more efficiently if we did a swop," said Johnston. "It wasn't a question of competition but of geography."

In fact the subject of an exchange had cropped up on numerous occasions at informal discussions between the two companies but as Reed expanded its interests in Lancashire it became clear that the Bury Times was a more attractive proposition to them.

And Johnstons were well pleased to add the Doncaster Free Press to their other interests in the region. In 2005 the paper sold nearly 40,000 copies a week while its stablemate, the Doncaster Advertiser, had a weekly free distribution of more than 79,000 copies.

However, disposing of the Bury Times was not on the agenda as the Eighties unfolded and the company's sights were now firmly set on growth in England, although it returned briefly to Scotland in 1984 to buy the North Lanarkshire weeklies the Motherwell Times and the neighbouring Bellshill Speaker for £101,000.

Both acquisitions were seen as a "filling in" exercise that helped to strengthen further the company's position to the east of Glasgow. The combined circulation of the two papers is now about 15,500 in an area that was once dominated by mining, heavy engineering and steel making – the latter remembered through the Motherwell football club's "Steelmen" nickname.

Far and away the most important purchase of the 1980s was the £3,630,000 paid for the Wakefield-based Yorkshire Weekly Newspaper Group (YWNG) in December, 1985. With the broadsheet Wakefield Express at its core, alongside the Pontefract and Castleford Express and the Selby Times, the company was the market leader in weekly newspaper sales in a swathe of West Yorkshire which was also the heart of Britain's coal mining industry.

YWNG had suffered badly during the miners' strike of 1974 but the infamous "Scargill Strike" of 1984 - 85 had an even more serious effect on business as the area's economy reeled under the effects of prolonged industrial strife.

The action was prompted by an announcement by the National Coal Board early in 1984 that an agreement it had reached after the strike 10 years earlier had become obsolete. It proposed to close 20 pits, shed 20,000 jobs and many communities in areas such as the North of England would lose their main source of employment.

Yorkshire Weekly Newspaper Group chairman Michael Robinson (front, third left) with colleagues at Wakefield

In the Yorkshire coalfield, strike action started on March 5 and lasted until March 3 the following year, when the National Union of Mineworkers conceded defeat, faced with an impoverished membership and a hostile government.

The effect of the dispute on business was one of the factors why the YWNG's founding family, the Robinsons, under chairman Michael Robinson, decided to look round for a buyer and had already spoken to a potential purchaser. With revenues falling and profits eroded the Wakefield directors had been forced to take stock of their future, even though in reality the effects of the strike were little more than a temporary difficulty from which the business would recover. Another unstated but obvious factor was the lack of a clear line of succession to the business within the Robinson family.

"My worst fears became a reality," Michael Robinson told shareholders in September, 1984. "The fourth quarter of our year's trading was disastrous. We were operating well below break even point."

In an attempt to increase business outside its core area YWNG had launched a new free distribution newspaper, the York Times, in 1983 but that was contributing little to profits. Fierce competition was being faced from other free newspapers started up in opposition.

The cumulative impact of the miners' strike was described as "severe" by Robinson in his annual report for the year ended September 27, 1985. "Even though the dispute has been settled for some time its effects are still being felt. Consumer spending power in some of our circulation areas was substantially reduced and this had its effects on our advertising volume . . . local businesses were affected and we in turn have suffered in the incidence of bad debt which we have no hope of recovering."

To make matters even worse VAT had been imposed on advertising from May, 1985. This had further affected volumes, being tantamount to a price increase to advertisers.

All told 1985 was a miserable year for YWNG with profits of £215,571 showing a reduction of £227, 311 on those of 1984.

Alerted to the situation, Freddy Johnston made an approach. Wakefield had already been high on his list of independent newspaper companies that he considered would probably be sold one day.

Michael Robinson was receptive, well aware of the Johnston reputation and impressed with the way in which it had handled the

First impressions of YWNG were favourable. The Johnston executives quickly realised that they had inherited a well-run company with a strong management and a sound editor

Derbyshire Times, although he confessed that he had not considered Johnstons as a likely buyer.

The initial meeting between the two men went well, just as Freddy had anticipated, for they were old friends who had first become acquainted as members of the Young Newspapermen's Association in the early Sixties. This was just one of numerous trade and professional organisations in which Johnston took an interest and which enabled him to build up an enviable list of contacts throughout the newspaper industry.

He took personal control of the negotiations, closely supported by Chiappelli and Bell. The sale was concluded, swiftly and smoothly, on December 6 – and thankfully with no referral to the Monopolies and Mergers Commission.

At that point Robinson retired and his number two, Denis Cooper was appointed managing director, continuing in that role until his own retirement. Cooper's son, Richard became company secretary at Wakefield and was eventually promoted to a similar position with Johnston Press in Edinburgh.

The Wakefield Express and its satellite weeklies were a perfect fit within the growing Johnston group – all highly respected titles and leaders within their own respective market places. They also had growth potential – YWNG results in 2003 were among the best in Johnston Press and reflected growth on growth for almost every year since acquisition.

First impressions of YWNG were favourable. The Johnston executives quickly realised that they had inherited a well-run company with a strong management and a sound editor in Dick Taylor.

The biggest worry was the performance of the web-offset and sheet-fed commercial printing business, Yorkshire Communications Group, which was to cause a succession of problems. For administrative ease this was split off from the newspaper business, a sound decision, as events were to prove. Even when a buyer was found for the business in 1994 he backed out of the deal and it was the end of the year before Johnstons were able to dispose of YCG as a going concern – "a successful solution to a protracted problem," shareholders were told.

As was usual Johnston practice, Freddy Johnston and Iain Bell visited the offices to meet the staff and make an initial assessment immediately once the acquisition was complete. And a little later finance director Marco Chiappelli arrived in Wakefield to examine the accounting systems, the latest trading figures and the current bad debts.

As Christmas 1985 approached Bell and Chiappelli were looking forward to joining their families and feeling a trifle sorry for themselves as they met up one evening at the Trusthouse Forte Hotel, on the outskirts of town.

After dinner they retired to the lounge for what they expected to be a relaxed business discussion. But Chiappelli's wandering eye caught sight of someone he was sure he recognised – an attractive girl he had noticed earlier in the accounts section of the Express.

Moments later the men were approached by two other girls they had met briefly that day.

"Mr Bell and Mr Chiappelli, why don't you come in and join us," they invited. "It's the staff Christmas party. No need to sit out here while we're all enjoying ourselves."

It was two o'clock in the morning when they climbed the hotel stairs to bed. A few hours later when they arrived at the Express for work, still tired and bleary eyed, word of their night out with the office girls was buzzing round the grapevine.

Chiappelli reflected that it wasn't the usual way of getting to know the workforce. "Iain and I cheered up no end after that. And it didn't do our street cred any harm either!"

IT WAS by the dim glow of gas light in March, 1852, that printer John Robinson produced the first Wakefield Express newspaper on a press powered by steam.

The price was four-and-a-half old pence and the broadsheet editions were created at Southgate, where the business is still based.

By 1923 the company was trading as the Wakefield Express Series following the launch of the Skyrack Express in South Leeds, which incorporated the newly-purchased Skyrack Courier and Rothwell Times. The title joined the Pontefract and Castleford Express, launched in 1880, and the Hemsworth and South Elmsall Express, founded in 1912.

The Selby Times was bought in 1942 and the Ossett Observer in 1956. The series became a group in 1979 when the YWNG title was adopted and continued to develop with the launch of a number of free titles. The paid-for Morley Advertiser, established in 1930 to serve the small West Yorkshire town, was acquired in 1988.

Ultimately 11 titles were published from Wakefield, which also became an important print centre for other Johnston newspapers as well as contract publications.

After the purchase of YWNG it was to be a further three years before Johnstons made the next significant acquisition, the West Sussex County Times in 1988. In the same year the company took the momentous decision to obtain a Stock Exchange listing and so end 143 years of direct Johnston family control.

But those three years saw considerable activity behind the scenes in an effort to expand the business beyond Scotland, the North Midlands and parts of Yorkshire and Lancashire.

The West Sussex County Times, published in Horsham had been a target as early as January, 1985, when Freddy Johnston met the managing director, Joseph Podlasinski, for exploratory talks. But two months later he was told the company was not for sale.

However, hopes were raised again late the following year when Johnston and Podlasinski shared a drink at a Newspaper Society conference and once again the possibility of a sale was discussed. Although the chairman of the County Times, Mrs T.H. Green, rejected Johnston's advances a second time she conveniently left the door open for talks at a future date.

Other weekly newspapers in South Yorkshire and Lancashire were among many considered as other potential additions to the group, as were five county magazines being sold by the Thomson Organisation.

Optimism mixed with setbacks characterised the mid-Eighties, with most of the bad news emanating from Bury and Chesterfield.

When the Bury Times lost all its property advertising the newspaper faced a shortfall of £300,000 in revenue. But just as worrying was the way in which the Bury management had been taken completely unawares when local estate agents decided to change their allegiance.

Although the advertising was eventually recovered the Times and the Messenger responded by publishing their own colour property supplement. Johnstons were anxious not to compromise the independence of their Bury editors but nevertheless they were politely asked not use their columns to attack estate agents – at least not for the time being!

Within a month the Johnston board was being warned that estate agents in Derbyshire were considering transferring their advertising to a new property freesheet with the potential loss of £400,000 revenue. Heavy discounting failed to impress the estate agents and in March, 1986, they pulled out of the Derbyshire Times – a move which prompted the newspaper to change from broadsheet to tabloid format. Until then it had adopted the clumsy arrangement of tabloid property pages contained inside the parent paper.

But despite the setbacks 1986 saw the group doing well overall – no doubt helped by the reduction of 36 employees on the payroll at Wakefield. Minutes of the board meeting in November painted a rosy picture of F. Johnston and Co and the finance director reported that results for October were the best for any month in the company's history.

The chairman said he considered the month's profits to have reached an optimum and that further growth would have to be achieved through acquisition or an expansion of present activities – contract printing and specialist typesetting, for example.

Under "any other business" the directors had a more thorough discussion on the future of the group. Freddy Johnston said that as things stood the potential for the company to increase its profitability were minimal and could indeed be difficult to sustain at the present level.

The company's success, he said, had lain in its expansionist policy and continued success depended greatly on its growth. There were three options available:

1. Consider and plan going public (the first reference to flotation)
2. A sensible amalgamation or merger with another company
3. Continue to try to expand organically and through prudent acquisition.

The directors favoured the third option and agreed that in 1987 they should seriously look for further acquisitions, preferably in printing and publishing. A fighting fund of £1.5 million was set aside, while the idea of flotation was put on the back burner until "a more appropriate occasion."

Freddy Johnston returned to the subject a few months later, when he presented a discussion paper to the board in which he earmarked summer 1991 as a possible date for flotation. In the meantime a pre-tax profit target of £2.3 million was set for 1987 with a goal of £3 million by 1990.

Both figures appeared well within reach and in the annual report for 1987 Johnstons recorded a pre-tax profit for the year of

£3,028,689. Business in May was exceptional with a new profit record of £461,997 (£282,999 in 1986) beating the previous October's profit, which in itself had been considered the pinnacle.

The year's performance would have been even better but for the disastrous performance of the Yorkshire Communications Group at Wakefield and in September the company's expected loss to December was £150,000. The Johnston board decided that if there was no improvement they would consider ceasing operations and selling the assets.

It is not hard to imagine what the reaction must have been when the subsidiary lost a £500,000 contract to print another publication after only five issues. Lack of proper costing, poor quality control, bad timing and bad management were given as the reasons.

However, commercial printing and typesetting was regarded as a worthwhile activity alongside the core newspaper business. In addition to the troubled Wakefield printers Johnstons were by this time also running typesetters Computer Typesetters Ltd., of Leeds, bought in 1984, and had set up a new specialist typesetting company, Huntingdon Typesetters Ltd., at Huntingdon, Cambridgeshire, in 1987.

Further continuing this policy of print-related interests, Johnstons dipped into its acquisition kitty again that year with the purchase for £400,000 of the established colour printers, Wood, Westworth and Co, of St Helens, who specialised in high quality colour brochures. The company was eventually sold as a going concern in 1994.

The south coast of England – long referred to as the "soft under belly" by Iain Bell – continued to attract attention as the company looked to expand its newspaper interests. An approach was made to T.R. Beckett's, an old-established business with its headquarters and main publishing centre in Eastbourne, and other weekly newspaper titles in Worthing, Shoreham and Littlehampton.

Freddy Johnston was "well received" and his interest noted – the response he had come to expect on his frequent visits to newspaper offices, an activity that had earned him the reputation as a stalking horse among other proprietors.

Patience was indeed a virtue, and it paid off when, after two previously unsuccessful approaches, the West Sussex County Times Ltd and its associated business, the Gooding Property Company Ltd, became part of the Johnston group in March, 1988. The £3.8 million acquisition also included the free distribution Horsham

Advertiser, which had been launched nine years earlier.

The Johnston directors were in no doubt that they had bought a successful, well-run and profitable business. The balance sheets showed a remarkable increase in profitability during the five years leading up to the sale – from £87,000 in 1983 to £200,000 in 1987. And in the 10 months to January, 1988, the pre-tax profit was an impressive £449,000.

It was not only the company's sound track record that attracted Johnstons but also the obvious prosperity of the south east of England and the affluent nature of the County Times' circulation area.

The West Sussex County Times has a claim to fame that is almost certainly unique among British newspapers – from June, 1894, until its acquisition by Johnstons it was run by a succession of women proprietors.

Staff of the Sussex Express, in Lewes, one of numerous titles owned by Johnston Press in Sussex, pictured in 2005. The title was acquired from Emap in 1996

Joe Podlasinski, whose talks with Freddy Johnston in 1986 initiated the sale of the West Sussex County Times to Johnston Press

Mrs Green exercised tight control from her home in the Sussex countryside. Her domineering and Victorian approach was strangely out of place in the late 20th century

The paper can trace its history back to 1869 and for the first 25 years with men in charge it struggled to survive under a number of different titles.

It was under the ownership of the delightfully named Edward Vere-Walwyn that the title County Times was adopted in 1893. Indeed, that appears to be the only noteworthy feature of his short and undistinguished stint at the helm.

In 1894 – at a time when "going into trade" for women was frowned upon – the bankrupt paper was bought for £25 as a present for Mrs Susannah Elizabeth Gooding from her husband, who was anxious that she had something worthwhile to occupy her time when he was abroad as a Government barrister in India. It remained in the family for the next 94 years – always run by the female line.

Mrs Gooding stayed in control as owner and editor for 34 years until her daughter Evelyn Banbury Gooding succeeded her. When she died in 1942 she was replaced by her niece Suzanne Gooding, later to become Mrs T.H. Green, who continued the family tradition until her death in 1987 at the age of 76.

Mrs Green rarely visited the County Times office in Market Square and became more reclusive as she grew older, but she nevertheless exercised tight control from her home in the Sussex countryside. Her domineering and Victorian approach was strangely out of place in the late 20th century.

Under her supervision sales of the County Times, which retained its broadsheet format in two editions, soared from around 10,000 copies a week to 28,000.

Local content was the lifeblood of the newspaper, believed Mrs Green. Not only did she like to suggest the leader topic for the week but she also insisted on a marked paper being delivered to her home indicating the source of every single story.

Although Mrs Green remained firmly in command of her business she left the day to day running of affairs to her trusty joint managing director, Joe Podlasinski, through whom previous Johnston approaches had been channelled.

"As far as I was concerned she could have been a figment of the imagination. I never met her, " recalled Freddy Johnston. "My only dealings with her were by letter, which either resulted in the brush off, or she didn't bother to reply at all."

One of the few people who was granted an audience with the reclusive proprietor was Tony Dubbins, general secretary of the

National Graphical Association, who discussed a local dispute involving his members with Mrs Green while she was confined to bed recovering from illness.

Several months after her death it was Podlasinski, by then chairman, who indicated that the business was for sale. Once this was concluded he continued as a director until his retirement in 1990.

Podlasinski's contribution was vital to the smooth transfer of ownership, his charismatic style adding colour to proceedings, as well as 40 years' experience with the Sussex company.

He had been taken on by Mrs Green in 1948 and quickly rose up the management ladder. A native of Poland, he had been forced to flee the country in the wake of the German invasion and arrived in England with the Polish forces from Italy in 1946. Then followed another 18 months with the Polish Resettlement Corps before joining the Horsham newspaper as a clerk speaking only broken English – a beginning that made his rise up the managerial ladder all the more remarkable.

While negotiations with Podlasinski were taking place for the acquisition of the West Sussex County Times negotiations were also underway for the purchase of the Chesterfield Gazette, a free distribution paper that had been launched in the town by Graham Bannister and Mike Cummings. At one stage this rival publication had succeeded in briefly "stealing" the property advertising from the Times. Eventually a sale price of £350,000 was agreed and this was completed on April 5, 1988.

Behind the scenes, however, far more significant developments had been taking place.

Although 1991 had been earmarked as a possible date for F. Johnston and Co to become a public company with a Stock Exchange listing the pressure to take this significant step earlier than planned had been mounting for a number of reasons.

Indeed, it could have happened as early as 1987 had market conditions been right, but the Black Monday crash of October 19 put paid to any such thoughts.

On that day, the Dow Jones Industrial average in America fell 22.6 per cent, the largest one-day decline in recorded market history. This one-day decline was not confined to the United States but was mirrored all over the world. By the end of October, Australia had fallen 41.8 per cent, Canada 22.5 per cent, Hong Kong 45.8 per cent, and the United Kingdom 26.4 per cent.

> "Joe Podlasinski joined the Horsham newspaper as a clerk speaking only broken English – a beginning that made his rise up the managerial ladder all the more remarkable"

Flotation was always likely to be a risky move and not something to be attempted in an atmosphere of uncertainty and when investor confidence was low. Within months, however, world markets showed signs of recovery and the Johnston directors again considered going public as a means of safeguarding the company's long-term future.

At quarter past nine on the morning of Friday, February 5, 1988, they met in the boardroom at Manor Place – Freddy Johnston in the chair, Iain Bell, Marco Chiappelli, Harry Johnston, Ian Dickson and Austin Merrills. A seventh director James Johnston, the chairman's brother, sent his apology for absence.

There were only two items on the agenda, the first a notification that the Hampshire Chonicle, at Winchester, might be for sale following the death the previous November of its owner, Mrs Monica Woodhouse. Freddy Johnston recalled that when he had last shown an interest in the weekly title Mrs Woodhouse's dog had attacked him.

But it was the second agenda item headed "Flotation – full listing Stock Exchange" that held the directors' attention.

The chairman reported on discussions he had held in London with the company's financial advisers, Hill, Samuel and Company, to consider Johnstons' future development and, in particular, whether it would be appropriate to seek a listing on the Stock Exchange.

The expert opinion was optimistic. The City merchant bankers advised that Johnstons was indeed suitable for a full listing and had offered their views on the likely range of price earnings ratios, yields and other relevant financial information.

The minutes record that a "full discussion" took place at the end of which Freddy Johnston moved that the company should seek a listing for its ordinary share capital. His brother Harry seconded the proposal and the other directors gave their unanimous approval.

The meeting ended at 10.30am – it had taken just 75 minutes to take the most momentous decision in Johnstons' 142 year history. Soon the family firm with its roots in Falkirk would head off in a new direction, with all the attendant risks and exciting opportunities this presented.

The West Sussex County Times: a newspaper of characters

Newspaper offices everywhere have a habit of throwing up characters, from the amazingly brilliant to the downright eccentric. Johnston Press is no exception.

But the West Sussex County Times, in Horsham, can lay claim to two of the most fascinating people to grace the history of the group – one of whom became a virtual recluse; the other a gifted refugee who defied the odds to rise from lowly clerk to chairman.

Miss Suzanne Gooding was 31 years old when she became owner of the County Times in 1942 and she continued to run it with ruthless efficiency until her death, aged 76, in 1987, all the while becoming more eccentric and reclusive. Some of her staff did not see her for years, if at all, but never a week passed by without which she made her presence felt.

Miss Gooding, later to become Mrs Terence H. Green, was the third generation of women to own the Sussex newspaper since 1894, inheriting the company from her unmarried aunt.

Her views on how a newspaper should be run were distinctive, to say the least, and she wasted no time in putting them into practice. And they worked. Circulation soared from around 10,000 copies a week at the end of the war to 20,0000 when the County Times celebrated its centenary in 1969, and then continued to climb.

The main plank of her policy was a high proportion of local news – never less than 50 per cent. It was not unusual for advertisements to be left out to make way for news – but that was in the days before finance directors and target-seeking ad managers – although a 70:30 ratio later became the norm.

To accommodate the high story count the pagination regularly reached 20 broadsheet news pages of eight columns, with no more than a couple of columns of advertising per page. It was a huge undertaking for the small editorial team.

The content of the paper was unmatched by any other publication in the region and led to a famous quote at a Newspaper Society meeting from the managing director of the Brighton Evening Argus. ⟹

> " Her views on how a newspaper should be run were distinctive, to say the least, and she wasted no time in putting them into practice. And they worked "

"Even if a mouse farts it will be in the County Times on Friday," he declared to applause and laughter.

In her first 20 years at the helm Mrs Green personally supervised every aspect of the newspaper but by the time David Briffett was appointed editor in 1977 she had already become reclusive and rarely ventured from her home at Buxted, a village 40 miles away in East Sussex. Yet nothing escaped her attention.

Her editors were required to mark up a paper each week with the name of every reporter and photographer against the stories and pictures they had contributed. She then drew up a league table, obsessed with volume and content.

Mrs Green took no account of circumstances so that a reporter who had, say, spent three days in court producing one story was marked down while those who spent their days, and evenings, producing scores of filler paragraphs were promoted up the league.

Briffett bore the brunt of her displeasure when the tally dropped, but even so he met her only four times in 10 years. Communication was usually by typewritten memo from her home – the reason for the resignation of a previous editor who had been warned that a dip in circula-tion would not be tolerated, even though this occurred in summer when sales traditionally fall.

But there were "brownie points" too, and Briffett knew that he had only to run a story on one of her three favourite topics, the postal service, refuse collection and the health service, to earn a commendation.

Mrs Green believed that her editors should become an integral part of the community, always on the front line. Thus when the offices closed for the day the telephone was switched through to the editor's home so that he could deal with complaints and queries, generally from advertisers and newsagents, and occasionally lorry drivers who had lost their way when delivering newsprint. Christmas Day was no exception and irate callers ruined several turkey dinners.

At one time the telephone number of the West Sussex County Times was also very similar to that of the local branch of The Samaritans. It was not unusual for the editor to be woken in the middle of the night to find a suicidal person on the other end of the line.

The wives of prospective editors and managers were not exempt from Mrs Green's attention, and she had been known to subject them to a most searching interview to ensure their suitability to accompany their husbands on newspaper business. Her moral standards were such that one manager was dismissed when she discovered he and his wife had divorced.

Marriage was important to Mrs Green, perhaps because of her own sad experience. Her fiance was killed at Arnhem in the second world war and when she finally married Yorkshire businessman, Terence Green, this lasted only 12 years before he, too, died in 1967.

From then on she rarely ventured from Orchard House, her country home at Buxted, a mansion with rolling lawns offering splendid views over the South Downs. There she lived in splendid isolation with only a chauffeur and a housekeeper to look after her needs.

However, an office at the newspaper's Market Square premises in Horsham was retained for her use, although she never visited it for at least the last 15 years of her life. "Mrs Green's Room", which included an en suite toilet, shiny board room $\Longrightarrow$

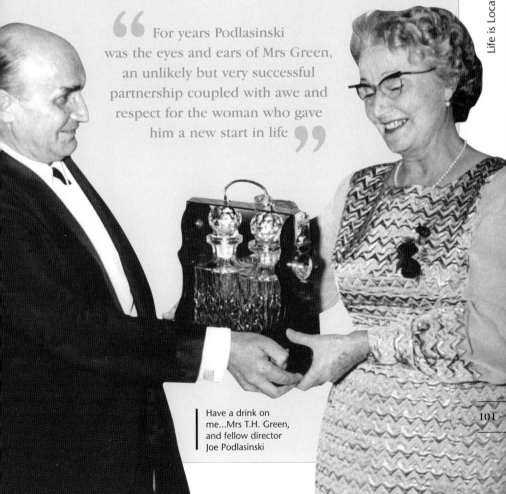

> For years Podlasinski was the eyes and ears of Mrs Green, an unlikely but very successful partnership coupled with awe and respect for the woman who gave him a new start in life

Have a drink on me...Mrs T.H. Green, and fellow director Joe Podlasinski

table and cocktail cabinet was cleaned and polished regularly, just in case the proprietor paid a surprise visit.

Mrs Green, who by then spent much of her time ill in bed, had only one regular contact from her newspaper – her joint managing director Joseph Podlasinski, who visited her every Friday to take along a marked copy of the paper and the week's trading accounts.

It was usually after one of those visits that she despatched her chauffeur back to Horsham with a memo to the editor, and woe betide him if the story count or the sales figures had dipped. For Mrs Green there was only one way – and that was up.

The most dramatic of Briffett's four meetings with his boss was when he and his fellow four directors were summonsed to Buxted for a crisis board meeting in 1979. Each was ordered to arrive at 15 minute intervals, unaware of the reason for the call, and interviewed individually by Mrs Green from her sick bed. No collusion between them was allowed.

There was only one topic: the Horsham Advertiser free newspaper that had been launched two weeks earlier to ward off competition from a new publication in the town.

"Close it down," she ordered with headmistress-like sternness. "My company does not trade in free newspapers."

The reply from each director was the same – like it or not a free newspaper was necessary to protect the West Sussex County Times, and in the end their wise counsel prevailed.

The impromptu board meeting ended in Mrs Green's sumptuous lounge, where she appeared from her bedroom and shared large glasses of whisky with her fellow directors. Time was called when Podlasinski pushed back his chair and knocked over the standard lamp.

"She was an amazing lady, strikingly good looking and very determined," recalled Briffett. "The Iron Lady of the provincial press – that's how I saw her."

Briffett maintained that Mrs Green always had a twinkle in her eye and that there was a softer, kinder person behind the autocratic exterior. He was proved right when she died and in her will left a small sum of money to every member of staff from her £3 million estate.

Her memory lives on in Horsham today thanks to the £1million she left in trust to be distributed to the elderly of the district. Since 1987 the

> **"** She was an amazing lady, strikingly good looking and very determined. The Iron Lady of the provincial press – that's how I saw her **"**
>
> David Briffett

> Joseph Podlasinski mastered the language within a year and passed an Oxford examination. Reading the West Sussex County Times was an essential part of his studies

Suzanne Green Charitable Trust had paid out thousands of pounds to those in need.

Another condition of her will was a clause requiring those remaining in charge of the company to retain control and continue its success. The directors decided the best way to honour her wishes was to negotiate a management buy-out from the executors, only to be pipped at the post when a London company submitted a better offer only hours before they were due to sign-up.

Acting chairman Joseph Podlasinski was alarmed and rang Freddy Johnston, with whom he had enjoyed a close relationship for years. A scrambled third bid was put together and in 1988, a year after Mrs Green's death, the West Sussex County Times became part of Johnston Press.

Podlasinski stayed on as chairman and managing director until his retirement in 1990 – the crowning achievement of a man who arrived with nothing and worked his way to the top.

For years he was the eyes and ears of Mrs Green, an unlikely but very successful partnership coupled with awe and respect for the woman who gave him a new start in life.

Podlasinski – "Mr Joseph" to colleagues who were unable to pronounce his tongue-twisting surname – was born Jozef Jan Podlasinski in 1920 in the large Polish county town of Bydgoszcz *(Bidgosh)*. He and his family were among thousands forced to flee in 1939 when Hitler's troops flooded across the border.

On their return they faced a very different life under the jackboot, Joseph forced into a labour camp to build roads. By 1943 he had had enough and with a friend made a daring and dangerous escape, ending up in Southern France – the start of an eventful journey that finally brought him to England in 1946.

Joseph's war saw him link up with the Maquis, the French underground movement, and take part in action in Italy with the Polish Army during the final days of hostilities.

Unwilling to submit to the Communists now running Poland, Joseph became one of thousands of displaced persons across Europe. Many of them arrived in England, and it was as part of the advance party of the Polish Resettlement Corps that he was sent to a new camp being set up at Five Oaks, on the outskirts of Horsham.

Joseph did not speak a word of English, but with the aid of camp lessons and a correspondence ⟹

The association between Mrs Green and Podlasinski, which began as the dominating female boss and the humble accounts clerk, developed into a formidable business partnership and a close friendship

course he mastered the language within a year and passed an Oxford examination. Reading the West Sussex County Times was an essential part of his studies.

Was it this that impressed Suzanne Gooding, in her fifth year of ownership, when in 1947 Podlasinski responded to her advertisement for a bookeeper and got the job?

His rise through the newspaper's ranks was ever upward – as an advertisement salesman, and by 1953 advertisement manager; general manager in 1964; joint managing director with the now widowed Mrs Green in 1974. He was a natural choice to succeed her as chairman when she died.

Podlasinski also became a happily married family man in his adopted country. He and his wife Halina, another refugee with an equally harrowing tale to tell, met and wed at the refugee camp outside Horsham. Their first child was born in 1953 while they were still living in a nissen hut. It was only a stroke of good luck that enabled them buy their first proper home – Joseph won £190 on the pools, enough for a deposit, and another £20 the week after.

When Mrs Green moved into her graceful, but reclusive retirement in the Sussex countryside, she looked to

Podlasinski to run her business, his persuasive nature and business acumen a perfect foil for her fabled intransigence. In return she showered him with shares until he owned about a third of the business.

The arrangement worked for 20 years – the weekly pilgrimage to Buxted, cocktails in the magnificently furnished drawing room, the orders conveyed back to the staff at Horsham, her comments noted and acted upon.

"He threw his whole life into the County Times. He had a passion for the paper and, like her, he believed it had to be the best in every respect," recalled Briffett. "He was a workaholic – always the first to arrive and the last to leave, Saturdays included."

Thus the association between Mrs Green and Podlasinski, which began as the dominating female boss and the humble accounts clerk, developed into a formidable business partnership and a close friendship. He and his wife were at her bedside when she died – loyal and faithful to the end.

Joseph died in 1995 at the age of 75. Halina later moved to Cambridge to be with her family.

"He wasn't a trained newspaperman but he just seemed to know what he was doing," said Briffett. "He was a natural."

Chapter Four

The City expects...

Friday morning in the City of London was even more hectic than usual, a sure sign that the weekend was only hours away. Blue skies overhead signalled the prospect of plenty of sunshine to come, but still the streets were in deep shadow as the warming rays struggled to rise above the towering edifices of stone and concrete.

The pavements echoed to the sounds of a thousand feet. Stockbrokers, bankers, analysts, secretaries scurried on their way to work – the start of another day, just like the one before, and they knew the routine well.

But this morning, April 29, 1988, there were two strangers in the crowd, insignificant and anonymous to those around them, those busy folk intent on their own business, heads down and wrapped up in their own thoughts.

Johnston Press managing director Iain Bell and finance director Marco Chiappelli strode out purposefully to the Moorgate offices of stockbrokers Phillips and Drew.

D-Day had arrived, the day on which a new name was about to join the other media companies already listed on the London Stock Exchange.

But there was still a vital, last minute decision to be taken – conditions had to be just right for the flotation and now all that was needed was a word of approval from the two men.

Weeks before the issue price for Johnston's 23,800,000 shares had been the subject of much discussion but had only been endorsed at 122p the previous evening at a directors' meeting with lawyers and financial advisers, valuing the company at £29 million.

But share prices are sensitive to many influences – overnight trading in New York, Tokyo or Hong Kong; poor results or profits warning from a blue chip performer; political decisions here and across the Atlantic; world events in far away places; even the weather.

That morning the signs were good, very good. There was nothing in the news bulletins or market reports to suggest that this would be anything but a normal business day.

Shortly before the Stock Exchange opened at 8am an excitable Chiappelli gave the go-ahead. "Press the button," he yelled, his Latin temperament getting the better of him for once.

Phillips and Drew did the rest, and within minutes the Johnston Press flotation had flashed across the Stock Exchange screens. Because of recent upheaval on the financial markets it was only the second flotation in two years involving a Scottish company of any description.

As expected, trading opened at the offer price of 122p and even improved slightly. Not exactly a brisk trade, but considering that the issue of four million new Johnston shares had been oversubscribed it was a fair performance on day one. In the years since the share price has never fallen below its issue level, even during the rocky years of the early 1990s, the most difficult trading period for the printing and publishing industry for more than a decade.

Freddy Johnston followed events from his office at Manor Place, trusting implicitly in the judgement of his two lieutenants. He had agreed to stay behind in Edinburgh to handle the public relations side of the flotation and now he had a good story to tell.

In numerous interviews with newspaper, television and radio journalists he related the Johnston story from its grass roots beginnings to becoming a significant player in both Scotland and England. It was, he said, a proud day and it was just the start of a new chapter.

Johnston, as we have seen, had been instrumental in raising the subject of flotation and persuading shareholders that this was in the best long-term interests of the company.

It was also very much in their own best interests. At last a true market value was placed on shares that until now had had a nominal value of a few pence each and could not be sold or exchanged beyond the confines of the Johnston family – a condition that had been laid down when the company was incorporated in 1928.

The core family – Freddy Johnston, his wife Ann and their two sons, Harry Johnston and his two daughters, and another brother, Jim – held about 70 per cent of shares and they had no intention of selling. But among the remaining 30 per cent of shareholders were those who had inherited their holdings, had no sentimental regard for the company or interest in working for it, and who would like the opportunity to realise their investment at a fair price.

Several of them had already expressed an interest in selling their holdings if the price was right although none of them was pressing to do so at the time. But Freddy Johnston was well aware of what had happened at another private company, Heart of England Newspapers (now owned by Johnston Press), where shareholders had eventually forced the sale of the business when they realised what their investment could be worth.

Freddy Johnston and his brother Harry had faced an ethical dilemma. Both felt that it would have been improper to buy shares themselves from those outside the immediate family circle in the knowledge that soon they might become much more valuable.

"That," said Johnston "would have been dishonourable. We did buy one or two small holdings when they were going to be sold anyway but we always advised people to hang on. Anything else would have been a form of insider dealing and that just wasn't our way of doing things.

"Ideally we wanted to create a situation whereby passengers who wanted to get off the bus could do so without damaging the vehicle."

There were good financial reasons, too, why the company's long-term interests would be best served by flotation. Alert to the plight of Heart of England Newspapers, the directors were anxious to secure the independence of Johnstons, enable it to grow and have easier access to finance for future acquisitions. It was considered important to reduce the gearing of the company – the relationship between assets and debt – which increased every time money was borrowed to support an acquisition. This is turn led to a clear reality that the expansion programme could not be supported indefinitely by remaining a private company saddled with expensive bank loans.

Once the restrictions of the 1928 articles of association had been removed the opportunity would also exist for making acquisitions involving new share issues. This was a factor that proved crucial a few years later in the purchase of T.R. Beckett Ltd, at Eastbourne, when it was clear that for tax reasons Johnston shares were preferred by some shareholders to straight cash.

All the signs indicated that early 1988 was the time to act, the time to move forward into a new era. Profits were rising, the acquisition of newspapers in Derbyshire, Yorkshire and Lancashire had gone well and by then the company had also established a base in the South of England.

Flotation made instant paper millionaires of some Johnston shareholders and even within the public company the immediate family retained a 58 per cent interest. But in a tough business

All the signs indicated that early 1988 was the time to act, the time to move forward into a new era

environment there was little room for sentiment – hereditary businesses were not without their problems and, as Johnston Press acquisitions have proved many times, were vulnerable to takeover.

"Most family companies, as generation succeeds generation, reach a point where the majority of shareholders no longer have a day to day interest in running the business," explained Johnston. "It was certainly true of Johnstons and many other companies that at least until the 1960s they were run as a form of occupational therapy – to provide jobs for members of the family, and not always the right ones.

"It was also quite difficult to motivate non-family people who worked for the company because they couldn't become shareholders under the restrictive articles of association – in our case that privilege was restricted to descendants of the original 1928 subscribers."

Once the Johnston directors had decided to go public they embarked on a consultation exercise among all the shareholders, large and small, and found an overwhelming majority in favour. But tracking some of them down proved difficult.

The quest to find Richard Neilson led to New York, where he had become a Catholic priest. Freddy Johnston's personal assistant, Norma Forbes, was given the task of speaking to him and in her soft Scottish accent asked if he could be brought to the telephone from the "seminar" that he was attending. "Lady," came back the American voice. "This is a seminary".

A succession of complex, technical meetings were arranged, taking Johnston, Bell and Chiappelli on a steep learning curve as they quickly familiarised themselves with the intricacies of the City and the strict rules and regulations surrounding a new initial public offering.

The main flotation team consisted of the issuing house (Hill Samuel and Co), stockbrokers (Phillips and Drew), stockbrokers to the placing (Bell Lawrie Ltd), solicitors to the company (MacRoberts), solicitors to the placing (Slaughter and May), auditors (Alexander Sloan and Co), reporting accountants (Ernst and Whinney), registrars and principal bankers (Royal Bank of Scotland) and financial public relations (Buchanans).

Frequent journeys to London for interminable discussions became routine during a frenetic period of activity. Not only were the Johnston directors endeavouring to run the business day to day but for part of the time were also involved in buying the West

Sussex County Times and the Chesterfield Gazette.

One of the most exhausting tasks of the flotation was the verification process insisted on by Glasgow lawyers MacRoberts, and London solicitors Slaughter and May, in drawing up the formal placing document – a spiral-bound, 50-page booklet giving precise information about the history, trading record and prospects of Johnston Press.

It meant that every entry, every date, every figure had to be double checked and authenticated, even to the extent of retrieving documents from the earliest days of the business.

The placing provided a valuable insight into the working of a successful newspaper company – information that pleased City analysts and persuaded investors that this was an opportunity worthy of serious consideration.

The three executive directors embarked on a hectic round of presentations to key figures in the City, but it was not just the past performance and future prospects of the company that were subject to critical analysis. Every bit as important was the calibre of the management team – in other words Johnston, Bell and Chiappelli had to convince potential investors of their own credentials to run the business and take it forward. It was a totally new experience being subjected to such public inspection, and all the more intense as newcomers to the scene.

"They liked the combination of the high Church of England, Presbyterian Scot and Roman Catholic. I always stressed that if the world could get on as well as we did there was hope for everyone," said Bell.

Their individual styles shone through – Johnston statesman-like and thoughtful, Chiappelli with sheafs of financial statistics and Bell speaking off the cuff – "just look into people's faces, the cynics, the old ones, the youngsters, the important ones and decide where they're all coming from."

Even on flotation day the busy round of presentations continued, something Bell and Chiappelli had almost forgotten the previous night as they over-indulged at the bar of their hotel near Piccadilly Circus. But a dawn telephone call from Philips and Drew reminding them of their busy schedule galvanised them into action before they were finally able to catch an early evening flight back to Edinburgh.

The principal reasons given for the placing were to enable the company to raise new equity capital to assist in financing the group's expansion and offer flexibility in financing future acquisi-

tions. It was also felt that a Stock Exchange listing would substantially enhance the group's status within the industry.

Of the 6,110,350 Ordinary shares being placed 4,000,000 were newly issued, aimed at raising £4.4 million – enough money to pay off the existing debts. The balance of 2,110,350 shares was being sold by existing shareholders, but not the immediate Johnston family who were not offering any of their 14,034,030 shares for sale.

In outlining the group's prospects the placing report was in bullish mood. "Johnston Press has been successful in making acquisitions . . . the directors believe that there are a number of privately-owned businesses to which the group could apply its proven skills," it was stated confidently.

The group's trading record over the preceding five years justified this optimism, with pre-tax profits doubling to £3,029,000 in 1987 on a turnover of £29,565,000, an increase of almost 25 percent since 1983. At the time of flotation Johnston Press comprised of 16 wholly-owned subsidiaries, of which the latest addition to the portfolio, the West Sussex County Times, had yet to make its contribution to group profits.

"Despite often strong competition the group has continued to grow and prosper," added the report.

It also recorded that investors were buying a stake in 50 newspaper titles, comprising 29 paid-for newspapers and 21 frees. Circulation of the group's paid-for local weekly publications had been ABC certified as 380,829 in the six months to June, 1987, while free distribution amounted to 800,000 copies weekly.

But in a national context Johnston Press was still a relatively small player, albeit an ambitious one. UK circulation of all paid-for weeklies in early 1988 was estimated at more than seven million while total free newspaper distribution was about 40 million.

On March 31, 1988, the group had 1,079 staff – 480 in production and distribution, 240 in editorial and photographic, 175 in advertising, 172 in administration and 12 others. There were also 109 part-time employees.

For the first time employees of Johnston Press were given the opportunity to buy shares in the company and many did so. In offices from Kirkcaldy to Horsham there was a sudden interest in the Stock Exchange prices in the morning papers, coupled with a new feeling of having a real stake in their employer's performance.

Just about everyone was well satisfied when the first day's "public" trading came to an end on April 29. There had been no hiccups and analysts were openly discussing the merits of Johnston Press as a well-run company with good prospects. That opinion was subsequently reiterated by brokers and institutional shareholders who attended a series of presentations in the months following flotation.

The financial media, too, seemed suitably impressed. The business page of the Yorkshire Post – later to become a Johnston title – said the flotation would recharge the group's financial resources, halving gearing to 25 percent, and pave the way for future acquisitions.

It quoted chairman Ted *(sic)* Johnston as already "chatting up" a number of possible takeover targets and advised investors that Johnston Press was "An attractive long-term share."

The group's performance during the remainder of 1988 fully justified this confidence. Within a week of flotation the bullish mood was reflected in a report to the monthly board meeting, which described business at the West Sussex County Times as "booming."

In May steps were taken to acquire the Morley Advertiser, a small weekly newspaper in West Yorkshire, at a cost of £50,000. Talks were also opened with father and son Ian and Nick Linney for their Nottinghamshire newspaper and printing company, W and J.Linney Ltd, publishers of the Mansfield Chronicle and Advertiser ("Chad") and the Worksop Guardian.

Although the Johnston overture was rejected it was deemed sensible to keep in touch in the hope of a future acquisition. (Patience finally paid off in 1995 when Linney's newspaper interests were acquired and they now form part of North Notts Newspapers.)

At an upbeat board meeting in October, 1988, various seemingly imminent opportunities to acquire other regional newspapers were identified, including the evening and weekly titles published by the Halifax Courier Ltd. in West Yorkshire. The possibility of expanding the group's activities to mainland Europe was also discussed at length.

The directors' enthusiasm was understandable on the back of trading results for the first nine months of the financial year, which showed a 38 percent increase in net operating profit to £3,044,814, compared with the same period in 1987. Most of the growth had come from operations at Chesterfield, Wakefield and Horsham.

By the end of the year the performance of the majority of the Johnston centres in England and Scotland was being described as "exceptional" – sweet music indeed to the ears of investors. But could the momentum be maintained?

The manner in which the budgets for 1989 were prepared was a new experience for the Johnston executives. Getting the sums right had always involved a mixture of sound judgment, intuition and a degree of crystal ball gazing. But if forecasts were inaccurate they had been answerable only to a small group of relatively passive and understanding shareholders.

Now many more people – City investment groups, analysts, stockbrokers among them – were looking to Johnston Press to live up to its flotation promises . . . "good prospects for growth in the current year and in the longer term."

Finance director Chiappelli had spent hours pouring over revenue projections from around the group before presenting his consolidated budget for the year ahead. Finally a pre-tax profit of £5.1 million was agreed as the target. Now all that remained was to deliver. They did, by a comfortable £700,000.

It had always been recognised that organic growth alone would not produce the profits that investors were expecting. Freddy Johnston knew that he must redouble his efforts on the acquisition trail and 1989 saw two additional newspapers join the group.

Of these the Belper News, established in 1896 to serve the thriving south Derbyshire mill town – home to the world's first water-powered cotton spinning factory – helped to further strengthen the company's growing influence in the North Midlands. Contiguous to the G.C. Brittain titles published in nearby Ripley, but not in direct competition with them, it proved to be a modest but successful acquisition and marked a return to the company from which it had been sold for £1 while under Wilfred Edmunds' ownership.

The acquisition of the Mexborough-based South Yorkshire Times from Reed Regional Newspapers, later to become Newsquest, was a convenient arrangement between the two companies which paved the way for the exchange of the Doncaster Free Press and the

Bury Times seven years later. The deal, for security reasons, was given the codename Terrier.

Johnstons brought a period of calm and stability to a newspaper that had had a succession of owners in recent years. In 1977, shortly after celebrating its centenary, it was bought by the American company St Regis International, which in turn sold it on to Reed International five years later.

When the newspaper, which was founded in July, 1877, was offered to Johnstons it was viewed as another useful addition to its interests in the region but in truth the business, which Reed had found difficult to make profitable, continued to face a series of external pressures that in turn resulted in its performance consistently failing to live up to early expectations.

Situated in the centre of the "coal triangle" formed by Doncaster, Rotherham and Barnsley, the mining town of Mexborough has seen much of its lifeblood drain away with the precipitous decline of the Yorkshire coalfield.

The reorganisation of local government in 1974 also robbed Mexborough of its administrative independence, while the creation of the new county of South Yorkshire only served to cause confusion over the circulation area of the South Yorkshire Times. This remained rooted in the close-knit area of Mexborough and surrounding villages, and not a county title as its name suggests.

Over the years scores of aspiring young journalists have been given their first taste of newspaper life at the South Yorkshire Times, pounding the streets of the surrounding mining communities in the search for snippets of news. Among those who had good reason to look back with gratitude at the weekly diet of district parish pump stories was broadcaster and chat show host Michael Parkinson, who began his career at Mexborough as a trainee reporter.

BY NOW Johnston Press had diversified its activities to include a number of print-related interests, most notably typesetting and commercial printing, but in 1990 it made a significant departure from its core activity with the purchase of the old-established firm of bookbinders and library

Broadcaster and chat show host Michael Parkinson began his career at Mexborough as a trainee reporter

In 1990 Johnston purchased bookbinders Dunn and Wilson Ltd

113

suppliers, Dunn and Wilson Ltd, of Falkirk.

To a large extent this additional diversification reflected the static state of the newspaper industry at the time with very few businesses for sale or even prepared to contemplate a sale. Repeated knocking on doors drew blank after blank with Johnstons merely joining a queue of other acquisition-minded companies.

It was becoming increasingly difficult to fulfil the flotation pledge of continued growth by acquisition even though finance was available to do so from year-on-year profits and the proceeds of the share issue at the time of going public.

Since its formation in 1909 Dunn and Wilson had grown to become one of the country's leading library book binders, journal book binders and suppliers of books to public libraries – a market that was estimated to be worth over £100 million in the United Kingdom.

It also operated a specialist operation at Morley to strengthen the binding of books before being sold on to public libraries, who required more robust bindings than those applied to standard editions found in shops, and a bindery in Huddersfield, also in West Yorkshire. Both had been acquired as the book re-binding industry grew to a peak of activity in the 1950s and the Huddersfield business occupied a niche corner of the market by concentrating on the binding of specialist journals and book conservation work.

In the 1960s Dunn and Wilson established its library book selling activities through the Morley Book Company Ltd, and this subsequently grew, in turnover terms, to represent the major part of the group's activities, accounting for about nine per cent of the UK market.

Throughout that time the business had been very much a family affair and for a period there were five Dunn brothers on the board of directors. But as so often happens, the family involvement had become fragmented with succeeding generations until in the late Eighties questions were being asked about its future direction.

Selling out was one option. Going public was another, but the company was judged to be neither big enough nor profitable enough for this to happen.

In 1977 Freddy Johnston had been appointed non-executive chairman of Dunn and Wilson, a move supported by the firm's auditors, the accountancy firm Deloitte, and he was the first person outside the Dunn family to hold that position since the company's foundation. But his credentials fitted the requirements ideally –

experience of running a family business and a considerable knowledge of the printing industry.

Prior to Johnston's appointment as chairman Hugh Dunn, a younger member of the Dunn family, had become chief executive and under the direction of the two the company enjoyed a renewed period of prosperity. Dunn later became a director of Johnston Press for several years. A bindery was opened in 1979 in Ireland, at Wicklow, south of Dublin, and existing links in Australia, where the company had had a joint venture since 1974, were also developed. This included the expansion of the Melbourne-based library book selling activities which had traded under the name of Dunn and Mason, and the purchase of a library bookbinder in Sydney.

After negotiations with the Australian partner, Bill Mason, it was eventually decided to end the joint arrangements and split the businesses. Mason took the bookselling operation while Dunn and Wilson assumed sole ownership of the Sydney bindery, which traded under the name of L.J. Cullen.

"I was keen on developing the Australian business because the British library market was quite clearly finite and was not going to be the recipient of unlimited amounts of public money," recalled Johnston.

With this in mind the Australian interests were developed further with the acquisition of two additional bookbinders in Melbourne, Apollo and Moon – names which caused a wry smile at the time of the American lunar landings – which were amalgamated on a single site in expanded premises. Both companies had been acquired before the Johnston purchase but after the split with Mason. For a brief period activities Down Under also included a bindery in Perth, Western Australia.

The company's overseas interests accounted for more than nine per cent of group turnover, with the Australian operation eventually making a substantial contribution to Dunn and Wilson's annual profits of around £1 million in the first year, on a turnover of £17 million. Bookbinding, especially, was a good business in which to be involved, requiring little in the way of expensive stock and with a steady flow of work rebinding books for public libraries and binding journals and periodicals for specialist customers such as universities and companies.

The purchase in 1990 of Dunn and Wilson, for £7.7 million, was the first substantial acquisition by Johnston Press since its flotation and was made all the easier given the close association between the two companies and the fact that they shared a common chairman, although Johnson himself took no part in the negotiations.

Talks with the Dunn family – codenamed Duke and Baron – were concluded quickly but ran into last minute problems when directors Marco Chiappelli and Ian Dickson travelled to Leeds in January, 1990, to sign the formal handover. New conditions for the sale were suddenly demanded by the Dunns and it was four o'clock the following morning when both sides finally put pen to paper. The Johnston team grabbed a couple of hours sleep at their hotel before catching the 8am flight to Edinburgh for a board meeting.

Shareholders were well pleased when profits were tripled within a few years and fully justified claims that the acquisition would not only broaden the group's base but would also enhance earnings.

Dunn and Wilson shareholders, too, reflected on the financial wisdom of the sale. They had received three new Johnston Press ordinary shares worth £1.50 each and £5.50 in cash for each of their own ordinary shares. Holders of preference shares were able to exchange these for an equivalent number of Johnston preference shares.

Nevertheless, the early trading results hinted at problems that had not been apparent before the takeover with the Australian operation reporting a hefty deficit when the quarterly management accounts to December, 1989, became available. The overall profit of £85,000 compared very unfavourably with the profit of £379,000 for the same period in 1988. Worse still, the news was received on the day Bell and Chiappelli were due to make an important presentation to investors, some of whom had been highly sceptical about the lateral diversification away from newspapers.

As a first step the bookselling and bookbinding operations of Dunn and Wilson were split into separate divisions, the Australian business was told to report directly to Bell and a management reorganisation was put in place in which the group managing director and finance director were high profile casualties. At the same time the Dunn and Wilson head office at Pegasus House, Leeds, was closed.

Bell, meanwhile, was sent to Australia to investigate. His report on his return said the company there was "in a financial mess" and the morale of employees at an extremely low ebb. The resignation of the managing director in Australia, Austin Dunn, a member of the Dunn family, followed this.

The turnaround was nothing short of spectacular and in June,

1991, a Johnston board meeting was told that results from Australia were "excellent", especially from the Sydney operation.

In 1997 all the group's book-related interests – now including a bindery in Bristol and another bookselling business in Huddersfield, Greenhead Books, which had been bought in 1992 – were sold as part of a major policy change to concentrate solely on its core activity of publishing newspapers. By then the Dunn and Wilson arm of the company had served its purpose of contributing materially to group profits during a period up to the mid-Nineties, when newspaper acquisitions had been difficult to come by. What's more, the City had been happy that profit growth and increased earnings per share had been maintained.

The bookbinding arm of Dunn and Wilson was the subject of a venture capital backed management buy-out, and continued to operate as Riley, Dunn and Wilson from the same site in Falkirk, which it shared with the Falkirk Herald. The library bookselling business was sold to a separate management buy-out team.

By then wholesale bookselling had become a far more competitive and less profitable activity with the ending of the Net Book Agreement, a registered restrictive practice that had operated since 1900 and which set the prices at which books could be sold. A bookseller who dared to sell a book at less than the agreed price was simply not supplied with any more books by that publisher – needless to say, only the foolhardy stepped out of line.

The agreement had been examined in 1962 by the Restrictive Practices Court, which decided that if the NBA did not exist the prices of most books would rise and fewer literary and scholarly books would be published.

The agreement had been considered again in 1984, but matters were brought to a head in 1995 when several major publishers unilaterally withdrew from the agreement and in 1997 the Restrictive Practices Court ruled that it was against the public interest and was therefore illegal.

The collapse of the agreement strengthened large bookstore chains and brought down book prices. The small independent bookshops were most affected – more than one in ten independent booksellers folded between 1996 and 2001.

It was not good news for Dunn and Wilson. Under the old agreement it had been allowed to give a maximum discount of 10 per cent to public libraries, which still left a healthy profit margin. Now new suppliers appeared on the scene, undercutting prices to

> The collapse of the Net Book Agreement strengthened large bookstore chains and brought down book prices... it was not good news for Dunn and Wilson

Joe Hale, the former chairman of T.R. Beckett who became a Johnston Press director

such an extent that the viability of the operation was thrown into question.

Freddy Johnston admitted to certain sadness when the business was sold. "But I recognised the commercial viability of the decision – times were changing.

"The company had been overtaken by advances in technology and a new regime in the world of books – funding made available to public libraries was restricted and more information was being stored electronically. The need to keep bound copies of journals and reports was much diminished."

Johnston Press had good reason to thank Dunn and Wilson for its contribution to the group, especially during a newspaper advertising downturn in the early-1990s, which saw revenue at many centres put under pressure. During that lean period good results from selling and binding books provided a welcome boost to profits.

In 1991 the group had added another small Derbyshire title, the 110-year-old Ilkeston Advertiser, to its portfolio in the county. But this was merely a prelude to a series of larger acquisitions that were to follow.

Freddy Johnston and his colleagues had developed a long-standing friendship with Joe Hale, the chairman of the Sussex newspaper group T. R. Beckett Ltd, of Eastbourne, and had already expressed a keen interest in buying the company if it came onto the market. The close relationship had been further cemented by participation in the annual Newspaper Society golf tournament with Iain Bell and Marco Chiappelli showing their prowess on the greens and Johnston, a non-golfer, dispensing hospitality at the 19th hole.

Johnston had the utmost admiration for the ageing Hale, a war hero who was awarded the Military Cross, mentioned in despatches, fought at Salerno and Anzio and saw action with Tito's partisans in Yugoslavia. In 2003 he was featured in a BBC television documentary, The Boys from 113, which told the story of the 113th Field Regiment and the Worthing "boys" from the 228 Field Battery.

The former London lawyer, who specialised in tax and trust affairs, subsequently joined the Johnston Press board and gave a number of years of distinguished service as a non-executive director and chairman of the audit committee.

"He was shrewd, dead straight and had a very good and forward looking attitude," enthused Johnston of Hale.

The Beckett corporate structure was far from simple with a diversity of shareholders who had inherited an interest in the company through the gradual dissipation of shares, including the family of Hale's wife, Gwen, who had acquired a major interest in 1958.

Unusually, one of the largest blocks of shares belonged to the Eastbourne Health Authority, which had been bequeathed a substantial interest in Becketts in the will of T.R. Beckett's eldest son, Arthur. This arose out of family squabbles and litigation, to the extent that when he died in 1943 the childless Arthur decreed that his 41 per cent of the company's equity was to go to the Princess Alice Cottage Hospital, Eastbourne, on the death of his wife or last surviving sister. This occurred in 1957 by which time the National Health Service was in existence and the shares passed to the local hospital management committee, and subsequently to the health authority.

The involvement of the authority had a further complication when Beckett's chief executive Derrick Platt was appointed as its chairman in 1980 and held the position for the next 10 years. Very wisely, he declared his interest before accepting the post and withdrew from meetings whenever the Beckett shareholding was discussed.

This proved vital when an attempt was made to discredit both the company and Platt by a renegade Member of Parliament, who threatened to ask a question in the House of Commons about alleged restrictions in the payment of Becketts' dividends. Platt called in a favour from his friend and Eastbourne MP Ian Gow, who was later murdered by the IRA, and after feverish behind the scenes activity the question was never raised.

"It was political dirty tricks," said Platt. "Whoever was behind it wanted to embarrass us and the Government. Mrs Thatcher was being sniped at all the time and this was just another example."

The shares were of little direct value to the health authority, other than the annual dividends they earned, but there was no thought of selling them until an offer was received that was simply too good to refuse. The surprise bidder was the Senews (South-east news) subsidiary of East Midland Allied Press (Emap), which already had newspaper interests on the south coast including Lewes, Hastings and Bexhill.

Clearly, the further purchase of newspapers in Eastbourne and Worthing was seen as a sensible and logical development by Emap, and with a 40 per cent share in Becketts would have meant it was

THE

Eastbourne Gazette

AND FASHIONABLE INTELLIGENCER.

EASTBOURNE, MONDAY, JULY 11th, 1859.

The first edition of the Eastbourne Gazette, July 11th 1859

ideally placed to take overall control of that company, in which it had been showing an interest for years. But in business such things do not always work out as intended.

The Monopolies and Mergers Commission was alerted to the situation, called in the deal for scrutiny and in a ruling that pleased no one allowed the Emap purchase to proceed – with strings attached.

Emap was barred from taking overall control of the company without a further MMC hearing. In addition Becketts directors made it clear that Emap representation on the company's board would not be welcomed and the group was not allowed to buy any further shares.

The cuckoo in the nest was thus rendered impotent for the foreseeable future, a situation that was unsatisfactory for all concerned, especially Emap. The group was denied a say in a company in which it was the largest single shareholder, with about 40 per cent of the shares, and now saw its expansion plans thwarted.

But in summer 1992 events took a surprise turn. Fed up and frustrated, Emap became prepared to sever its links with Becketts. Chief executive Robin Miller was well aware of Johnston Press's ambitions to expand its south-east interests and also alert to the competition with its own Senews operation that would result, but nevertheless he responded favourably when approached about a deal.

Business dealings aside, Miller was curious to meet Freddy Johnston, about whom he had heard a great deal from his fellow

Emap board member, Richard Winfrey, a Newspaper Society colleague of the Scot. At one time there had even been talk about inviting Johnston to join the Emap board. "He had the reputation as a smooth-talking, charming, urbane character – a master seducer who made things happen," recalled Miller.

Although Miller left most of the negotiations to the director of Emap's newspapers division, Martin Lusby, his discussions with Johnston – "a formidable competitor" – formed the basis of a healthy mutual respect for each other that was to be tested several times in the years ahead.

In parallel discussions, Freddy Johnston talked at length with Beckett's chairman Hale and reached an agreement to buy the remaining issued share capital of the Eastbourne business, which by then was publishing seven paid-for weekly newspapers and three free distribution newspapers in East and West Sussex. The paid titles had a combined audited circulation of 73,123 and the distribution of the frees was more than 200,000.

The complete deal, codenamed Lord, was worth £12 million and suited all concerned – "The existing shareholders were getting a good price – it seemed at the time like a very good price – and it got everyone off the hook," recalled Johnston.

T.R. Beckett, chairman of the Eastbourne Gazette, 1908-1916

"We were well pleased with the acquisition, which brought with it some excellent titles and more than doubled our presence in Sussex. But by at last getting rid of that difficult shareholders' situation we had also removed a factor that had been inhibiting the development of Becketts."

While Hale was adamant that he would not sell the company to Emap he was far more favourably inclined towards Johnston Press. "But by then Emap had accepted the situation and co-operated fully in the sale," he said later.

Johnston's inititial offer was

well below what Hale and other principal shareholders considered a fair price for their company but when Freddy Johnston increased his bid by £3 million several weeks later this was accepted.

By then behind-the-scenes discussions had taken place in, of all places, South Africa. Coincidentally Joe Hale and his chief executive Derrick Platt were on holiday in Cape Town at the same time as Johnston's Iain Bell and the three combined business with pleasure at two evening meetings at the Mount Nelson Hotel, Cape Town.

"The broad terms of an agreement were thrashed out in total privacy a long way from home," recalled Platt. "We then went our separate ways."

It took just one further meeting at Hale's London club, the Army and Navy, to iron out the final detail. Hale extracted promises that there would be continuity of existing businesses, that the editorial policy of fairness and integrity that he had laid down would not change, and that staff contracts would be honoured.

Unexpectedly, he was invited to continue as chairman of Beckett's and also offered a seat on the Johnston board. "We've already been to the Stock Exchange and they think it's a very good idea," explained Freddy Johnston to the surprised 72-year-old.

It was agreed that Hale would shadow Iain Bell on his travels round the group's centres. "I had no intention of being a director of a company I knew little about," he said. "It was a very salutary experience. He's a very good hearted man, but also very hard. We used to leave the people we had seen quaking in their shoes."

Beckett's operations in the south east were centered on the fashionable and well-to-do seaside resort of Eastbourne, where the production facilities were also located. Its main publication, the Eastbourne Herald boasted the highest weekly paid circulation in Sussex and had been founded in 1920, having previously been an edition of the Sussex County Herald, in which the company had acquired an interest.

The Beckett family connection began in 1871 when a Yorkshireman, Thomas R. Beckett bought the Eastbourne Gazette and Fashionable Intelligencer and set up a printing and publishing company in the town. The Gazette had been established in 1859 by one Cyrus Grant and can proudly claim never to have missed a publication day since. The Gazette, with a circulation of around 12,000 in the Eastbourne, Hailsham and Seaford areas, is the only midweek paid-for weekly in a UK seaside town.

The Beckett acquisition also included the free distribution

Eastbourne Advertiser and the newspapers based a few miles further down the coast at Worthing, the scene of bitter rivalries for many years.

In 1924 the Worthing Herald had been started to challenge the old-established Worthing and Littlehampton Gazette and it was not until 1962 that the papers merged. Among Worthing's claims to fame are the town with the highest ratio of women to men in the country and also the town with the highest number of people aged over 80 – a fact which explains why retirement homes form such a significant part of the local economy.

Another Worthing newspaper, the free distribution Worthing Guardian which had been established in 1984, was also acquired in 1992 and run from Johnston's base in Horsham.

In 1950 the Shoreham Herald was launched as an extra to the Worthing Herald and in 1953 Beckett's bought its only remaining rival, the Eastbourne Chronicle, and combined it with its main Eastbourne title.

From 1926 until its closure in the 1960s Becketts also published the Sussex County Magazine, a high quality monthly journal with a somewhat highbrow readership which was the forerunner of the glossy county magazines of today. When a lack of advertising forced its demise the Duke of Edinburgh expressed his sadness at the need to close "such an excellent publication."

As a result of the Becketts deal Johnstons also found themselves the owners of a subsidiary company in Sussex, Shoesmith and Etheridge Ltd, wholesalers in stationery, toys and fancy goods for sale to small shops such as newsagents. The company, which remained in Johnston hands until 1999, had been bought by Becketts in 1969 and supplied scores of customers from its Uckfield warehouse in an area extending to Southampton to the west, Reading to the north-west, the Thames to the north and Kent to the east. Subsequently this activity was extended further with the purchase of the Ipswich wholesalers F.W. Pawsey and Sons and William B Harris Ltd, of Northampton.

In the three years before the takeover Becketts had, like most regional newspapers publishers, experienced difficult trading conditions, largely due to economic recession and a consequent decline in advertising revenues, mainly as a result of the collapse of the housing market in the south east of England

This had seen pre-tax profits fall from a high of £1,523,000 in 1989 to £1,024,000 in 1991. But the position would have been

> **As a result of the Becketts deal Johnstons found themselves the owners of Shoesmith and Etheridge Ltd, wholesalers in stationery, toys and fancy goods for sale to small shops such as newsagents**

markedly worse but for the splendid performance of Shoesmith and Etheridge – a situation reminiscent of the way in which Dunn and Wilson had come to the rescue of Johnston Press profits during the same period.

While the operating profit on Beckett's newspaper publishing and printing had almost halved in three years – the unprecedented collapse of the property market had seriously undermined confidence – its stationery activities had grown by 27 percent in the same period, resulting in an operating profit of £106,000 on a turnover of £2.4 million. Johnston shareholders were told of a similar trend in 1992 and of the potential for future profits growth from this sector of the business if they approved the acquisition.

In recommending the Becketts purchase to them, Freddy Johnston remarked that recession should be regarded as a fact of life for the foreseeable future. But while belt-tightening and strict cost controls were the order of the day the long-term target was for growth, and the value of linking the adjoining geographical markets of the West Sussex County Times and Becketts was regarded as crucial to this.

The deal, completed in September, 1992, was a cash and shares combination in which Becketts shareholders were alloted new Johnston Press shares worth £3.5 million as part of the £11.95 million package. The principal beneficiaries were chairman Joe Hale and his immediate family, who owned 15.5 per cent of the company, and Emap plc, who by then had a 37.1 per cent stake. As already noted, Hale was invited to stay on as non-executive chairman of Becketts for three years and was also given a non-executive seat on the Johnston board.

Yet another adjunct to the Becketts deal were two specialist publications, forming Outbound Newspapers, which had been part of the Eastbourne operation since the late 1980s. Both had been started in Bexhill and were aimed at people who were thinking of emigrating to South Africa or Canada.

Under Johnstons the Outbound activities have been expanded to five publications, also covering New Zealand, Australia and North America, and moved into new areas such as conferencing and services to the travel trade. In June, 1998, the acquisition was announced of Amberstock Publishing Ltd, publishers of two magazines, World of Property and Focus on France, which were merged with Outbound.

The acquisition of Becketts was a good piece of business and achieved additional geographical diversity for the group – now it was entrenched on the South Coast (much further than Bonnie Prince Charlie had penetrated, observed a cynic, reflecting on the cutting remark years before that the Scottish leader had never made it further south than Derby).

At a presentation to investors Iain Bell upset one of them by speaking openly about the "soft underbelly" of England, a description he vigorously defended. "While Scotland and Northern England had struggled against poor advertising revenues the south was still a bonanza," he asserted. "The managements of newspapers there never knew what hard times were. Suddenly, when things turned they just couldn't cope with it.

"Analysts used to ask why we were so successful, but it was quite simple – since the Act of Union in 1707 Scotland had been in permanent recession. We had been to hell and back and survived."

AMONG THE new additions to the Johnston payroll as a result of the Becketts acquisition was the company's West Sussex marketing director Danny Cammiade, who was destined to become a key figure in Johnston Press in the years to follow as the group chief operating officer.

This important role was a far cry from local boy Cammiade's humble start in newspapers as a telesales rep at Worthing in 1978. From there he progressed to field sales and a number of supervisory positions in classified and display advertising. Within five years Cammiade was promoted to advertising manager at Worthing before being given wider responsibility and a directorship in 1988.

Johnstons liked his no-nonsense, businesslike approach and earmarked Cammiade for promotion – managing director of the West Sussex County Times in 1994, North Midlands divisional managing director at Chesterfield in 1996, a similar role in the new South Division at Portsmouth in 1999, and a group position of director of operations based in Edinburgh in 2001. His climb up the ladder was completed in 2005 when he was appointed as an executive director of the group with the position of chief operating officer.

As Robin Miller had suspected, the sale of Emap's interest in Becketts to Johnston Press not only affected the balance of newspaper publishing in the south east but also whet Freddy Johnston's appetite for more acquisitions in that part of the country.

"He seemed to be expressing interest in all our newspapers all of

> Managements of newspapers [in the south] never knew what hard times were. Suddenly, when things turned they just couldn't cope with it
>
> Iain Bell

the time, dropping hints, occasionally throwing a price into the conversation, showing a dogged persistence," recalled Miller. "We were under no illusions that Freddy was a predator on the prowl."

One title that attracted Johnston was the paid-for weekly, the Crawley Observer, a business that he regarded as having considerable growth potential in an area of new-found wealth from technology companies and well-paid jobs at Gatwick Airport. He also saw Crawley as a logical extension of the West Sussex operation in nearby Horsham.

But Emap wasn't going to give up the boom town that easily although it was engaged in a bitter struggle with the rival Crawley News. At the same time both papers were being played off against each other by vigorous estate agents, with a consequent effect on yields and profits, despite turning out up to 160 pages a week.

UNTIL NOW Johnston's publishing interests had concentrated solely on the weekly newspaper sector. But its commitment to growth, embodied in its assurances to shareholders at the time of flotation, meant that sooner rather than later a reappraisal of its acquisition strategy was called for.

Provincial evening newspapers were the natural progression – flotation had provided the financial strength that this would need, and this in turn was providing increased confidence to break out of the weekly paper mould.

But for a time the Johnston board remained unsure about entering an area in which it had no expertise in dealing with the disciplines of six-day publication, a revenue structure which relied heavily on a higher proportion of income from newspaper sales, and titles serving large urban and city areas.

An abortive attempt to buy the Huddersfield Examiner, the old-established evening paper serving Huddersfield and the larger Kirklees metropolitan district, highlighted this dilemma and brought with it the first real difference of opinion on acquisitions faced by the Johnston board.

Group managing director Iain Bell, who by then was approaching the age of 55 and the time he had set himself for early retirement, had serious misgivings about pursuing the Examiner, owned by Joseph Woodhead and Company, on technical and financial grounds.

The Examiner had been high on the Johnston list of potential targets for some time and its chairman, Ivan Lee, and managing director, Christopher Dicks, were both well known to Freddy Johnston, Dicks especially through his membership of the Newspaper Society. While both Lee and Dicks were in firm operational control of the business they did not have a majority interest in the shares. Indeed, Woodhead's was yet another example of a family business with a diverse share ownership – shares owned by a variety of people with no direct involvement in the business and with no opportunity to capitalise their holdings.

Johnston realised that here was a business showing all the classic signs of being highly vulnerable to a takeover attempt and what's more he wanted a slice of the action. The Examiner, he argued, was a sound, independent company that would fit in well with the group's other Yorkshire interests. Its modern press could also print all the group's titles in the region and save the expense of installing a new web-offset press at Wakefield – an investment that, in the light of events, was subsequently agreed at a cost of £1 million.

Dicks and Lee agreed to exploratory discussions about a possible sale while showing no great enthusiasm. Johnston made it clear that while he would prefer any offer to be with their blessing that would not preclude him approaching the other shareholders, who collectively owned the majority of the shares.

Tedious and protracted negotiations eventually stalled on price, but by then the Johnston interest had cooled somewhat when it was accepted that although the Examiner could boast a new offset press it would also present technical difficulties.

"Once we knew that it had the wrong cut-off, which restricts the size of newsprint that can be used, it diminished its value in our eyes," said Johnston. "It meant that problems would arise if we wanted to transfer some of our county printing to Huddersfield."

The Johnston indicative offer – a figure of around £11 million had been mentioned, although with justification this could be raised – was left on the table without agreement on the understanding by both parties that discussions could be resumed if either changed their minds. But they never did, although Johnston still believed that with patience and time on his side the Examiner would become the first evening title to join the group.

In the summer of 1993 Johnston put business thoughts to one side and took his wife on holiday – a safari to Namibia on the south west coast of Africa. Here their base was a hostel offering only basic facilities in the country's former German colonial capital, Swakopund. This is a remote location, approached through the

endless expanse of the Namib desert and within constant earshot of the booming surf on the notorious Skeleton Coast.

The Johnstons were spending their time exploring the dramatic and towering sand dunes and soaking up the eclectic mix of Teutonic architecture that is Swakopund's legacy from its original German settlers. One destination for the carefree family was the extraordinary Moon landscape just outside the town – a seemingly never-ending series of bizarre hills reminiscent of pictures from the Sea of Tranquility.

Meanwhile office staff in Edinburgh were making frantic efforts to locate their chairman and eventually did so through his holiday tour company and the caretaker of the hostel, who gave him the message to ring head office urgently. Dressed in shorts and sun hat, Johnston eventually located a coin-operated telephone in the village laundry and phoned home to be told that the Examiner had been sold to Liverpool-based Trinity International Newspapers for £12.5 million.

Johnston could hardly conceal his disappointment – it was, he said, the biggest corporate setback since his failure to buy the Stirling Observer in 1973. He had to wait another eight years before finally getting his hands on the Examiner – a symbolic framed front page was presented to him by Trinity (by then Trinity Mirror) chief executive Philip Graf to mark his 65th birthday. Graf was all too well aware of Johnston's continuing interest in the paper – only two years after the Trinity purchase he had made a speculative approach to the new owners.

Failure to buy the Examiner was the second disruption to expansion plans that occurred within weeks in 1993 – and once again Trinity were involved. For months a consortium of Johnstons,

Tindle Newspapers and the Guardian and Manchester Evening News had been negotiating to buy Argus Newspapers Ltd, publishers of a number of local weekly papers, mainly in the London and Thames valley areas.

But in July 1993 it was reported that Trinity had stepped in with a successful bid of £23.5 million, some £3 million more than the consortium had offered.

The sale of the Huddersfield Examiner also caused disappointment to directors of the Halifax Courier Ltd, eight miles away and separated only by a lofty fold in the Pennine hills. Chairman Kingston Macaulay and managing director Edward Wood believed they had a reciprocal agreement with Lee and Dicks that if ever either company was for sale the other would have first refusal on its purchase.

Like Johnston, they were taken by surprise when an announcement was made on the Press Association newswire that a deal had been agreed with Trinity. Wood was incensed and mounted a last-ditch counter bid that involved his own staff delivering offer documents to far-flung Examiner shareholders, many of whom were baffled and bewildered to be awoken from their slumbers by the nocturnal drivers from Halifax.

The advice the shareholders received from Huddersfield was to reject this last-minute approach, which they did, with the Courier directors being painted as "a bunch of cowboys" who were simply interested in creaming off the Examiner profits and riding roughshod over the staff.

Within 12 months Halifax Courier Holdings Ltd – owners of the Evening Courier, several weekly newspapers, and all the newspaper interests on the Isle of Man – was itself sold, to Johnston Press.

The addition of the Evening Courier to the group portfolio was of considerable significance – it was its most expensive newspaper acquisition at that time (equivalent to the flotation value of Johnston Press), its first evening title, a source of

The Halifax Evening Courier office's distinctive art deco clock

129

new skills and expertise, and a highly profitable operation. More especially, once it had been realised that the culture gap between weekly and evening newspapers was not as great as had been imagined confidence to repeat the exercise soared.

The Courier's circulation area matched that of the Calderdale metropolitan district, which had been stitched together with a population of 200,000 during local government reorganisation in 1974. With an overall household penetration of more than 40 per cent, and 70 per cent in the core Halifax area, it was by far the leading evening title available locally and unfazed by the limited opposition posed by its neighbouring rivals from Huddersfield, Bradford, Leeds, Blackburn and Manchester.

The three paid-for weekly papers – the Brighouse Echo, and the two small Calder Valley titles the Todmorden News and Hebden Bridge Times – published and printed from Halifax and market leaders, too, in their respective circulation areas – together with the free distribution Calderdale News completed the coverage. In Hebden Bridge and Todmorden especially it was said that nothing moved without a mention in the papers, which probably explained their market penetration of around 80 per cent and 90 per cent respectively!

The acquisition of the newspapers ideally matched the Johnston Press template of community involvement and affinity with their readership. Johnstons also admired the character of the Yorkshire wool and engineering town with its record of stability and thrift, exemplified, of course, by the growth of the Halifax Building Society into the world's largest mortgage lender and trusted haven for savers.

In Halifax the Courier was so much a part of the fabric of the town that its sale to Scottish owners prompted debate and questions at a meeting of Calderdale Council.

A Labour member expressed concern at the growth of newspaper groups and declared them to be against the public interest, while a Lib-Dem councillor said he had lodged an objection with the Monopolies and Mergers Commission because "I don't want to see control of our newspapers pass to Scotland." The Conservatives took a more pragmatic view – "If people do not like the way the paper is run in future they can always decide not to buy it."

Councillors were not the only ones surprised by the sudden and unexpected sale of a piece of Calderdale's heritage. Managing director Edward Wood knew that his staff and readers would be concerned and took steps to allay their fears by sending editorial director Edward Riley to London to interview Freddy Johnston

> With an overall household penetration of more than 40 per cent, and 70 per cent in the core Halifax area, it was by far the leading evening title available locally

before the takeover was made public.

"When the interview was published it was a great opportunity to let everyone know what the new owners stood for and what sort of people were running Johnston Press," said Riley, who had taken an oath of secrecy to prevent insider dealing or leaking news of the company's annual results, which were both announced to the Stock Exchange on the same day.

"Freddy and I met in the City, at the offices of merchant bankers Hill Samuel, and believe me it was the most nerve racking interview of my career – blow it and that would have been curtains with Johnston Press!

"But it didn't work out like that. I knew straight away that in Freddy I was talking to a real newspaperman and immediately we struck up a wonderful rapport."

Johnston stood by his pledge to retain the fundamental local character of the titles he had bought and to invest in them for the future, but the marriage between the weekly newspaper group and the evening paper got off to an uncertain start. The pace of a six-day operation and the number of employees required to sustain it initially bemused Johnstons. For their part the remaining Courier directors and managers quickly realised that their evening paper pedigree did not entitle them to special privileges or status within the group – publication of an internal newsletter that proclaimed "We are the flagship of the fleet" was stopped on orders from Edinburgh. That title was reserved for the Falkirk Herald.

Edward Wood, who had agreed to stay on as managing director and had also joined the Johnston Press board, was appointed non-executive chairman of the local company. His replacement as managing director was Graham Gould, who transferred from a similar position at Wakefield and was also in charge of the North of England division. Gould himself stepped down in 2003 when he took on a new role overseeing group IT strategy.

The impact of the Halifax and Manx acquisitions was obvious immediately – in 1994 the two businesses contributed to a 31 per cent rise in group profits and in 1995 helped profits rise by a further 15.7 per cent to £17.5 million.

The Evening Courier has its origins in the intense political rivalry of the early 19th century. First the Tories launched the Halifax Guardian in 1832 and the Liberals followed with the Halifax Courier in 1853, the two businesses eventually merging in 1921, by which time they were also publishing evening editions. In time the long-winded Halifax Evening Courier and Guardian became simply the Evening Courier.

The Brighouse Echo, founded in 1887, was acquired in 1923. The former textiles and engineering town was on everyone's lips in the 1970s when its famous brass band, the Brighouse and Rastrick, shot to No 2 in the music charts with its version of "The Floral Dance".

During the 1960s both the Hebden Bridge Times, founded in 1881, and the Todmorden News, founded in 1853, joined the Courier group. It was at the Hebden Bridge Times that Prime Minister Margaret Thatcher's gruff and forthright press secretary Bernard Ingham started his newspaper career – a link of which he was extremely proud, writing a regular column for the paper long after his retirement. Mill town Todmorden, too, has its claim to fame as the birthplace of two Nobel prizewinners and two England test cricketers.

For some time the Evening Courier and its associated titles had been on the Johnston list of possible takeover targets and the group's performance had been monitored closely for several years. Thus the two disappointed suitors for the nearby Huddersfield Examiner were drawn together as if fate had taken a hand, and when Freddy Johnston made his interest known the response was more optimistic than he had dared imagine.

The Courier directors, he speculated later, had probably become somewhat demoralised following the Examiner affair and from a position of fiercely proclaiming their prized independence were prepared to contemplate a somewhat different future for their own business.

Managing director Edward Wood was well practised in fending off approaches from other newspaper groups, private companies and venture capitalists who all saw the Courier as an attractive proposition. He joked about rejecting offers every other week, but the truth was that speculative bids, some with a price attached, were received several times a year.

Newspaper Society gatherings were the worst and Wood knew to be on his guard in readiness for the interest that was inevitably shown by fellow members during the social chit chat over cups of tea or other drinks.

It was following one such meeting at the Newspaper Society offices in Bloomsbury Square that Johnston made his first tentative move by inviting Wood to his company flat in Earls Court Road.

During coffee and biscuits the discussion turned to the future of their respective companies, at which point Johnston showed his hand – what were the chances of the Courier being for sale? It was not the first time he had raised the subject but since the last approach the two men had struck up a closer relationship through a mutual interest in presses and Wood had visited Edinburgh on several occasions.

Wood, who all along had suspected that the invitation for coffee had been more than a purely social gesture, showed no great enthusiasm, but he promised to discuss the inquiry with his fellow directors.

Johnston raised the issue yet again when he took Wood out for lunch to the upmarket Wilton's restaurant, in London's fashionable St James, where they dined on delightfully cooked Dover sole. The canny Scot was well prepared and at his most charming.

"He was very flattering," recalled Wood. "He told me what a fine company we had, how well managed it was, how profitable it was. Just the sort of business he wanted to add to Johnston Press.

"Freddy's timing and judgement were perfect – he knew full well that the directors were approaching retiring age, that the shareholding was widely split

Tim Bowdler, who sat in as an observer during the company's purchase of the Halifax Courier Ltd, shortly after joining as group managing director

134

and there were considerations about who would run the business in the next generation."

Johnston then played his trump card – an offer of about £23 a share that he knew Wood would be duty bound to report to his fellow directors and eventually place before the 50 or so shareholders dispersed around the world.

"If it's worth more than I'm offering all you have to do is convince me and we'll pay what it's really worth. We don't buy companies on the cheap – we just pay a fair value," he explained.

Wood and his chairman decided to call Johnston's bluff. Their accountants, Ernst and Young, had valued the company at substantially more than his offer but Johnston was undeterred when presented with the figure and a series of meetings followed at which a sale was agreed in principle on Valentine's Day, 1994.

Wood and Johnston called a final meeting to iron out the details at the offices of bankers Hill Samuel, where Iain Bell and Courier chairman King Macaulay and their respective advisors joined them. Tim Bowdler sat in on the group as an observer.

Macaulay took a tough, uncompromising stance – not only was he intent on obtaining the best possible price for his shareholders but, as a man who greatly valued tradition, he was determined to ensure that the Courier's ethos of service to its community would be safeguarded by the new owners. So adamant was he on these issues that on more than one occasion the negotiations appeared to be on the brink of collapse.

It was well past midnight and the two sides called yet another recess to consider their positions. By then Bell's patience was at breaking point. He confronted Macaulay and Wood and in a heated exchange told them that unless they were prepared to put the Johnston offer to shareholders he would go behind their backs and do so himself, confident that the offer price was just too good to turn down.

After that negotiations quickly reached a conclusion. Exhausted and battle weary, the two sides shook hands on a complex deal worth £36 million in cash and a new shares issue, of which £29.4 million was for the eight titles owned by the Courier group. The remainder came from the realisation of property and other investments and a special dividend payment.

At the time this was not only the most expensive acquisition ever made by Johnstons but twice as much as the valuation they had placed on the neighbouring Huddersfield Examiner, so similar in many respects. But although Johnstons now had their first provincial evening newspaper, a landmark in itself, the frequency of publication was secondary to the quality of the business they had bought and the further geographical consolidation in West Yorkshire.

The Courier deal – codenamed Watch – was announced on the same day as the Johnston Press results for 1993, which showed record profits of £12.5 million, an increase of 28 per cent on the previous year. In the same period the Courier, with sales of £9.97 million, had made a pre-tax profit of £2.7 million. The City liked the combined news, which was reflected in a modest rise in the price of Johnston shares.

Press reaction to the deal was also favourable. UK Press Gazette described the Courier titles as "something of a prize" while the Financial Times remarked "Halifax Courier is a rather better managed company than most of Johnston's recent targets."

Three months later the acquisition became official when the Monopolies and Mergers Commission gave its unconditional approval – it had been called in to investigate because the purchase had taken the combined circulation of all Johnston Press newspapers to more than half a million per edition.

There was also concern during the MMC hearing that the addition of another West Yorkshire title would create an unacceptable overlap with the titles based in Wakefield, and so restrict competition.

Edward Wood was called to give evidence and quickly put the issue to rest. "The only common readership I can think of is among the inmates of Armley Gaol, in Leeds," he declared. It was a rare lighter moment that broke the tedium of the proceedings.

Acquisition of Halifax Courier Holdings brought with it a little gem in the form of the newspaper publishing interests on the Isle of Man. The offshore tax haven and financial centre had never figured on the Johnston Press list of areas for expansion – indeed, on the face of it the growth potential on an island with a population of 76,000 would appear to be limited.

"We never realised just how good the Isle of Man was until we had bought the business," reflected Johnston. "The operation was extremely well managed and the three papers were all market leaders in the community.

"They had never attracted our attention before – my only interest in anything Manx had been kippers and the steam railway on the island."

Chiappelli, too, was lukewarm about the Isle of Man acquisition – until he discovered just how well run and profitable the business was.

Far from being a finite market, Johnstons were soon aware that the development of the financial services industry on the island was also creating growth potential for its titles, the only traditional newspapers printed and published there. Weekly paid-fors and frees they may be, but as mouthpieces of island life they enjoy the status of national newspapers in the eyes of the staunchly independent and patriotic Manx people.

Indeed, it was against this somewhat unusual background that the amalgamation of a ragbag collection of poorly-run and unprofitable titles into one successful company took place thanks to the commitment and vision of the Halifax Courier directors, and Edward Wood in particular.

"It was a remarkable and largely under-estimated feat," extolled Johnston.

The national strike by provincial journalists belonging to the National Union of Journalists in the autumn of 1979 was a gloomy time for everyone connected with the newspaper industry. But the black cloud that settled over evening and weekly papers had a silver lining in Halifax.

Local members of the NUJ so upset their print union colleagues that rather than working strictly to rule members of the NGA and Natsopa offered maximum co-operation with the management – and that included unloading unlimited supplies of newsprint. Thus continuity of publication was ensured for as long as the hard-pressed editors could manage to bring out their papers virtually single handed, and there was newsprint to spare.

But in Llandudno, North Wales, it was a different story and as the contract printers there struggled to eke out their dwindling stocks of paper they decided they could no longer print the Isle of Man Courier until the strike was over.

Publisher John J. Christian, without a press of his own on the island, turned to other mainland printers without success until his call for help was answered in Halifax. It was a decision that Wood soon began to regret. Rumours about Christian's tardy payment of bills soon turned out to be true and he was left with no choice but to issue an ultimatum of cash up front before the next week's edition was printed. The furious Manxman – a well known politician, hotelier and lawyer – reluctantly agreed and promptly took his business back to Llandudno when the newsprint shortage there eased.

Months later, in 1980, he put the Isle of Man Courier up for sale. Wood sent his evening paper editor Edward Riley and advertisment manager Stephen Quick on a scouting mission and it was thanks to their favourable report that the Halifax company made a bid for its namesake Courier and sister paper Mona's Herald, both of which were founded in the 19th century.

The Halifax offer of £100,000 was accepted, a package that included the titles, premises in Douglas and Ramsey, machinery and equipment – and more problems than anyone could have imagined.

Long standing grievances with the NGA print union quickly surfaced while the island's printing employers' federation appeared only too willing to side with the union if it meant embarrassing the off-cumdens from Yorkshire.

Even the local joiner in Douglas made life difficult after the front door of the Ridgeway Street office blew off in a gale. Not until a debt incurred by the previous owners was paid was he prepared to lift screwdriver and chisel to carry out repairs.

The main opposition to the Courier was provided by the long-established Isle of Man Examiner, owned since 1956 by Henri

Leopold Dor, a highly unpredictable and eccentric Frenchman. He, too, set out to make life as uncomfortable as possible for the newcomers to the island, just as he had done to John Christian for years. The two newspaper publishers had been at constant loggerheads since Christian beat him to the purchase of the Courier in the late 1960s.

Christian was determined to keep the paper in Manx hands and regarded Dor as an unwelcome intruder on the island, spending a small fortune on premises in Douglas and new equipment to keep him at bay.

Dor, widely regarded as the first high profile millionaire to settle on the Isle of Man, had fought with the French Resistance during the Second World War and then went on to amass a fortune through marine insurance. A staunch Roman Catholic, intellectual and fascinated with the paranormal, he also published the naturist magazine Health and Efficiency, much sought after by schoolboys for its nude images.

The head to head between Dor and Christian plumbed the depths at times. Dor would attack his rival through a column ostensibly written by his collie dog, Strog, and on one occasion printed the classic headline: "Christian – your Courier lies" when challenging the latest sales figures.

As if Dor's antics were not enough for Wood to contend with the launch of the Isle of Man Gazette by former Examiner editor and talented photographer Bill Dale further complicated the newspaper scene. For fourteen months it gave the islanders a choice of news media that simply could not have been sustained in a mainland town with a similar population.

Desperate measures were called for. Wood made two thirds of the Courier staff redundant – after first consulting with the island Governor – and turned the Isle of Man Courier into an all-island free distribution newspaper. From that point onwards the company's fortunes started to improve – indeed, the new free paper was so popular that long queues of readers anxious to obtain a copy would form outside the Ridgeway Street offices, even though those same people would have a Courier pushed through their letter box later the same day.

But still the logistical problems of printing in Halifax remained. On occasions thick fog at Ronaldsway Airport prevented the aeroplane from taking off to fly the pasted-up pages to Manchester or Liverpool for collection. At other times the weather forced the

> *The new free paper was so popular that long queues of readers anxious to obtain a copy would form outside the Ridgeway Street offices*

plane to divert from Manchester to Birmingham or other airports – leaving the collection driver from Halifax stranded. And on the return trip, by sea, storms prevented the ferry sailing on time from Heysham.

On numerous occasions baggage handlers at Ronaldsway forgot to load the slender box containing the pages, while at the other end they were not taken off the aeroplane and flown on to its next destination, which once included Jersey. Even the use of bright orange Kodak film boxes failed to guarantee that the precious cargo was dealt with. One solution suggested, but never tried, was to include a loud ticking device in the package!

A press of their own on the island would make all the difference. And out of the blue one became available in yet another twist in the Isle of Man newspapers saga.

The Courier found itself unchallenged when a round-the-clock, sit-in strike at the rival Examiner in 1987 halted its publication for 16 weeks, following a disagreement between Henri Dor and his editor. It was typical of his unpredictability when out of the blue, and during the dispute, he agreed to sell his publishing interests - including titles and assets – to the Courier group.

The tip off that the paper was for sale came via a phone call to Courier managing director Trudi Williamson from the office of mainland newspaper entrepreneur Eddie Shah who offered her a job with the Examiner, which he was hoping to buy.

Another phone call – this time to Edward Wood, who was on holiday in Tenerife – set the alarm bells ringing. A counter offer was submitted and accepted, much to the chagrin of Shah whose own negotiations had been well advanced and seemingly about to end in success.

Wood's elation was short lived. Unknown to him the National Union of Journalists and the National Graphical Association had decided to start their own newspaper, The Manx Independent, using existing staff and supported financially by the Isle of Man branch of the Bermuda-based Mercantile Overseas Bank. Initially it was a 28-page broadsheet, published twice a week, and printed off the island. Within a short time a third edition was added, and in 1989 the paper was converted to tabloid format and printed on a second hand press on an industrial estate.

"What we ended up with at the Examiner," said Wood "was an empty shell – a title, premises and a press but no one to work there. The unions put a black on the entire operation."

Not to be outdone, Wood mothballed two minor titles, the Star and the Times, and resolved to print the Examiner with or without union co-operation. After all, the paper founded in 1880 on a revolutionary democratic platform, had been through difficult times before. He rolled up his sleeves, drafted in willing staff, including the advertising team and office girls, and flew in his press room manager from Halifax. Between them they ran the press with not a printer in sight, week after week.

By the time normality had been restored the Courier group was showing a healthy profit and growing in confidence – enough confidence to buy a site in Peel Road, Douglas, for new offices and a new press at a cost of £2 million.

The Times, published on Tuesdays and with an emphasis on the island's financial life, and the sports orientated Star, never reappeared and the establishment-minded Examiner was switched from Friday to Monday publication – one of very few weekly newspapers to appear so early in the week.

"It was all very unorthodox, but we didn't want the Courier and the Examiner to clash at the end of the week. We simply did what we thought was best for the Isle of Man," recalled Williamson.

Readers liked the change, and so did the Newspaper Society, which made an award to the Examiner for its circulation growth. Not to be outdone, the Courier was named best free newspaper in the North West, an accolade it won again in 2002.

But on the Isle of Man nothing could be taken for granted. A storm of unprecedented ferocity broke in 1993 when Wood bought up the rival Manx Independent, by then owned by Morton Newspapers, of Lurgan, Northern Ireland, to give the Courier group control of all the island's newspapers – only Manx Radio provided any form of opposition.

Opposition to the sale came from every quarter – the Manx government, the unions, and the business community. A full-scale parliamentary debate in the House of Keys reflected the public concern, not only at the monopoly that had been created but also the ownership by a company from mainland Britain.

But, despite all the fulminating, the deal stood. The opposition gradually subsided and the perceived threat to balanced news coverage proved to be unfounded. For the first time in years the newspaper wars that had been fought out on a most unlikely battle-ground were over.

Peace reigned when Johnston Press acquired the Isle of Man

interests in 1994. After years of hovering between annual losses and small profits the outlook was healthy, even though the Johnston directors did not immediately appreciate the true merit of the Manx business they had acquired as an adjunct to the Halifax Courier deal.

The group continued to print the three main titles on the island – the Courier, published on Fridays and with a 36,000-copy distribution to 95 per cent of Manx homes; the paid-for Examiner, published on Mondays with a circulation of about 15,000 copies; and the Independent, which is published on Thursdays with a circulation of about 13,000 copies.

Although the Johnston titles predominate they face opposition from several radio stations, numerous quality free distribution magazines and localised newsheets. Advertising income, while buoyant, is still below half of the total island spend.

Even so, the first ten years under Johnston ownership was a period of unprecedented growth and rising profits – and another prestigious award when the Examiner was named Newspaper Society Community Newspaper of the Year in 2002. A key factor was the strength of the management team, which remained unchanged throughout that time and comprised managing director Williamson, editor Lionel Cowin, production director Jeff Black, sales director Helen Byrne and company secretary Christine Oates. Together they brought stability and order out of the turbulent situation that had existed previously. The team remained together until 2005 when Cowin retired.

Fortunately economic conditions on the Isle of Man were also beginning to improve at the same time as Johnstons were making their own investment. The company not only contributed to the financial upturn but reaped the benefits from it, as double figure growth in the gross domestic product was reported every year for a decade. House prices more than doubled in three years alone and Manx salaries rose from 70 per cent of those on the mainland to 120 per cent.

Equally important, the foundations were laid for future prosperity with the island diversifying beyond its kippers and motor bikes economy to became a major offshore finance centre and the home to a burgeoning film making industry.

Within 18 months of the Courier/Isle of Man deal further titles were added to the Johnston portfolio, but one that eluded them at the time was the Spenborough Guardian, another West Yorkshire

weekly newspaper which was sold to United Newspapers, publishers of the Yorkshire Post, for around £1 million – £300,000 more than the Johnston valuation, which the directors declined to increase.

In 1995 Johnstons turned their attention to the newspapers published by W & J Linney Ltd, at Mansfield, Notts, which for years had been printed on the Derbyshire Times press at Chesterfield.

This arrangement had continued after the acquisition of the Chesterfield centre in 1978. It was a contract of some significance, so much so that concern had been expressed some years before when the rumour mill suggested that Linneys might be sold and the newspapers printed elsewhere.

But there was a certain inevitability that perhaps one day Linney's, too, would become part of the Johnston group and already the two companies enjoyed extremely cordial relations – father and son Ian and Nick Linney not only among Chesterfield's most loyal customers but also friends with most of the senior managers.

For a town of its size Mansfield had been well served by weekly papers. In 1858 the Mansfield Reporter made its debut, courtesy of founder John Langley. It was his devotion to duty that cost him his life when in 1875 he was reporting a mill fire for the paper when a wall collapsed and buried him.

A second paper was launched in 1871, John Linney's Mansfield and North Notts Advertiser, followed by Fred Willman's Mansfield, Sutton and Kirkby Chronicle in 1895.

In 1952 the Chronicle and the Advertiser joined

Putting together the front page of the Mansfield Chad (above) are editor Jeremy Plews, seated, and deputy editor Tim Morris; the paper in 2004 (below)

143

forces to become the somewhat wordy Mansfield and North
Nottinghamshire Chronicle Advertiser, soon abbreviated to the
Chad, by which title it has been known affectionately ever since. In
1956 Linney's bought the rival Reporter to complete Mansfield's
newspaper evolution.

By 2005 the Chad was the top-selling weekly newspaper in the
county and one of the largest in the country with a circulation of
more than 46,000, boosted by the conversion of the free Ashfield
edition to a paid-for in 2003. Its classified section won the
Newspaper Society award for weekly newspapers on 14 occasions
and was runner-up seven times.

In 2004 the Chad was the fastest growing newspaper in the group
and improved its sale in the first half of the year by an impressive 22
per cent, an achievement that also topped the Newspaper Society
rankings.

The Linneys also ran a substantial commercial printing business
and finally decided to concentrate on this and dispose of their
newspaper interests – the Chad, the Worksop Guardian (paid-for,
1896), Dinnington and Maltby Guardian (free, 1975), Retford and
Bawtry Guardian (free, early 70s), Mansfield and Ashfield Observer
(free, 1969)and the Hucknall and Bullwell Dispatch (paid-for,
1903).

The titles, and other free newspapers that have been acquired
since, provide unrivalled coverage of events in North
Nottinghamshire, also the location of Sherwood Forest and forever
associated with Robin Hood.

Johnstons' offer of £20 million in cash – codenamed Ceco – was
sewn up with the minimum of fuss and financed through a
revolving credit facility from the Royal Bank of Scotland. The titles
changed hands in December, 1995, the formal transfer being
completed in Brussels to take advantage of a loophole in the law,
since closed, that enabled Johnstons to avoid the payment of stamp
duty. A private aeroplane was chartered to take the Linney team to
Belgium while the Johnston directors and lawyers took a scheduled
flight from Edinburgh.

The deal was examined by the Department of Trade and Industry,
who raised no objections having been satisfied that consumer
choice would not be affected and that there was no significant
overlap with other Johnston interests in the area.

Although the Linney acquisition had been straightforward it
assumed additional relevance within Johnston Press as one of the

earliest deals involving the company's new group managing director, Tim Bowdler, who had joined in January, 1994, and had spent the time since learning about the Johnston business and the newspaper industry in general.

It was a steep learning curve for a man with an engineering background whose closest link to newspapers until then had been reading the Daily Telegraph and the Financial Times each day.

Bowdler also had the task of filling the considerable void left by his predecessor, Iain Bell, who formally retired at the company's annual meeting in April, 1994. Ten years before that Bell had signalled his intention to step down at the age of 55, and while no one seriously believed he would do so by the middle of the previous year his resolve was unshakable.

"It was clear he was going to leave a big gap," recalled Freddy Johnston. "For 20 years since the mid-70s he had been involved in every aspect of company life and the key figure in our move into England."

His impending departure was put on the agenda as early as November, 1992, when directors were told of a meeting between Johnston and bankers Hill Samuel at which the implications in the City of Bell's retirement were discussed. In Edinburgh, half a day was set aside to consider the issue.

Johnstons had been fortunate in the past in finding the right people within their own ranks to fill this important position – first Tom McGowran and latterly Bell. This time a review of the available talent failed to identify a logical successor from a number of potential candidates and so, reluctantly, the decision was made to look outside the company to make an appointment.

The criteria were simple: a tough and effective management style coupled with the ability to develop Johnston Press from the position it had reached as a public company of some significance.

Several executive recruitment agencies – the headhunters – were approached and the task of narrowing down the search was handed to the London-based firm of Heidrick and Struggles, with offices at 100, Picadilly, and which for 40 years had specialised in chief executive, board member and senior-level management search assignments for a wide variety of clients,

After a trawl of senior executives within the newspaper industry, none of who ideally fitted the Johnston Press model, the headhunters were told to widen their search.

The spotlight was turned on 46-year-old Timothy John Bowdler,

> The spotlight was turned on 46-year-old Timothy John Bowdler, at the time a divisional managing director with Cape plc

married with two daughters and with an impressive track record as a production engineer, managerial appointments in commercial and marketing roles and, at the time, a divisional managing director with Cape plc in charge of the group's building and architectural product companies.

Reluctantly Bowdler, who was unsure about his own career prospects at Cape, which was facing a string of claims because of its asbestos activities, agreed to let his name go forward – partly at the insistence of his Swedish wife, Margaretha, who was more attracted to living in Edinburgh than him – and was one of six candidates interviewed by a committee of three Johnston directors – Freddy Johnston, Austin Merrills and Joe Hale.

One interviewee was eliminated quickly during a session of close questioning. "What do you think the company's principal problem is?" probed Johnston.

"You," came back the reply.

"He might have been right, but needless to say he didn't get the job" quipped Johnston later.

When the number of candidates had been whittled down to two both were taken out individually by the committee for lunch and dinner, after which Johnston and Hale expressed their support for Bowdler. Merrills declined to give an opinion until after the two hopefuls had been interviewed by the full board but also backed Bowdler when the appointment was put to the vote on October 22, 1993.

Delighted with the choice, Johnston left the meeting to telephone the good news to an equally delighted Bowdler. It was agreed that he would start work the following January.

The final, crucial interview could not have got off to a worse start. Bowdler joined the directors round the highly polished table in what is now his office at Manor Place. They sat him next to Marco Chiappelli's "good side" so that the partially deaf finance director could hear what was being said.

Chiappelli asked the first question: "And tell us, Mr Bowdler, exactly how many companies are you responsible for at present?"

"Six or seven, I think."

Iain Bell, the man Bowdler was hoping to replace, exploded, as only he could.

"Six or seven – does that mean you don't really know?"

Bowdler's answers were more precise after that uneasy beginning. Later he and Bell became firm friends as the two visited every Johnston Press office as part of Bowdler's three-month induction.

But he was to suffer at the hands of Bell yet again, this time when his predecessor was called upon to present the awards at the golf competition that formed part of the Scottish Newspaper Publishers' Association annual conference.

Bowdler was pleased with his performance on the testing course at Ladybank, near St Andrews, and proudly stepped forward to collect the prize as runner-up, just one point behind the winner.

"Second place, Tim Bowdler of Johnston Press," announced Bell. "But we didn't bloody well employ you to come second!"

His business record alone was not the only factor that won him the job. The selection panel liked his winning manner, which would carry people with him, an inner strength behind a non-confrontational exterior and his lively, forward-looking attitude. They were also conscious that the eyes of the City would be on the person they appointed – it had to be someone who could maintain confidence in Johnston Press.

Bowdler for his part was impressed with the honesty and high moral tone set by Freddy Johnston and his co-directors. The prospect of running a publicly quoted company that, he reckoned, had a bright future excited his ambitious streak.

This was the man who had rung Johnston to cancel an initial interview because he really couldn't be bothered after a tiring business trip abroad and who knew next to nothing about the newspaper industry.

"They couldn't find anyone who knew less than me but that seemed to please Freddy," he recalled. "He was looking for someone with a fresh approach who could come in and manage the business.

"What did I bring to the job? I could offer management skills, a well organised approach and I had experience of acquisitions and disposals."

Once the formalities of the appointment were completed Bowdler set about moving his family north from their home in Ilkley and soon found a Georgian house near the city centre in Edinburgh's New Town. The kindly Johnstons provided a warm welcome to the city and an invitation to join them at their home for dinner.

Bowdler remembered the day well. After leaving Wakefield early in the afternoon in his car he endured a nightmare journey up the

A1 in blinding snow, arriving in Edinburgh with only minutes to spare before the taxi arrived to take him and Margaretha to join Freddy and Ann.

The blizzards of the A1 were nothing compared with the short ride across Edinburgh – first the cab driver lost his way and then collided with another car. Bowdler, dazed and concussed, struggled free and hailed another taxi to complete the trip.

"Sorry we're late," apologised Bowdler to a beaming and forgiving Johnston. "I've driven all the way from Wakefield and then been involved in a crash on the way here."

"Oh, my god!" exclaimed Johnston, clearly concerned about the new company Jaguar. "Is the car all right?"

Bowdler was not given a specific brief other than to continue to grow the business. He had been made aware from the outset that the Johnston family and the board of directors were keen to be acquirers of further companies and were placing their faith in his expertise to make that happen.

Minutes of the monthly board meetings reveal a succession of opportunities for expansion that were discussed, rejected or ended in disappointment following his appointment.

"A lot of it was to do with timing," he said. "We could, for example, have bought the Yorkshire Post four years earlier than we did (in 2002) but it was too big and at the wrong time in our development."

Within a short time in the job Bowdler identified changes he considered necessary for the smoother operation of the company, the first being to tighten up Iain Bell's wide management structure under which a large number of people had reported directly to him. Instead Bowdler created four publishing divisions, which have been expanded since to accommodate new acquisitions.

"For me, with my obvious lack of publishing experience, I needed a relatively small number of senior people on whom I could rely for their publishing judgements."

Bowdler also initiated the disposal of non-newspaper activities, a process that was to take five years to complete when the wholesale stationery business was sold for £2.5 million in 1999, having failed to reach an optimum size to become a significant player in a highly competitive market. The loss-making commercial printing plants at Wakefield and St Helens were almost immediate casualties, followed soon after by the bookbinding and bookselling operations, where profits were being squeezed by changing trading conditions.

"Companies tend to be slow at exiting businesses even when it is hard to see a bright future," reflected Bowdler. "Disposing of our non-core activities was absolutely the right thing to do."

UNTIL HIS appointment his knowledge of newspapers had been confined mainly to reading his favourite nationals and childhood memories of the Express and Star, in Wolverhampton.

He was brought up in the shadow of the famous Molineux football ground and close to his father Neville's business, Bowdler's Sweets, makers of humbugs, mints, pear drops and other boiled sweets. Neville's passion for golf meant that he often enjoyed a round with the chairman of the Express and Star business and it was after one such occasion, when Tim had acted as his father's caddy, that he was invited to look round the newspaper offices.

It would be untrue to say that it created a lasting impression, but Bowdler always remembered how he was given the traditional slug of type bearing his name, still hot from the Linotype machine.

Three years after his appointment Bowdler became chief executive when Johnston stepped down from that role on reaching the age of 62. By then he had learned to juggle the insatiable demands of developing Britain's fifth largest newspaper group with his other interests of playing golf, sailing, fishing and escaping to his summerhouse in Sweden with his wife and daughters.

But he was also winning friends and admirers within the newspaper industry and his growing stature was recognised in 2002 when he was elected national president of The Newspaper Society, followed by chairmanship of the Political, Economic and Regulatory Affairs Committee. He had already been appointed a director of the Press Standards Board of Finance, becoming its chairman in 2005, and a non-executive director of the Press Association, and in 2004 he was chosen as Scottish Chief Executive of the Year.

By now Bowdler could lay claim to be a true newspaperman and observers were amazed at the extent of his knowledge and feel for the industry. From the outset he had set about learning the tricks of the trade – initially by following Iain Bell's advice to play the "daft laddie" and asking what must have been seen as naïve and elementary questions. This tactic worked well until Bowdler arrived in Kirkcaldy and was shown round by a senior manager, who was not impressed by his new boss's lack of knowledge. "It reminded me of being part of a group of school kids – I was made to feel very much

> "
> Tim Bowdler's growing stature was recognised in 2002 when he was elected national president of The Newspaper Society. In 2004 he was chosen as Scottish Chief Executive of the Year
>

like a kid myself," said Bowdler.

Bowdler felt more at ease among the pressroom crews of the centres he visited, his engineering background more easily helping him to understand the complexities of the roaring machinery. But for a long time he was baffled and perplexed by the role of his group's many editors and the freedom and independence they enjoyed within the Johnston structure – "the unique relationship between management and editor was quite different from any of my previous experience. It took me a while to accept that the product you put into the market place is in the control of somebody who has absolute discretion on its content and the way it will look."

Away from the office, Bowdler set about meeting all the group's suppliers, from computers to ink, and this was a practice he continued in order to keep abreast with the latest developments and technology. Most weeks he spent an average of three nights away from home and used the evenings to meet industry friends and contacts over dinner, much in the same way as Freddy Johnston turned frequent networking to his advantage.

That all formed part of a 70 to 80 hour working week that included about 150 internal flights a year and countless train journeys on the East Coast line – a routine that led to speculation that Johnston Press was intending to buy a newspaper at every stop along the route!

After his initiation Bowdler rapidly became engrossed in the day to day running of the company, but in 1996 his management skills were put to their biggest tests yet – the exchange of Lancashire and South Yorkshire titles with Reed Regional Newspapers, and an acquisition that sent shock waves around the industry.

Having already co-operated with Reeds on one strategic realignment of publishing interests with the acquisition of the South Yorkshire Times, Johnstons now found attractive the more significant exchange of its interests in Bury with those of Reeds centered on Doncaster.

Since 1978 the Doncaster Free Press and other associated titles had been part of an ownership merry-go-round that had seen control pass from the descendants of founder Richard "Dickie" Crowther to America's St Regis International in 1978, to Reed International (later to become Reed Elsevier) in 1982, and to a Reed management buy-out backed by a New York investment institution, in January, 1996.

Within four months of the buy-out the South Yorkshire portfolio, which also included the frees Doncaster Courier and Goole and Thorne Courier, was transferred to Johnstons, with a cash adjustment in Reed's favour of £10 million. It is an investment that has been amply repaid as Doncaster has developed into one of the group's main weekly newspaper profit centres. Its potential had been recognised years before by the man who started it all – Dickie Crowther was a keen race-goer and even named one of his racehorses Profit from Print!

"Both ourselves and Reeds had a common problem with titles that were geographically isolated from the rest of the business. It made a lot of sense to rationalise our interests," concluded Freddy Johnston.

Johnstons had initiated negotiations over an exchange of titles with Reeds in the summer of 1995 at a meeting attended by Johnston, Bowdler and Chiappelli. Good progress was made but soon afterwards the discussions were put on hold when Reed International announced that all their UK newspaper interests were being offered for sale. Furthermore, Reeds intimated that they were not interested in a piecemeal disposal of their titles.

The North of England newspapers belonging to Reeds were especially attractive to Johnstons and with this in mind the company entered into a consortium with Guardian Media Group, Southnews and Midland Independent to buy all the Reed titles and share them out on a regional basis.

When the Guardian withdrew from the consortium the remaining three agreed to pursue their interest on the understanding that Southnews would acquire Reeds business in London, Midland Independent the Midlands titles and those in Essex and Johnstons papers in Cheshire, Merseyside and Yorkshire.

The consortium's indicative offer of £220 million was made up of London £63 million, Essex £27 million, Lancashire £32 million, Cheshire £42 million, Midlands north and south £45 million and Yorkshire £11 million.

But the consortium's attempt to obtain exclusivity and be treated by Reeds as their preferred buyer was strongly opposed by Reeds bankers, Warburgs, whose competition lawyers warned of considerable difficulties with the Monopolies and Mergers Commission. The Reed directors also felt the joint approach was against their own personal interests.

The Johnston position cooled somewhat at the news and also following an indication that details of the consortium's offer had been passed on to a third party who was also interested in buying the Reed business.

The initial optimism of pushing through a substantial acquisition was fading fast and Johnston board minutes of November, 1995, rated the chances of success as slim. It came as no real surprise when shortly afterwards it was announced that the Reed newspaper interests were being sold to a management buy-out.

Jim Brown, chief executive of the new owners – Newsquest – and a long-time acquaintance of Freddy Johnston, wasted little time in resurrecting the Doncaster/Bury exchange now the last obstacles had been removed. The deal, codenamed Driver, was discussed at a meeting in January, 1996, and sewn up within three months. A valuation of £15 million was placed on the Doncaster operation and the Bury titles were valued at £5.75 million.

Doncaster was assimilated into the North of England division with Nick Perella moving from Mansfield as managing director once the acquisition was approved by the Department of Trade and Industry in April.

Bowdler remembered the transfer as one of his most successful early business experiences with Johnston Press, but a more vivid memory was dealing with the print unions at Bury when it was decided to close the out-dated press there and transfer printing to Wakefield.

At first the militant members of the Graphical, Paper and Media Union (GPMU) were having none of it and escalated their opposition by bringing in national officers. The conclusive negotiations took place in a hotel at Preston where Bowdler came face to face with the firebrand GPMU leader from Liverpool, Arnie Martin.

Realising that further resistance was useless, and increasingly frustrated at the outcome, Martin finally conceded. "If I'm going to be f***** ah wanna be kissed," he growled at the genteel Bowdler.

Within weeks of sewing up the Doncaster-Bury exchange Johnston, Bowdler and Chiappelli were engaged in what proved to be not only the group's largest single acquisition at the time but a deal of epoch-making proportions. The purchase of all the regional newspapers published by Emap, formerly East Midland Allied Press, almost doubled the size of Johnston Press and propelled it into the top five of regional newspaper companies in the UK.

And it came out of the blue . . .

Chapter Five

Eastern promise

·

As we have already seen, expansion by acquisition had been a central theme running through the Johnston Press story since the very early days in 19th Century Falkirk. But after the company obtained a Stock Exchange listing in 1988 the quest for growth assumed new impetus, more than ever strategically controlled and planned from a broader financial base.

While Johnston directors were ambitious to develop into new areas of weekly and daily newspaper ownership they were level-headed enough to realise that the group was still only a medium-sized player in a market dominated by the likes of Northcliffe, Westminster Press and Trinity.

As potential takeover targets were identified and discussed the name of East Midland Allied Press (Emap) had been discounted initially. Firstly, it was considered unlikely that the Emap titles would be for sale and, secondly, even if they were, the financial commitment would stretch Johnston Press to the limit.

Nevertheless, the Peterborough-based company was the subject of much industry speculation and discussion and Johnstons was not the only interested party observing from the sidelines. A significant change was taking place in the structure of the regional press, and this had already resulted in the Thomson Corporation and the Anglo-Dutch company Reed Elsevier disposing of their newspaper interests to Trinity International Holdings plc and Newsquest Media Group Limited respectively.

Chairman Johnston touched on these developments in his annual report for 1995. "The Johnston Press board is watching the situation carefully and believes that such change is an ally in the pursuit of future growth," he advised shareholders.

Emap was clearly developing a new role as a multi-faceted media group with magazine, exhibition and radio interests to add to its core newspaper business – but what everyone wanted to know is where this would take Emap and how, in turn, they would be affected.

Freddy Johnston was well qualified to indulge in crystal ball gazing. Some years before he had been invited to Peterborough to meet Emap chairman Sir Frank Rogers, who made clear his desire to buy Johnstons, and more recently he had struck up a good working relationship with chief executive Robin Miller when Emap agreed to sell its stake in T.R. Beckett Ltd, at Eastbourne.

Johnston noted that as well as selling its Beckett's shares Emap had also sold some of its Senews titles in Kent, including those at Dover and Folkstone, to Harry Lambert's Adscene. Based on this he concluded that further peripheral disposals were a possibility.

The remaining Senews titles in south east England – at Rye, Bexhill on Sea, Hastings, Lewes and Crawley, for example – were an attractive proposition and would dovetail well with other group publications in the region.

Johnston also reckoned that of all the Emap titles that might be sold these were the most likely as they were physically detached from the rest of the group in the East Midlands. He was also attracted to Emap's East Yorkshire titles at Scarborough, Bridlington and Whitby.

A telephone call to Robin Miller, who had started his publishing career as a trainee journalist on his home town weekly newspaper in Penrith, was all that was needed to arrange a meeting and this took place at the Great Northern Hotel, in Peterborough.

Johnston and Bowdler found Miller an agreeable individual and the discussions were held in a friendly and relaxed atmosphere, but the response to a possible sale of Senews was lukewarm, although Miller promised to put the proposition to his board of directors. However, a more extensive disposal of Emap's newspapers was not even discussed at that stage.

Undeterred, Johnston requested a further meeting following Emap's acquisition of a number of magazines in France and increased industry speculation about the future of the group's newspaper division. By now Johnston's horizon had widened beyond Senews and Scarborough and he made sure that Miller was aware of this.

Nevertheless, his answer a few weeks later astounded Johnston Press.

"We are not prepared to talk about selling Senews in isolation. But we are prepared to discuss the sale of all our regional newspaper interests," said Miller.

"All of them?" stammered Johnston.

"Yes, all."

Unknown to Johnston, his

approach had brought about the single most important decision ever made by Emap – to think the unthinkable and turn away from newspaper publishing, on which its very existence had been based. It was, said Miller later, akin to selling the family silver.

But for years Emap had been moving towards this major change of direction – ever since it launched its first tabloid magazine, on newsprint, to fill spare capacity on its press at Peterborough. Under Frank Rogers the magazine business had been expanded in the 1970s and this process accelerated further during the 1980s, with more magazines and newspapers acquired – Heart of England Newspapers, Senews and titles at Grantham among them.

Emap also looked to grow in new areas such as business exhibitions and local radio stations, which, together with magazines, slowly overtook newspaper publishing in size and profitability, so that by 1996 newspapers accounted for only 25 per cent of profits yet employed half of the 4,000 workforce.

Ever since taking over as chief executive in 1976 the economics of publishing newspapers had become increasingly less attractive to Miller who, despite his local paper upbringing, had seen greater profit opportunities in other activities.

Several factors combined to convince Miller that he should share his views with his fellow directors before inviting them to reach a decision on which direction to take. One of these was the abortive attempt to buy the Nottingham Evening Post in 1994 when Associated Newspapers easily bettered Emap's bid of £75 million.

Had Emap taken the Johnston approach, which was then still to buy market-leading weekly titles, the defeat might have been more palatable. Instead, having failed to move up a gear, Miller began to question the future involvement in newspapers.

The Johnston Press board in 1996, with newly-appointed director J.S. Gordon (second right) and company secretary P.R. Cooper (far right)

Miller was also concerned about the high capital cost of newspaper production and, as an example, felt uneasy at the prospect of spending £20 million on a new print facility between Kettering and Northampton, knowing full well that in the blink of an eyelid it would soon be overtaken by more advanced technology.

Investment on that scale, he reasoned, was probably better directed towards the new areas in which the company was doing well rather than the traditional business of producing newspapers – labour intensive and operating on margins of only 15 per cent or less.

Finally, Miller worried about the cyclical nature of newspaper advertising, over which publishers had little control as the national economy went through its inevitable boom and bust undulations.

Emap, he concluded, had better things to do with its time and money than publish newspapers. On the other hand magazines were cheaper to produce, had fewer overheads and could contract out production and printing at competitive rates. Similar advantages could be applied to radio, television and exhibitions, too.

More frequently, or so it seemed, Miller was asking himself if the time had come to make a clean break from newspapers. Unwittingly Freddy Johnston was the person who helped him reach a conclusion when he asked about buying the Senews titles in Sussex.

This was the worst performing part of the newspaper division, yet to sell it would send out all the wrong signals about Emap's commitment to the printed media. "Rather than sell a bit we now had to contemplate whether we wanted to be in newspapers at all," said Miller.

The Emap board supported this view and authorised Miller to put the idea of buying the entire division to Johnston. Apart from the reasons already discussed the timing, too, was right – the directors had looked on as other newspaper groups had changed hands for high prices and reckoned that their own conservative valuation of their company, of £195 million, could probably be exceeded.

Freddy Johnston, meanwhile, had the task of convincing his own board that an acquisition on this scale was in the company's best interests. In April,1996, the chairman set out the reasons in a detailed report.

● There was, he said, a similarity of titles with those of Johnston Press; these enjoyed a high market share within their circulation areas; acquisition would provide Johnstons with further geographical expansion.

● Emap, he explained, had four print centres which would provide the group with additional capacity and more flexibility in printing Johnston Press's existing titles. Over the previous two years the pressrooms had benefited from an £8 million investment.

● Closing the group's extensive newspaper division head office at Stamford and other central costs could pave the way for significant savings after acquisition.

● The net profit margin of Emap's newspapers, at around 13 per cent, were on the low side compared to Johnston Press and as such a significant opportunity would be available to increase percentages.

● There were few large newspaper groups of the quality of Emap available.

Next it was Bowdler's turn to spell out the areas of cost savings that had already been earmarked by the executive directors. These were: Head office – £800,000; Training – £200,000; Central costs – £20,000; Accounting reorganisation – £450,000; Printing consolidation on the south coast – £75,000; Newsprint – £100,000.

"These estimates are highly conservative," Bowdler told the directors. "The opportunity for further savings could be significant."

The future management structure of Johnston Press was also an issue that needed addressing. Bowdler said Scarborough would become part of the existing North of England division, with the Senews titles joining the South of England division. Two new divisions would be created, one to accommodate the South Midlands publications based on Northampton and the other based on Peterborough for the East Midlands.

The Johnston board was impressed. There was unanimous agreement that an indicative offer of £205 million should be made for the entire newspaper interests of Emap, including its fixed assets. It was also decided that this should be financed by a one-for-two rights issue of shares to raise about £100 million, with bank borrowings to cover the balance.

Johnston, this time accompanied by finance director Chiappelli, met Miller again at a hotel near Stansted Airport to discuss the indicative offer, but it became clear immediately that an exclusive deal had already been ruled out by Emap. Instead Miller said the company intended to invite offers from other interested parties, of which there were likely to be several.

Initially Johnston Press found itself bidding against two other groups – Newsquest, who later withdrew, and Chris Oakley's Birmingham-based Midland Independent Newspapers. Separate data rooms were set up at the offices of the Emap lawyers, identically supplied with information about the company so that each prospective purchaser could carry out its own due diligence process – essential factual and financial research.

Although sooner or later news of one of the industry's biggest deals for years might leak out on the grapevine, the immediate concern was for total secrecy, even if that meant going to extraordinary and expensive lengths.

The Emap negotiations were given the codename Drucker, but if that was not enough to throw other publishers off the scent Freddy Johnston resorted to trans-Atlantic subterfuge.

He had already agreed to attend a conference in Washington organised by the Federation Internationale des Journeaux, now the World Association of Newspapers, and knew that his British contemporaries would ask questions if he failed to show up.

Johnston put in a token appearance, glad-handed his colleagues in an up-front show of conviviality and then caught Concorde back to London to resume negotiations.

"It was all happening at the right time in the business cycle," he recalled. "It was just after the recession of the early Nineties and right at the beginning of the boom that took place in the late Nineties. No one could possibly have known this but from Emap's point of view, and with the benefit of hindsight, it might have been the wrong time to be getting out of newspapers."

Johnstons tabled a formal bid of £205 million for the Emap portfolio, together with a further £6.1 million for its net working capital, and emerged victorious when Newsquest discontinued its interest in favour of pursuing the Pearson-owned Westminster Press group, and Midland Independent Newspapers also eventually withdrew. The City showed its approval of the takeover as the Johnston Press share price surged and a rights issue of new shares to finance the deal was fully subscribed.

Few people were aware at the time of the nail-biting finale to the negotiations, which were concluded within three months. Just days before the deal was due to be signed the directors of Johnston's merchant bankers, Hill Samuel, announced that they had sold their corporate finance division to bankers Close Brothers Ltd.

Johnston and Chiappelli were furious – angry that bankers with whom they had enjoyed a long and amicable relationship had not entrusted them in confidence with the news, and worried that a now inaccurate name on all the documents would render these legally invalid. Luckily, it didn't.

But there was more drama to come. The following morning Johnston Press and Emap teams of directors and advisers met to conclude negotiations at the Cheapside offices, in London, of merchant bankers Schroeders. Emap's Robin Miller sprung another surprise.

"I have to tell you," he informed a nonplussed Freddy Johnston "that there has been another offer – and it could be bigger than yours. Do you wish to reconsider your offer?"

Johnston declined. He knew that the rival bidder was Midland Independent but it had already been decided that the bid on the table was a fair reflection of Emap's worth.

Miller and his colleagues withdrew to meet the other group, promising to return with a decision within the hour. "It was," reflected Chiappelli "the longest sixty minutes of my life."

It was an anxious time, too, for the Emap team, headed by Miller and Chris Innes, the group's corporate director, who had handled most of the detailed negotiations. They knew that a foot put wrong at this critical stage could force Johnstons to amend their bid or, worse, withdraw and for the whole sale to collapse. They also had to be sure that negotiations with an eager Midland Independent were concluded properly and that they were given every chance to finalise their best offer.

Anxiously the Johnston team paced the room, those who smoked drawing nervously on their cigarettes, the others drinking coffee and tea and talking in small animated groups.

When Miller returned to break the tension there was a smile on his face. "Freddy," he announced. "We've met the other party and they could have problems. Is your offer still on the table?"

Johnston did not bother to answer. Instead he stood up, leaned across the table and shook Miller's hand. Then everyone shook hands. Chiappelli and Bowdler slapped each other on the back before Chiappelli walked away to the end of the room, looked out across the London skyline and wiped a tear from his eye.

Both sides were satisfied with the outcome; both of them emerged as winners. In the years that followed Johnston Press improved the performance of the newly-acquired business while Emap used the money from the sale to expand into France, launch new consumer magazines and build up its radio interests.

But it did not forget its loyal newspaper employees, many with 25 years' service or more, and £1 million was set aside to share among them in recognition of their contribution to the group's success.

Miller, who enjoyed two spells as chief executive of Emap between 1985 and 2003 and was also non-executive chairman for three years between 1998 and 2001, received a knighthood for services to industry in June, 2003.

The immediate aftermath of the acquisition for the Johnston team was a hectic round of presentations, in London, Edinburgh and Glasgow, to explain the biggest single transaction in the company's history to existing investors and potential new ones. Many considered that Johnston Press had paid too much for Emap newspapers and needed convincing of the benefits that would accrue – the £3 million savings that could be achieved, the economies of scale, how the numerous printing presses could either be sold or better utilised.

When the first year's results came out, showing a whopping increase in operating profit of 59 per cent, the critics were silenced once and for all. The more perceptive investors realised that Johnston Press had created for itself a platform for future acquisitions on a similar or even larger scale. Now the company was attracting growing interest from the City with pension funds in particular, including some from Europe, keen to buy shares.

But a pause for breath was needed before Johnstons moved forward again. Thus when Westminster Press, the regional newspaper operation of Pearsons, came on the market and with Newsquest already in talks, the group decided it was not in a position to bid for this sizeable business.

In a historical context the Emap acquisition was another defining moment, on a par with the purchase of the Derbyshire Times in 1978 or the flotation ten years later. The significance of buying the Halifax Courier also became more apparent. Freddy Johnston later conceded that without the experience of running a daily newspaper that this provided the group would probably have hesitated over taking on a venture the size of Emap.

At a stroke the deal added a further 65 titles to the Johnston portfolio: four evenings – at Peterborough, Northampton, Kettering and Scarborough – 30 paid-for weeklies and 31 free weeklies. Together they had a total circulation/distribution of more than two million copies per week.

Midlands/East Anglia acquisitions from Emap

- Northamptonshire Evening Telegraph Series
- Northamptonshire Citizen Series
- Chronicle & Echo (Northampton)
- Northampton Mercury
- Northampton Image
- TV Advertiser Northamptonshire
- Peterborough Evening Telegraph
- Peterborough Citizen
- East Cambridgeshire Town Crier Series
- West Cambridgeshire Town Crier Series
- Stamford Mercury
- Stamford Citizen
- Grantham Journal
- Grantham Citizen
- Melton Times
- Melton Citizen
- Market Harborough Mail
- Spalding Guardian
- Lincolnshire Free Press
- Daventry Weekly Express
- Rugby Advertiser
- Rugby Review

- Lynn News
- Norfolk Citizen Series
- Fenland Citizen
- Bury Free Press Series
- Bury St. Edmunds Citizen
- Diss Express
- Haverhill Echo
- Newmarket Journal
- Suffolk Free Press
- Milton Keynes Citizen Series
- Leighton Buzzard Citizen
- Bedford and Kempston Times and Citizen
- Biggleswade Chronicle
- Luton and Dunstable Herald and Post
- Bucks Herald
- Aylesbury Local TV Guide
- Bucks Advertiser
- Thame Gazette
- Bucks and Winslow Advertiser
- Banbury Guardian
- Banbury Citizen
- Hemel Hempstead Gazette
- Hemel Hempstead Herald Express
- Leamington Spa Courier
- Leamington Spa Review

Emap's former Yorkshire titles	
● Scarborough Evening News	● Bridlington Free Press
● Scarborough and District Trader & Weekly News	● Bridlington Leader
	● Driffield Times
● The Mercury Series	● Beverley Guardian
● Whitby Gazette	● Wolds Weekly Trading Post

Sussex acquisitions from Emap	
● Mid-Sussex Times	● Bexhill-on-sea Observer
● Mid-Sussex Citizen	● Hastings & Bexhill News Series
● Crawley Observer	
● Weekend Herald	● Sussex Express
● Hastings and St. Leonards Observer	● Rye & Battle Observer

Emap never stated publicly why it had decided to sell such an extensive regional newspaper business. However, it caused widespread surprise, not least among the workforce, who first became aware of the sale a few days before it was concluded, when the Sunday Times published a story based on City rumours.

Even then there was no hint that Johnston Press or Midland Independent Newspapers were the likely buyers and media speculation centered around the Northcliffe arm of Associated Newspapers and Newsquest.

Emap declined to comment on the rumours, and were more than happy for the financial press to be beavering away down a blind alley.

Although the group had been harbouring doubts about its future in regional newspapers for some time these had been confined to the higher echelons of management who were well aware of the devastating effect a leak would cause. However, staff on the newspapers had begun to feel increasingly sidelined as Emap's other interests blossomed. Even so investment in the titles had been maintained and no one believed that the group would ever dessert its roots.

After the Sunday Times disclosure the office grapevines moved into overdrive and there was only one topic of conversation when printers, journalists and sales people met over drinks at their local bars. Inevitably names were bandied around, but Johnston Press was considered a rank outsider.

When the announcement was made it left them speechless. Managers broke the news of the sale in turn to small groups until everyone in every Emap centre was informed.

The group's senior editor David Rowell, then in charge at the Kettering Evening Telegraph, told his journalists before leaving for a family holiday, apprehensive at what the future held for him and his colleagues.

"Johnstons had this fierce reputation of being a cost cutter, and that hadn't been an Emap trait," he said. "The first reaction was that we had been sold to a company that was going to slash budgets and everything else.

"That never happened – at Kettering the first thing that Johnstons did was to build new premises to replace the old ones that had been falling down around our ears."

Senior managers at Johnston Press had always made a practice of visiting newspaper offices and print centres on a regular basis. That way they knew just about everyone who worked for the company and learned of local success stories, and problems, first hand,

New acquisitions merited special treatment – always a visit from Freddy Johnston along with his group managing director and

The Kettering Evening Telegraph's fleet of delivery vans in Dryland Street in the 1950s

Richard Pattinson Winfrey and (far right, below) his father Sir Richard Winfrey

finance director on a familiarisation and fact-finding mission.

Now Johnston, Bowdler and Chiappelli embarked on the grand tour of all the main Emap centres, from Whitby in the north east to Hastings in the south.

At each office they faced robust and searching questions. It was an exhausting schedule but the hearts and minds approach convinced the somewhat bewildered former Emap employees that their jobs were safe and in good hands.

PRIVATELY, THE observant Johnston team concluded that further savings were possible as a number of activities appeared to be over-manned. One such area was in pre-press where it became clear that Emap had not invested sufficiently in labour-saving and cost-saving systems.

The group's considerable success in the early days was almost entirely due to the diligence and commitment of the Winfrey family, three generations who carefully nurtured the group's development from one small weekly newspaper in rural Lincolnshire.

Sir Richard Winfrey bought the Spalding Guardian in 1887 and remained the company's father figure from Victorian times until his death in 1944. He was succeeded by his son Richard Pattinson (Pat) Winfrey, chairman until 1973, who in turn handed over to his own sons Richard John Winfrey and Francis Charles Winfrey.

For many years Sir Richard was a Liberal Member of Parliament for South-West Norfolk, and later Gainsborough, and there is little doubt that his efforts to build up a newspaper empire were inspired at least partly by a desire to propogate the Liberal cause, and that of Mr Gladstone in particular.

Surprisingly, in 1936 Sir Richard sold the Spalding Guardian, along with the Boston Guardian that had been started in 1925, to Westminster Press, who published them with their other local title, the Stamford Mercury.

Pure sentiment led Pat Winfrey to seek to bring the Spalding Guardian back into family control after the death of his father. The Westminster directors were sympathetic but insisted that the package should comprise the Spalding, Boston and Stamford titles.

The deal concluded in 1951 has subsequently led to Johnston Press owning all three titles and the distinction of publishing the

Rutland and Stamford Mercury, Britain's oldest surviving newspaper title – a fact recognised by the Guinness Book of Records. Founded in 1695, it also rivals the Worcester Journal for the honour of being the country's oldest surviving newspaper. Alas, with a sale of around 22,000 it can no longer lay claim to be the best selling provincial paper in the land – but that record was set in the 1850s when the readership was very different!

The Mercury's archive of bound volume copies covers nearly 300 years and is a unique record of local life. Its significance was recognised in 2005 when the National Lottery Fund awarded a £300,000 grant to carry out crucial restoration on the old papers – so fragile after constant handling that public access had been barred for eight years.

The restoration, together with a complete microfilm record, once again allowed researchers to delve into Stamford's colourful past. One of the most unusual news items is that of a man who sold his wife for four shillings at Stamford market – an incident that is said to have been the inspiration for a scene in Thomas Hardy's novel, The Mayor of Casterbridge.

By the time of its sale Emap was the eleventh largest regional newspaper publisher by circulation. Although its original business was based in Peterborough, Kettering and East Anglia it had developed into three broad geographical areas: Yorkshire, the Midlands/East Anglia and Sussex and operated four printing plants at Scarborough, Peterborough, Northampton and Burgess Hill.

Much like Johnston Press at the time, its portfolio of titles was focused on smaller provincial centres. Based on its own market share estimates, Emap could claim to be the leading title in more than 70 per cent of the markets in which it operated.

Space and time mean that it is neither feasible nor practical to analyse each title individually – indeed such a publication already exists, *Men of Mark* by David Newton, which tells the Emap story up to 1977. But if we are seeking examples of market leaders then we need look no further than King's Lynn, in Norfolk, and Bury St Edmunds, in Suffolk, where the paid-for weekly papers are an integral part of the fabric of the towns they serve.

The Bury Free Press was founded in 1855 and acquired by the Winfrey family in 1903. It fitted their political template, having been started to satisfy the Liberal readers among a population

of 17,000, who until then had to make do with the Conservative-leaning Bury and Norwich Post.

Now part of Anglia Newspapers, the Free Press had in 2004 a circulation of around 31,000 copies per week, drawn from a population of 90,000 based on Bury St Edmunds, Stowmarket, Mildenhall and Thetford.

As so often was the case in the politically turbulent 19th Century, local newspapers were launched as much as mouthpieces for the Conservative or Liberal parties as for their local news content.

Kings Lynn was a typical battleground with the strongly-entrenched Tory paper the Lynn Advertiser, founded in 1841, up against the Liberal-minded Lynn News, founded in 1859. As the Winfreys extended their East Anglian interests they acquired the News in 1893 and the Advertiser in 1922, merging the two titles as the twice-weekly Lynn News in 1945.

The Tuesday and Friday editions have a combined circulation of around 52,500 copies in the largely agricultural areas of Kings Lynn, Hunstanton, Downham Market and Swaffam with a population of 130,000. People in very high places are among the readership – the Queen's Sandringham estate is within the circulation area and a constant source of Royal news.

Among the newly-acquired Sussex titles was the weekly Sussex Express, based in Lewes, which had been founded in 1837 but in recent years had undergone a succession of ownership changes. The title passed out of family hands in 1975 when it was bought by Morgan Grampian, who sold it on to Westminster Press the following year. In 1984 Yorkshireman Robert Breare took control and after spending a small fortune on a new colour press and computerised typesetting disposed of the business to Emap in 1987.

Breare's wealth had been inherited from his father Will Breare, principal of the Harrogate Advertiser series, now also a part of Johnston Press. He had assumed control of the company following

a domestic upheaval and eventually sold out to United Newspapers for £3.4 million – much of which he then reinvested in Sussex.

At one time Will Breare's business in Harrogate had also interested Freddy Johnston and the possibility of a sale had been discussed when both were members of the Press Council. But Breare was more interested in passing on the business to his son, even though the relationship between them seemed strained.

Newspapers wouldn't be the same without the seemingly endless supply of anecdotes about people and events, but one of the most arresting tales from the Emap stable concerns the Hemel Hempstead Gazette, which can probably claim to be the only paper in Britain to be delivered by the police!

For 71 years the title was published by the Needham family and during all this time could boast never to have had a strike or missed an edition. Even when the printing unions called a national stoppage the Gazette's staff did not take part, which lead to heavy picketing to stop the papers being distributed.

Luckily the police station was located next door to the print works and with the help of the local constabulary a plan was hatched. The horse and cart, which normally delivered the Gazette around the town, was put out front as usual and it appeared as if it was being loaded.

But round the back copies of the Gazette were bundled into two police cars, which drove out of the station unnoticed to make the deliveries to newsagents.

Of the 31 free titles acquired by Johnston Press from Emap the

The launch of the tabloid format Lynn News in 1989

Milton Keynes Citizen is a perfect example of how newspapers of that genre can provide a superior service to advertisers and readers alike. Not only can it claim to be one of the biggest and best free newspapers in the United Kingdom, it has the trophies to prove it!

For four years in succession, in 1993, 1994, 1995 and 1996, the Citizen won the Newspaper Society accolade of Best Free Newspaper in Great Britain. In 1998 it was judged the NS best free newspaper in the south east and again won the national award in 2000. The same year the trade magazine UK Press Gazette also named the Citizen as the best free in the nation. When Johnston Press began its own internal awards for excellence the Citizen, inevitably, was among the winners, as group free newspaper of the year in 2002 and 2003.

The Citizen was founded in 1981 – 32 pages printed in black and white and delivered to 60,000 homes. The readership was spoiled for choice and at the time of the launch there were already four other newspapers in Milton Keynes – the Wolverton Express, Milton Keynes Mirror and the Weekender, all published by Westminster Press, and the Milton Keynes Gazette, published by Home Counties Newspapers. Of these only the Citizen, which was acquired by Emap in 1987, remains.

The Milton Keynes Citizen's marketing manager Sarah Jamieson with awards from the bulging trophy cabinet

The Milton Keynes Citizen, which in 2004 was delivered free to more than 100,000 homes and businesses every week, has titanic proportions – typically a main section of approximately 80 pages, motors 64 pages, property 168 pages, entertainments 24 pages, plus a 28-page monthly business insert.

The title heads a product range that also includes the free Tuesday Citizen, formerly the Sunday Citizen (90,000 delivery, 60 pages), Leighton Buzzard Citizen (16,000 distribution, 88 pages) and the paid-for Leighton Buzzard Observer (8,500 circulation).

As a result of the Emap acquisition Johnston's lone evening paper at Halifax now found itself joined by another four evening titles.

Sir Meredith Whittaker, who expanded the family business in Scarborough across East Yorkshire

The smallest of these, indeed one of the smallest in the country, was the Scarborough Evening News with a circulation at the time of around 17,000, mainly in the East coast resort towns of Scarborough and Filey.

Until the title and several associated weekly papers were bought by Emap in 1986 it had been published for 104 years by five generations of the Whittaker family, a dynasty that began with Thomas Whittaker, a campaigning teetotaller who came to Scarborough to manage a temperance hotel in the town.

The family's abhorrence of strong drink was never more apparent than when the company's granite-faced offices were nearing completion in the late 1800s. A gang of experienced stonemasons had been drafted in from Scotland to carry out the work, but they turned out to be hard-drinking men who downed copious amounts of ale as they worked. The embarrassed Whittakers sacked the lot and replaced them with a more abstemious team!

For a short period after the launch of the Evening News in 1882 the town, with a population of only 30,000, had no fewer than six newspapers, two of them dailies. These included the Whittaker-owned Mercury, which continued until 1998, having for many years replaced the five-days-a-week Evening News on Saturdays.

Gradually the Whittaker influence extended over a wide area of East Yorkshire, much of the growth being down to the unflagging

energy of Sir Meredith Whittaker, who was still at the helm when he died at the age of 90. He was knighted for services to the newspaper industry, having been a leading negotiator for the proprietors over wages and conditions.

In 1989 the group changed its name from Scarborough and District Newspapers to Yorkshire Regional Newspapers, an operating title that has been retained by Johnston Press. This more accurately reflected its wider activities that included the Bridlington Free Press (bought in 1897), Whitby Gazette (1978), and East Yorkshire Newspapers (1987, from United Newspapers and including the Driffield Times, Beverley Guardian and Pocklington Times).

Subsequent acquisitions have been the free distribution Trader and Weekly Post (1995), and the Bridlington Gazette and Herald (free), Pocklington Post (paid-for) and Driffield Post (paid-for) which were bought in 1997 for £1.3 million. The Mercury name lives on at Filey, Malton and Pickering.

While Scarborough had always been out on a limb geographically in the Emap portfolio, the other evening titles were all located in the group's heartland. Of the three the Northamptonshire Evening Telegraph at Kettering had been part of Emap, as it became, since 1901.

The paper was founded in 1897 by a group of county Liberals to serve the shoe-making towns of Kettering, Wellingborough, Rushden and Thrapston. But only four years later Richard Winfrey was called in to save the ailing enterprise when the bank became restive about the size of the overdraft and the chief executive was suspended for accounting irregularities.

Winfrey did rescue the Evening Telegraph, and 43 years later he was still there as managing director, but only by maintaining an unrelenting grip on spending. Waste, he told his staff, was wicked.

Kettering remained at the core of the Emap operation for most of the 20th century, both as a print centre and, until 1961, as the home of its only evening title. Under the guiding hand of the Winfreys it benefited from investment in new technology and in 1976 made the transition from hot-metal to web-offset printing.

A new Goss rotary press was installed in purpose-built premises as the original Dryland Street premises in Kettering were all but abandoned. To mark the occasion one of Northamptonshire's top rose growers developed the new Evening Telegraph rose and a bed of these was presented to each major town within the circulation area.

In its centenary year the Evening Telegraph moved home again, to Rothwell Road, Kettering, as Johnston Press set about reorganising the South Midlands division, with divisional control centred at Upper Mounts, Northampton. This also led to the closure of the Kettering press when Upper Mounts was established as the print centre for both the Telegraph and the Northampton Chronicle and Echo. In 2000-2002 the presses there were updated and enlarged at a cost of £20 million.

At Peterborough the evening paper tradition is less than half that of the Kettering title that spawned it and it was not until 1961 that the rapidly growing town had an evening paper it could call its own.

Until then Peterborough had been served by the Emap weekly titles the Advertiser, which it acquired in 1897, and the Citizen, founded in 1898, and a slip edition of the Northamptonshire Evening Telegraph.

Newsprint shortages after the war forced the merger of the weekly titles in 1946, but as the supply situation improved the potential for evening paper sales was recognised by the Emap directors and in 1949 they decided to introduce a Peterborough edition of the Evening Telegraph.

The idea was not a new one and had been discussed before the outbreak of war. What prompted the idea this time was the competition posed by the two London evening papers, the Evening Standard and the Evening News, which were both rushing papers to Peterborough containing up-to-date racing results.

If they can do it, so can we, argued managing director Pat Winfrey. The solution was to utilise the Advertiser press in Broadway – a complete set of cast rotary plates of the Kettering paper was driven over each day and stop press racing results inserted.

This worked fine until on one trip the van carrying the plates was involved in an accident and its cargo so badly damaged that all the plates had to be recast. After that only the papier mache flongs were taken to Peterborough and plates cast on the spot.

The arrangement proved its worth in 1952 when the death of King George VI was announced. A special edition printed in Peterborough sold 30,000 copies, after which the Peterborough content was increased to six or eight inside pages daily.

The stand-alone Peterborough Evening Telegraph was born on May 15, 1961, and quickly built up a daily sale of 7,000 copies. If the readers liked it, so too did the country's leading newspaper design experts.

Before the end of that year the judges in the annual Newspaper Design Awards, which had been started some eight years earlier, hailed the Evening Telegraph as "a newspaper of real typographical personality" and placed it third behind papers in Glasgow and Sheffield. In 1963 it came second to the Belfast Evening Telegraph, making it England's best-designed provincial evening.

By then sales had already doubled to 14,000 and by the mid-1970s had climbed to more than 30,000 to make the Telegraph the country's fastest-growing evening. No one doubted the quality of the product, but such phenomenal sales were spurred on when in 1969 the Development Corporation chose Peterborough for expansion to accommodate the London overspill population. When the title was acquired by Johnston Press sales had slipped back to 29,000.

The Emap evening titles had been stablemates for a mere four years when they were bought by Johnston Press, the last of the quartet, the Chronicle and Echo at Northampton, typifying the constantly changing nature of regional newspaper ownership. Having been bought by Provincial Newspapers in 1931, the daily and its sister weeklies eventually became part of the great United Newspapers empire before being acquired by Emap in 1992.

A sale of 30,000 at the time of the Johnston acquisition was a clear indication of the Chronicle and Echo's place in the fabric of Northampton, a town that had built its wealth on boot and shoe manufacturing – yet another of Britain's traditional industries that has gone into sharp decline in the face of foreign competition.

It has been Northampton's only evening paper since November, 1931, when the Daily Echo and the Daily Chronicle were merged. Both had been founded within a week of each other in 1880 – the Echo supporting the Anglican church and Conservatism and its rival Nonconformity and Liberalism.

The evening titles were preceded by well-established weeklies, the Mercury and the Herald, which also merged in 1931. Today the word Herald has been dropped from the

Early copies of the Stamford Mercury dating from from 1715

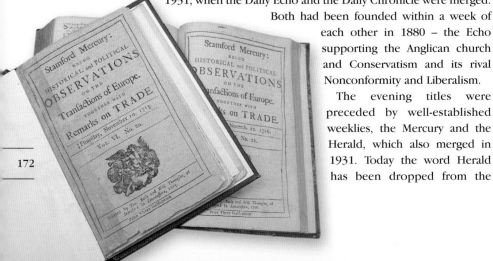

weekly masthead but the Mercury lives on as a free distribution newspaper and is delivered to about 60,000 homes in the Northampton area.

The Mercury was founded in 1695 and is one of the oldest continuously published newspapers in the UK – and to prove it every copy is on file with the local library service. The original proprietors were Robert Raikes and William Dicey, who were already seasoned newspapermen when they left the Stamford Mercury to try their luck on their own in Northampton. An early scoop for the Mercury was the news of Bonnie Prince Charlie's retreat on December 6, 1745.

At the other end of the scale, Northampton could also boast one of the country's newest publications, the free distribution Northants on Sunday, which was launched by Johnston Press in 2001. It is delivered to about 74,000 homes in the county and offers a comprehensive roundup of sporting action, regional news and features.

The idea for a Sunday free paper arose out of discussions between editorial director Mark Edwards and the then managing director, Peter Walker, who were looking for ways to revitalise their ailing weekend TV Advertiser, a freesheet that had been bought by Emap to capitalise on a sudden upsurge in demand for listings magazines and supplements.

They were also looking for a publication to reflect reader interest in the success of the area's two premier sporting clubs – Northampton Rugby Union, the "Saints", and Northampton Town FC, the "Cobblers".

The project received new impetus when rumours began to circulate that Frank Branson's Bedford-based Local Sunday Newspapers, publishers of Bedford on Sunday, were about to launch a new publication in Northamptonshire.

The decision was taken to launch Northants on Sunday with all possible speed and to give it an orange-red masthead to distinguish it from other titles already printed in Northampton.

What happened next made local newspaper history. Local Sunday Newspapers reacted by mounting a High Court challenge and seeking an injunction to prevent their rivals using the words "On Sunday" or the chosen colour in the masthead, claiming that both were similar to their own.

After a hearing lasting several days the judge threw out the challenge, in effect giving Northants on Sunday the green light.

> " Local Sunday Newspapers reacted by mounting a High Court challenge and seeking an injunction to prevent their rivals using the words 'On Sunday' "

Within days the new title was being pushed through letterboxes after a supreme effort by everyone involved at Northampton. Many of them had little sleep for this was also the week of the General Election in June 4, 2001, and they had already worked round the clock three nights earlier producing special editions of the two evening titles.

But it was worth it. The rival publication from Bedford never materialised and Northants on Sunday claimed its niche in the crowded county newspaper market.

IN THE 20 years prior to Emap's decision to sell its newspaper interests the company had expanded on all fronts, especially its magazine activities. But only a year before the sale to Johnston it had bought yet another newspaper, the Luton and Dunstable Herald and Post, a highly successful weekly free started in 1973.

The launch pad for this growth was the creation in 1947 of a group structure for the operation of the four individual newspaper companies controlled by the Winfrey family. The idea was not a new one – Sir Richard Winfrey had toyed with such a move before his death in 1944 and discussed it at length with his son, Pat.

Pat Winfrey wasted little time in putting the consolidation plan on the agenda despite the post-war difficulties that seriously hampered thoughts of expansion – newsprint was rationed, and remained so until 1956, and power supplies were so erratic that on occasions presses could not run and Linotype machines were unable to operate. If electricity cuts lasted too long hot metal in the Linotype pots solidified and took more than an hour to heat up again when power was restored – a calamity on publication days!

But Pat Winfrey argued that by combining the resources of the family's four newspaper companies there would be opportunity for economy and growth. A financial study appeared to support an amalgamation, and by the end of 1946 the directors and shareholders – 180 in total – of all the component companies had given the scheme their approval.

The result was East Midland Allied Press Ltd, which was incorporated on May 27, 1947.

The initials EMAP were already familiar in the newspaper world. It had been a convenience title when negotiating national advertising and also represented the East Midland Allied Paper Company, which had handled newsprint supplies for all four companies.

The businesses that combined to create the new group were:

- The Northamptonshire Printing and Publishing Co Ltd,
  Kettering, publishers of the daily Northamptonshire Evening
  Telegraph and weeklies Kettering Leader and Guardian,
  Wellingborough News, Rushden Echo and Argus, Thrapston
  Raunds and Oundle Journal, and the Market Harborough
  Advertiser and Midland Mail;

- The Peterborough Advertiser Co Ltd, publishers of the
  twice-weekly Peterborough Citizen and Advertiser;

- The West Norfolk and King's Lynn Newspaper Co Ltd, of King's
  Lynn, publishers of the twice-weekly Lynn News and Advertiser;
  and

- The Bury St Edmunds Printing and Publishing Co Ltd,
  publishers of the weekly Bury Free Press and Suffolk and Essex
  Free Press and printers on contract of the Newmarket Journal.

Despite the ongoing newsprint restrictions, which more or less
precluded any meaningful expansion, the first year's operation of
Emap was a successful one with profits of the new group higher
than the average profits of the previously independent companies.
By 1952 the group's combined circulation had increased from
200,000 to approaching 250,000 and the original 12 titles had
increased to 16.

This story of growth was repeated many times in the years that
followed and the paths of Emap and Johnston crossed several times
as each eyed up potential acquisitions. Among them were the titles

published by Stanley Clarke's Heart of England Newspapers at Leamington Spa, Aylesbury, Banbury and Rugby, all of which fell to Emap.

Staff working on those newspapers took some time to get over the change in culture that resulted. From Clarke, the self-important but likeable control freak, who involved himself in every part of the business and carried so many papers that he burdened himself with three briefcases, to the devolved style practised by Emap, in which managers were given greater individual responsibility.

Stamford was one of the centres that quickly came under the Johnston Press spotlight as the home of Emap's newspaper division head office, primarily a "think tank" function that was closed, bringing with it a number of redundancies. Elsewhere human resources and administration staff were trimmed. On the positive side, the newly acquired accounts centre at Peterborough was found to be so well structured that it was expanded to take on the whole of the Johnston Press accounting function.

BOWDLER PAID special attention to the group's considerable printing capacity with the aim of ensuring that any titles that were printed by outside contractors were now brought in-house, resulting in substantial savings.

A necessary bi-product of the Emap integration was the change in the structure of Johnston Press itself that Bowdler had foreseen, the creation of new operating divisions redefining the company's management style.

No matter how hands-on Bowdler and Chiappelli preferred to be it was obvious that they could no longer visit each centre with the same frequency as before or pay such close personal attention to all the semi-autonomous companies that comprised Johnston Press.

The divisional structure that had already started to evolve in Iain Bell's day was now refined and expanded. Divisional managing directors (d.m.d) and finance directors were appointed above the individual managing directors with a direct reporting line to head office in Edinburgh.

By 1997 the newspaper divisions comprised Scotland (with Stuart McPherson as d.m.d), North of England (Graham Gould), North Midlands (Danny Cammiade), East Midlands (Chris Pennock), South Midlands (Peter Walker), and South of England (Mike Pakes). The Isle of Man was managed by Trudi Williamson, although nominally part of the Scotland division.

Life is Local: The History of Johnston Press plc

At a lower management tier there was promotion and restyling from within – advertising managers became directors, some advertising managers became managing directors, finance controllers were redesignated finance directors . . .

ALTHOUGH THE absorption of Emap and the changes this necessitated occupied a great deal a senior management time this was not at the expense of further progress and growth for Johnston Press. However, it was to be another three years before the group made its next significant acquisition. In the meantime several smaller developments took place.

In January, 1997, one of the Emap titles, the Cambridge Crier, a loss-making weekly free newspaper, was sold to Yattendon Investment Trust. The same year also saw the purchase of three small weekly titles in East Yorkshire which fitted in comfortably with the group's existing activities there. They were the Pocklington Post, a paid-for weekly started in 1988, the weekly free Bridlington Gazette and Herald, and the weekly paid-for Driffield Post.

There was also further consolidation in Derbyshire with the purchase in October, 1997, of North Derbyshire Newspapers Ltd, publisher of the weekly free newspaper the Chesterfield Express, and the fortnightly free newspapers, the Matlock and Peak Express and Dronfield Express. The acquisition was made through the Johnston subsidiary, Wilfred Edmunds Ltd, of Chesterfield.

The prosperous south east of England was a key target area in group strategic planning and the purchase of London-based Home Counties Newspapers was seen as a mouth-watering prospect, "an attractive opportunity" as chief executive Tim Bowdler described it.

What proved so enticing was not only Home Counties' geographical spread of 27 paid-for weeklies and 21 free weeklies (which included slip editions of its main titles) in Essex, east London, north London, Hertfordshire, Buckinghamshire and Bedfordshire, but also the way in which the business was run.

This had been so inefficient that Johnstons reasoned there was tremendous scope for improvement if better managed.

At one time Freddy Johnston had been a director of HCN but resigned in frustration at the way in which it was being operated. "I didn't want to be associated with a company that I thought could fail at any time," he recalled. "They had an unfailing knack of getting things wrong, an uncanny way of always missing the boat."

Typical of the flawed thinking of HCN was the failure to perceive the threat posed by weekly free newspapers to existing paid-for titles, instead wrongly identifying the new evening titles being launched by Lord Thomson – nearly all of which failed – as the greatest danger.

On another occasion the substantial and successful paid-for Herts Advertiser was converted to a free distribution weekly when a more sensible decision would have been to protect the Advertiser by launching a defensive freesheet to supplement it.

In December, 1997, Johnston Press made an offer to acquire HCN's share capital and the following January announced that its bid of approximately £52 million had been accepted. It was on the verge of moving up from fifth to fourth place in the ranking of regional and local newspaper publishers with eight per cent of the national market.

However, the interest in HCN had first been expressed more than 16 months previously when Bowdler reported back to a board meeting on talks he had had with chief executive Bill Coppen-Gardner about the possible exchange of titles in Bedfordshire. Subsequently he revealed that the intention was to buy Home Counties' loss-making operation in Leighton Buzzard, Milton Keynes and Bedford for about £1.5 million, which would be increased to £5 million if the Luton operation was also available. But he warned that the businesses would need significant restructuring to make them profitable.

The deal had already been verbally agreed informally so there was both surprise and annoyance in the Johnston camp when a letter arrived rejecting the offer. What's more, the Johnston print division also lost a contract with HCN worth £860,000 to print some of its titles, although the loss was offset by bringing in house a number of newspapers printed externally.

Milton Keynes, especially, was viewed as an area with considerable growth potential and Johnstons were not prepared to sit back and do nothing while the HCN affair rumbled on. The company's answer was bold and decisive – the launch of a new free Sunday newspaper, even though this would run at a first-year loss of £200,000.

Spring, 1997, was set as a target date for the Sunday Citizen, but these plans were thrown into some disarray when news of the launch leaked out and rivals Bedfordshire on Sunday pre-empted the launch with their own Sunday paper for Milton Keynes. The appearance of the Citizen was advanced to February with a 70,000 distribution, compared with 40,000 for the competing Milton Keynes on Sunday, which contained very little local advertising but was strong editorially. In 2004 the Milton Keynes Tuesday Citizen replaced the Sunday Citizen.

While this diversion was taking place the unpredictable directors of Home Counties put the future of their company back on the agenda in a written offer to sell their loss-making titles, although it was to be the end of 1997 before a substantive offer for all of the group's titles was made.

The business, which started out as a family concern in 1891, was a listed company with a turnover of £38 million and a payroll of 600. It had expanded, mainly by acquisition, since the 1960s but for some time had been achieving unsatisfactory profits of around £1 million, due mainly to losses incurred by its newspapers in Luton and Milton Keynes. Herald Newspapers at Luton, for example, had annual losses of around £800,000. The group also had a tandem business for the manufacture and sale of customised envelopes which contributed £7 million or 8 per cent of turnover

The HCN directors, led by chairman Bill Gibbs, made a rational decision when they concluded that they did not have the resources or the capability to improve performance unaided and that the best course of action would be to sell the whole of the company.

Of the potential purchasers, Johnston Press was preferred because it was considered well placed to secure a viable future for the greatest number of the loss-making titles.

However, the sale was subject to the consent of the Minister for Consumer and Competition Affairs. Euphoria turned to dismay when she withheld approval and in February, 1998, she formally announced that the purchase was being referred to the Monopolies and Mergers Commission. Among the reasons were possible concerns about the effect on newspaper advertising rates in Bedfordshire, Buckinghamshire and Hertfordshire.

Despite Johnston Press's extensive geographical spread in the United Kingdom this was not an area of the country where a significant overlap with other group newspapers would occur and there had been confidence that formal approval would be forthcoming.

The delay caused by the MMC inquiry had serious repercussions and although the offer had been conditionally accepted by more than 95 per cent of Home Counties' shareholders it sadly lapsed because of legal constraints. There were, however, hopes that the Takeover Panel of the Stock Exchange would allow a new bid to be made after three months.

The Competition and Consumer Affairs Minister published the MCC's report in June, 1998. This concluded that the proposed acquisition would not operate against the public interest and should be permitted.

But it was all too late, for by then HCN had been bought by another group, Eastern Counties Newspapers, of Norwich, now known as Archant. Seizing the opportunity that had arisen by the unfortunate turn of events, Eastern Counties weighed in with an offer slightly above that made by Johnstons. In April it announced that the holders of 60.9 per cent of HCN shares had given irrevocable undertakings to accept the offer.

Under the circumstances the MMC inquiry was largely academic, but it was concluded nevertheless. When the official report was published it said that had the sale to Johnstons gone ahead this would not have been against the public interest, there would have been no adverse effect on regional or national advertisers and the transfer would not have threatened the accurate presentation of news or the free expression of opinion.

The failure to acquire the whole of HCN cast a temporary air of gloom over the Johnston Press boardroom. Hundreds of hours of research, due diligence and financial and legal arrangements had in effect been wasted. Bowdler's reaction on hearing the news of the sale was to pick up the telephone and complain bitterly to Coppen-Gardner, but this was more out of frustration than anger.

Freddy Johnston reflected that although HCN was not pivotal to the company it would have been a very useful addition to the portfolio. "But subsequently this setback left us with the capacity to expand elsewhere – it was like history repeating itself, going right back to 1973 when we failed to buy the Stirling Observer but bought better businesses shortly afterwards."

Within months, however, parts of Home Counties were again on the market – although Eastern Counties were keen to retain their new titles in, for example, Hertfordshire and Greater London, they were less interested in the loss-making titles in Bedfordshire and Buckinghamshire.

Such a scenario had been recognised by the MMC, which in effect cleared the way for Johnston Press to successfully complete the purchase for £8 million of eight of the original Homes Counties' titles from Eastern Counties.

Bowdler made the first move in a call to the chief executive of

Eastern Counties, Peter Strong, who had previously been in charge of Emap's newspaper division at the time of the Johnston takeover.

The new titles acquired were the weekly paid-fors the Luton News, Dunstable Gazette and Leighton Buzzard Observer, and the weekly frees, the Luton Leader, Milton Keynes Herald, Bedford Herald, and the Biggleswade and Sandy Herald and the Mid Beds Herald.

Although the MMC had not ruled out the possibility of another publisher making a bid for the loss-making businesses it considered this an unlikely outcome given the local market conditions and the scale and persistence of HCN's losses in those areas.

"We believe that, if not transferred to Johnston, all HCN's titles in Luton, Dunstable and Milton Keynes would close," was the Commission's verdict.

The newly acquired titles presented the kind of challenge that Johnston Press had come to relish over the years – the deal had been codenamed Angel and some wag even suggested that this was a heaven-sent opportunity.

Luton was found to have been especially poorly managed and haemorrhaging cash at an alarming rate, fully justifying the MMC's assessment. Johnstons had been prepared for just such a situation and embarked on a programme of reorganisation and capital investment. At the sharp end the task of reviving Luton was entrusted to Mike Richardson while the chairman's eldest son, Michael Johnston, was promoted to managing director of Bedfordshire Newspapers, having impressed during his previous stint at Hemel Hempstead.

Their brief was simple: to turn an annual loss by the eight titles of £1.2 million, on a turnover of £5 million, into a profit of £800,000 in the first year.

They did.

A by now rare acquisition in Scotland followed when, in January, 1999, Johnston Press announced the purchase for £1.8 million of the Arbroath Herald, a title which for years had been printed by Strachan and Livingston at Kirkcaldy. Other titles included in the deal were the Broughty Ferry Guide, Carnoustie Gazette, and Monifieth Advertiser, all of which were incorporated into the group's newspaper division in Scotland.

For years the business had been run by two elderly bachelors, George Lowe and George Shepherd, who was also the editor of the paper. Negotiations for the sale took place with Shepherd, now the

The brief was simple: to turn an annual loss by the eight titles of £1.2 million, on a turnover of £5 million, into a profit of £800,000 in the first year. They did.

sole proprietor after Lowe's death, and were held in his flat near the office.

Though small, the Arbroath Herald was a profitable operation that had been serving the Arbroath, Carnoustie, Monifieth and Broughty Ferry areas since 1884. Its claim to fame was as the last Scottish newspaper to devote its front page entirely to classified advertising, a tradition that finally ended in 2004.

This left editor Craig Nisbet with a problem not faced by any of his predecessors – finding a page one splash story every week. Throughout its history important local events – one of Scotland's worst rail disasters and a lifeboat tragedy among them – had been consigned to inside pages while church and public notices greeted readers of the Herald on Fridays.

This addition to the Johnston Press portfolio, which then comprised 155 titles, was merely the hors d'ouvres for the scrumptious main course that was to follow later that year when, in June, 1999, Portsmouth and Sunderland Newspapers were acquired in a deal worth £254 million.

Chapter Six

Daring dawn raid

The addition of new titles to the ever-expanding Johnston Press portfolio was always a roller coaster of emotions for those directly involved.

The thrill of the chase often gave way to frustration, disappointment, nail-biting delay and tedious formality. But nothing could match the sweet smell of success, the final adrenaline rush when the deal was closed.

The takeover of Portsmouth and Sunderland Newspapers in 1999 had all these ingredients in abundance, an often-bumpy ride with the bruises to prove it. Agreement was the culmination of protracted and difficult negotiations that had begun some 12 months earlier, initiated after Freddy Johnston had shrewdly identified the group with, as its name suggests, extensive interests in the North East and on the South Coast, as a potential takeover target.

P&SN was an attractive proposition, at that time publishing 35 evening and weekly newspapers, in the North spreading from Hartlepool to the Scottish Borders and in the South concentrated on East Hampshire and West Sussex, as well as operating a successful chain of convenience stores. Its flagship evening titles were The News, Portsmouth, with a daily sale of 71,700 copies, and the Sunderland Echo, selling 57,400 copies daily, while the weekly sector was led by the Chichester Observer series (31,200) and the Northumberland Gazette (10,700).

The company also published 21 free weeklies with a combined distribution of 655,000 copies. The total sale of the four evenings was 178,000 and for the 10 paid-for weeklies 86,000.

For many years P&SN, a publicly quoted company, had been controlled by its colourful chairman Sir Richard Storey Bt, a prominent figure in the newspaper industry who had served on the Press Council and was a former president of the Newspaper Society. A substantial landowner around Malton, in the East Riding of Yorkshire, he was also a staunch supporter of the Conservative Party. Storey had high political ambitions and unsuccessfully contested the parliamentary elections at Don Valley in 1966 and Huddersfield West in 1970, where he lost by a mere 193 votes after slashing the previous Labour majority by more than 4,000.

A disagreement within the Storey family led ultimately to the sale

Sir Richard Storey: reported disagreements with his sister over the future of P&SN may have led to the company's sale

of the family business. This is believed to have centered around who should run the group, with Sir Richard favouring his son Kenelm to succeed him – a seemingly logical line of succession given that this would provide a fifth generation of Storeys at the helm. However, the idea was said not to have appealed to Sir Richard's sister, the Hon Jacquetta Cator and her husband Francis, who were believed to have been advised not to let that happen.

Although Kenelm had a successful publishing career outside P&SN in charge of international sales of The Guardian, the split had a damaging effect among the board, which led to Storey giving up the cherished chairmanship although he remained as a non-executive director.

He was succeeded as chairman by Sir Stephen Waley-Cohen, a former Lord Mayor of London, theatre entrepreneur and owner of the St Martin's Theatre, home of the long-running Agatha Christie thriller, the Mousetrap, and a non-executive director since the mid-1990s.

Johnston met Storey at a Newspaper Society function the day after he had formally resigned as chairman, an event made all the more poignant as it fell exactly 25 years since he was appointed and 125 years to the day since P&SN was founded by his great-grandfather.

"He had a face like thunder," Johnston recalled. "I thought to myself, some day that business will be sold."

He shared his thoughts with fellow directors at a board meeting in August, 1998, and a lengthy discussion ensued on the implications of Storey's defeat. Three months later Johnston Press made its move with a formal approach to the chairman of P&SN and, as a courtesy, contact with the Storey family to ensure they were fully informed of developments.

The crucial meeting of Johnston directors at which the bid attempt – codenamed Pilot for security reasons – was agreed was also attended by three experts from the company's main financial advisors, N.M. Rothschild and Son, led by Bill Staple.

He addressed the board at length, giving a comprehensive summary of the options available, tactics and risks. As subsequent events were to prove, his reading of the situation was masterly.

Staple warned that a referral to the Monopolies and Mergers Commission was inevitable but considered that clearance would be given as the only overlap between Johnston and P&SN was in a small area of West Sussex. Competition from other bidders was a near certainty with Newsquest, Regional Independent Media and possibly Southern Newspapers (Newscom) as the likely candidates.

The risks, advised Staple, were the danger of over-paying for the business, given market volatility at the time, a repeat of the Home Counties scenario, or the blocking of a bid by the MMC.

Johnston and chief executive Bowdler met Waley-Cohen at another of his theatres, the Victoria Palace, near London's Victoria Station. The hit rock 'n' roll musical Buddy was playing there at the time, but the reception they received after climbing nearly 100 steps to an office at the top of the theatre was anything but upbeat.

Bowdler was still recovering from a sleepless night, when he had been kept awake by his wife's hacking cough, and a crack-of-dawn train journey from Castle Combe, in Wiltshire, where they had been staying. Johnston meanwhile had arrived fresh and eager but was visibly panting for breath by the time he had completed the long climb up the staircase trying to keep up with his younger companion.

Waley-Cohen, charming as usual, and his chief executive, the tall, affable, Oxford University educated Charles Brims, were unmoved by the distressed state of their visitors. Both were experienced businessmen, Brims having honed his management skills with the brewing giant Courage, including six years as retail director before being head hunted by P&SN in 1986 to utilise his marketing expertise.

The tenor of the brief meeting was polite and civilised but lacking in warmth. It had been arranged four days earlier in a telephone call from Johnston to Waley-Cohen, who had every reason to feel pleased after announcing a healthy set of trading figures the following day.

"We weren't at all surprised when the two of them arrived on November 20 to say they would like to make an indicative offer for the company," recalled Brims. "But this was nothing new – we had had a queue of people knocking on our door for years. The only difference this time was that Johnstons actually put a price on it."

Waley-Cohen, whose first job after leaving Cambridge University was as a financial journalist at the Daily Mail, and Brims, listened politely to the Johnston overtures but said they were neither timely nor appropriate. Under the circumstances they were not even prepared at that stage to notify shareholders of the interest that was being shown – a stance that could not be maintained in the light of subsequent developments.

That afternoon Waley-Cohen telephoned Johnston to say that he had spoken informally to all his directors and the company's financial advisors and they shared his view that the £15 per share offer that had been tabled was "quite unacceptable."

Despite the boardroom reshuffle the directors had never envisaged selling their business and certainly had no pressing financial reasons for doing so. As recently as September, 1998, the board had confirmed its strategy to remain independent and considered that after recent investments it was still on the lower slopes of a very strong profit growth. Indeed, quite recently it had made an approach to buy two newspaper companies, although P&SN realised it was in the strange middle ground of being prey to the very big predators and a predator itself to smaller groups.

After the initial rebuff Johnstons concluded that different tactics were required. Buying Portsmouth and Sunderland shares on the open market was an option, but unlikely to be very productive since there was little liquidity in the stock, so much of which was held by the Storey family.

Bill Staple and his Rothschilds colleague, William Spurgin, joined a meeting of the Johnston directors again in December, 1998, and even though this took place a few days before Christmas the festive spirit was not much in evidence.

It had always been accepted that the Storey family, with a 40 per cent shareholding, was the key to any deal and Tim Bowdler told the meeting that dialogue had begun with an advisor to some of them. It was also noted that of the remaining 60 per cent of shares in P&SN the majority was held by a number of institutions and an approach to three of these was considered as a next possible step.

But Staple was not in a hurry. He produced an action plan that proposed . . . no action. Johnstons, he said, should not be rushed into a next move, and certainly not before Christmas.

"We need to give the clear impression of being a reluctant suitor," he said. "In January we should contact the family, expressing surprise that their directors had rejected a friendly approach at a good price. And if that doesn't open the door to negotiations then an approach to the institutions should be considered."

The Storey family was not interested in playing mind games. Indeed, they were disdainful of the Johnston wooing and twice delayed meetings with the company. Freddy Johnston's efforts to break the deadlock were also unsuccessful when he invited Richard Storey for dinner at a Kensington restaurant in the hope of

receiving some positive feedback. But the P&SN director was having none of it and insisted that any attempts to negotiate should be done through Waley-Cohen.

Selling the sports news in Portsmouth

The largest single shareholder outside the immediate family circle was stockbrokers UBS (formerly Philips and Drew) with a 14.9 per cent holding, an investment they had held for some time but which produced only moderate returns and showed little sign of improving in value. Investment managers Aberforth also held another significant minority block of shares.

UBS, with whom Johnston Press had dealt on numerous occasions, were only too happy to consider an approach for their shares, especially at a premium price of £16 per share, and quickly agreed to sell after meeting with Bowdler and Chiappelli. The Johnston offer represented a substantial gain on the price they had paid for the shares originally and released capital for new investment elsewhere, principally in bonds rather than equities. It made good business sense, especially when soon afterwards the Stock Market slumped from a FTSE index high of almost 7,000.

The dawn raid cost Johnston Press £29 million but its 14.9 per cent stake in P&SN was to prove crucial in the serious takeover talks that were to follow. It was also a deterrent to other potential suitors who would now have to pay considerably more than Johnston's £16 per share to gain control – and provide Johnston's with a tidy profit if they succeeded.

At the same time Johnstons further made their intentions clear by seeking permission under the Fair Trading Act 1973 to acquire up to the whole of the P&SN share capital. This was a legal formality that, as expected, prompted the Competition and Consumer Affairs Minister to refer the matter to the Monopolies and Mergers Commission for a detailed investigation.

This procedure was a source of some annoyance as Johnstons and other major publishing groups considered the Act to be increasingly anachronistic in a world of e-commerce and digital communication, particularly as its strict conditions applied only to newspaper publishers.

But the 1973 Act was quite clear in its requirements – the Secretary of State's consent was needed before Johnstons could acquire an interest of 25 per cent or more in P&SN because the aggregate per issue circulation of the titles of both groups was more than 500,000 copies. Furthermore, because P&SN controlled two titles with a circulation of more than 50,000 copies the Act also required a report by the Monopolies and Mergers Commission.

Portsmouth and Sunderland directors reacted with fury when news of the pre-emptive strike emerged. Brims reckoned he knew his institutional shareholders well and only a short time before had visited most of them to discuss the company's annual results. All of them had appeared to be supportive of the business strategy and pleased with the trading performance.

As a courtesy Bowdler had attempted to contact Brims ahead of the official announcement but, having failed to do so, left a message on his mobile phone. It was not until much later in the day that Brims, who had been attending a board meeting of Northeast Press in Sunderland, switched his phone back on and learned of the dawn raid in messages from Bowdler and his company secretary.

The news compounded the misery he was already suffering, for by then he was at a fog-bound Newcastle Airport for his return journey to London and the tannoy had just crackled to announce that all deapartures had been cancelled. Brims abandoned his flight plans and instead caught the first train south to the capital, where he spent the weekend discussing tactics with advisors.

In the gloom of that January afternoon Brims had ample time to digest the full implications of the surprise shares swoop.

He was surprised that a major institutional shareholder had decided to sell its stock without prior consultation and even more taken aback by the apparent about face by Johnston Press.

Brims thought back to his meeting with Johnston and Bowdler when the figure of £15 per share had been floated and how Johnston had said he was not prepared to enter into a bidding war. "We're not interested in an auction, in fact we won't even pull on our rugger shirt for an auction," he had declared metaphorically.

The P&SN team wrongly assumed that was the end of the Johnston Press approach. "As a board we had always agreed that if ever we sold the company it would be at top price, and the way you achieve that is at auction," said Brims. "When we rejected £15 it seemed like Johnston Press was saying take it or leave it, that they were not interested."

Brims and Johnston were good friends and had spent hours together on Newspaper Society fact-finding trips to the United States and, more recently, Malaysia. But it had been presumptuous to write off the wily Scot that easily, even though Johnston had initially opposed the backdoor approach for P&SN shares and was only persuaded to agree after much soul-searching and cajoling from fellow directors.

Later Bowdler appreciated the extent of the P&SN displeasure while attending a Newspaper Society conference in Dublin for directors and chief executives, at which Brims, in his office as president, was one of the speakers.

In a hard hitting and analytical address – an "outspoken tirade" according to Bowdler and described as "calm and measured" by Brims – he discussed the relationship between companies and their shareholders and the different agendas to which they were both working. By selling shares cheaply at £16 Philips and Drew had, he declared, in turn let down their own shareholders in order to comply with the company's policy of getting out of equities and raising capital.

The audience knew exactly to whom the comments were directed, but Bowdler took it on the chin and smiled as those around him winked and raised their eyebrows. His smile also concealed the secret that Johnston Press was on the verge of buying more shares from two other small institutions!

Of these Aberforth later agreed to sell its holding of 2.36 per cent of the P&SN share capital at a price of £17.50 per share. This is turn raised the Johnston holding to 17.35 per cent, although the company anticipated having to pay up to £20 per share in future as the bidding increased.

Bowdler and Brims had what can, politely, best be described as "an exchange of views" after the latter's comments from the conference platform. Brims was also unhappy with another Johnston tactic that had been employed before the purchase of Aberforth's interests – a tender offer to shareholders with a view to acquiring a further 10 per cent of P&SN shares. This would have taken the Johnston holding up to the permitted maximum at the time of 24.99 per cent, although the Secretary of State for Trade and Industry was asked to waive this rule.

Ultimately, Brims could derive some satisfaction that the tender offer had been unsuccessful – it did not even reach one per cent – after a vigorous campaign mounted by the P&SN board.

Chairman Waley-Cohen had urged his shareholders to spurn the offer in a strongly worded and emotive letter in which Johnston's action was described as opportunistic and something that should be ignored. What's more, he said the procedure was unusual and allowed only five business days for them to make a decision.

"Johnston is trying to buy P&SN on the cheap," alleged Waley-Cohen. "Johnston has furtively acquired a significant 14.99 per cent stake in P&SN and is now trying to bounce you into selling your shares through its tender offer . . . we recommend that you take no action."

Apart from the ethical considerations, there were other reasons why shareholders accepted the advice of their chairman. The initial approach to buy P&SN had attempted to lay down conditions, one of which would have precluded a third party making a competing offer for the company within a defined period – the auction that Freddy Johnston had been anxious to avoid.

Not only had this been rejected, but when Johnston Press failed to improve on its initial indicative offer all discussions had been terminated. Since then, said Waley-Cohen, other approaches had been made to buy the company – a clear indication that by sitting tight shareholders could eventually expect to receive far more than the £16 a share that they were now being invited to accept.

Waley-Cohen went even further. "The board would be perfectly prepared to recommend an offer from a party offering a price reflecting the underlying growth prospects and strategic value of P&SN."

Once news of the Johnston Press approach had become common knowledge the flood gates opened. Many of those companies who had previously been tapping politely on Brims' door now telephoned him to ask if he was considering bids and, if so, they would like to make one.

Among the groups who indicated they would submit realistic proposals were Newsquest and Newscom. Another bidder, and one of the first to express an interest, was the former director of Scottish Radio Holdings, Charles Villiers, who also had the luxury of not having to obtain clearance from the Monopolies and Mergers Commission. He had been instrumental in 1973 in setting up SRH's Score Press business of 45 weekly newspapers in Scotland, Northern Ireland and the Republic of Ireland, all of which became part of Johnston Press in 2005.

P&SN now had the luxury of being able to draw up a shortlist of potential buyers in the certainty that if a sale was negotiated their shareholders would receive a realistic price way above the indicative £15 first mentioned by Johnston Press.

In the meantime the prospects of an all-out bidding war receded. The purchase of the UBS and Aberforth blocks of shares had, as expected, had the effect of sidelining the ambitions of some would-be purchasers. These included Newsquest, who, after being alerted to the likely sale of the P&SN group, had begun carrying out due diligence in preparation for a formal offer.

Detailed discussions between Johnston Press and P&SN recommenced at the beginning of May, 1999, and led to a formal offer being tabled the following month after an extraordinary general meeting of shareholders at Manor Place, Edinburgh. Only a handful bothered to make the journey north and the majority signified their approval of the offer terms by proxy voting.

By then it would have taken an upset of seismic proportions to knock the acquisition off course. Johnstons had already spent £33.7 million buying shares and now proposed investing a further £220 million to obtain the remainder. This valued the shares at £22.25 each – a premium of 88 per cent over the mid-market price of P&SN shares of £11.85 at the close of business on January 21, 1999 (the day before Johnston Press announced its dawn raid). In addition shareholders were to receive a second interim dividend per share of 18.03p, representing a total consideration of £22.43 per share, which was 40 per cent higher than the opening formal Johnston offer of £16.

66

...the flood gates opened. Companies who had previously been tapping politely on Brims' door now telephoned him to ask if he was considering bids

99

191

At the time no one on the Johnston Press side knew they had been a whisker away from losing to another bidder. Events of May 10, 1999, were to prove decisive.

The great and the good of the regional newspaper industry descended on the London Hilton for the annual lunch of the Newspaper Society. It was the highlight of Charles Brims' year as president and to top it all the Prime Minister, Tony Blair, was the guest speaker. Brims also had another important entry in his diary that afternoon – a meeting at Charterhouse Bank at which P&SN were almost certain to agree a sale.

Johnston Press had remained discreetly in the background while Brims and Waley-Cohen had talked with potential buyers but at four o'clock that afternoon Bowdler made his move. Brims was on the verge of signing a deal when the telephone rang – it was Bowdler with an 11th hour offer, so good that it simply could not be ignored.

"If you're serious you had better come round now," said a stunned Brims.

After the initial acrimony the final stages of negotiations were extremely cordial and not only were P&SN directors recommending acceptance of the "fair and reasonable" offer but irrevocable undertakings to do so had been given by 52 per cent of shareholders – binding commitments even if a last-minute competing offer was received from another newspaper group.

Although Johnston Press knew it would have to wait some weeks for the Monopolies and Mergers Commission to report it never doubted the outcome. The Portsmouth end of the business had little overlap with existing titles on the South Coast and the North East was virgin territory with no clash of interests.

When the verdict was announced this was done under the name of the newly-created Competition Commission, which had taken over the functions of the MMC on April 1, in compliance with Section 45 of the Competition Act 1998. That, however, had no bearing on the scope or purpose of the inquiry, which also embraced the likely effect if P&SN was transferred to Johnston's potential competitors, Newsquest and Newscom.

All three groups passed the public interest test with flying colours. The Commission examined four main areas where the best interests of the public might be compromised and found no grounds for concern. It concluded that accurate presentation of news and free expression of public opinion would not be jeopardised; the further concentration of newspaper ownership at a national level would not adversely affect advertisers or cover prices, given the importance of retaining readers to maximise revenues; where an overlap would be created with existing group titles this would not work against the public interest by unfairly restricting reader choice; and public interest on grounds of efficiency and employment would not be put at risk.

Johnston's evidence to the Commission was given in writing and at a formal hearing held at the Commission's offices in Carey Street, London, when the company was represented by Freddy Johnston, Bowdler and Chiappelli. The panel of five was chaired by Graham Corbett, who later became regulator for the Post Office, with a group of around 10 advisors ranged behind them. A stenographer was also present to take a verbatim note of the proceedings.

The four-hour hearing, which was repeated for each of the interested parties and for P&SN, was followed by a site visit – by all accounts this went better than the site visit to Halifax five years before when one member of the panel consumed too much red wine at lunchtime and fell asleep!

Bowdler later likened the hearing to a game of mental chess, the inscrutable panel probing and searching and the respondents trying to tune in to their thought process, while at the same time not giving misleading or inaccurate answers.

First, Bowdler set out to put the proposed P&SN acquisition in a national context. For a number of years, he said, P&SN had been regarded as a company which, in due course, was likely to be taken up in the process of industry consolidation that had affected the local and regional press.

This had been driven by two main factors: the need for capital investment in order to remain competitive, and the long-term decline in daily newspaper circulations caused by social changes and growing competition from other media.

Bowdler said that in his opinion the future of local newspapers in the UK, especially those with high-quality news and editorial content, was dependent on further consolidation. He agreed with the Newspaper Society view that concentration of ownership had been necessary to ensure a vigorous, well-resourced and effective local and regional newspaper industry.

The real danger was that competitors from new forms of media would not feel obliged to provide good editorial material and would merely be interested in targeting advertising revenue without regard to the quality of content.

The Commission was keen to know why Johnston Press was attracted to P&SN and how it intended to manage the new business if its bid was successful. These were crucial questions when considering if the deal was in the public interest and the Johnston team had thought long and hard to ensure that its response was honest and convincing.

Without beating about the bush, Bowdler said the main reasons for its bid was to obtain a portfolio of titles in North-East England, where it then had no presence, and to extend its existing operations in the South of England. It was also interested in acquiring P&SN's relatively modern printing presses, which would enable it to print more group titles in-house and to include more colour pages in a number of newspapers.

Bowdler dismissed the notion that a slight overlap of interests in West Sussex would be detrimental and said this would not adversely affect advertisers' interests or the diversity of editorial content.

"Owning both titles in an area of overlap does not change the way in which we behave," he declared. "Whether it be cover price or advertising rates, these are driven by the local communities at their core."

Much of the debate centered round seven common advertisers in the Arundel area, one of them the Black Rabbit pub. It appeared incongruous to the Johnston team that such an important acquisition as P&SN could hinge on such a relatively trivial issue.

In its own evidence, P&SN also dealt with the issue of competition and it soon became obvious to the Commission that in both areas of the country there was a healthy choice of media outlets – a growing number of local radio and television stations, a significant number of Trinity titles in the North East, and Newsquest, Newscom, Trinity, Northcliffe and independent titles in the South.

Commercially, Bowdler said Johnstons intended to maintain and develop all the titles but the Commission was told that savings would be sought. He indicated that synergies were expected to arise by reducing corporate and administrative overheads, the ability to purchase services and materials more economically, and through more efficient use of the enlarged printing capacity.

The Commission also asked about the degree of local autonomy that was allowed within the Johnston Press framework –were there head office rules on how advertising rates were to be charged, what was the degree of editorial independence?

The team was well prepared to deal with just such questions. For weeks the lives of advertisement directors and editors had been turned upside down as they were bombarded with urgent requests for information from Edinburgh – how had they responded to the advent of free classified advertising publications, how did their rates compare with neighbouring paid-for and free titles, what was their relationship with Mediaforce and other agencies, what packages were available to advertisers, had neighbouring Johnston newspapers adopted different editorial approaches to the same common issue, could editors provide examples of local campaigns they had conducted?

Bowdler's evidence to the Commission was emphatic and unequivocal – life under Johnston Press really was local. "Every one of our publishing businesses is a local enterprise operating in a specific market," he stressed.

By the time Competition Commission clearance to proceed with the purchase was received negotiations had progressed at a rapid pace, and with only this hurdle to clear both sides felt confident enough to announce the deal to the newspaper industry at large.

Johnston chairman Freddy Johnston was his usual charming and diplomatic self. "Johnston Press has long regarded Portsmouth and Sunderland as one of the most prestigious newspaper publishers," he enthused. "Their splendid range of both daily and weekly titles are a vital part of the communities which they serve and have always maintained the highest standards.

"We greatly look forward to working with the staff of P&SN and have every confidence that together we shall succeed in developing this fine business further as we enter the new millennium."

Waley-Cohen issued a more subdued statement to the media. "We believe we have achieved a very fair price for P&SN, reflecting the strategic importance of its publishing businesses," he said. "The quality of P&SN has been demonstrated by the level of interest shown by a number of parties.

"We have always respected Johnston Press as a company and believe that it will prove a worthy custodian of what we have built up over 126 years."

By the end of June the deal was finally ready for signing and the two parties and their advisors met at the offices of N.M. Rothschild and Sons, the merchant bankers to Johnston Press, in St Swithin's Lane, London.

Theatre entrepeneur and chairman of P&SN Sir Stephen Waley-Cohen

195

Unusually in such circumstances, the celebrations had started before either side put pen to paper, but as the champagne flowed the Royal Bank of Scotland threw a spanner in the works.

Because of the size of Johnston's borrowing to finance the deal – a facility of up to £360 million had been agreed – the bank had decided to syndicate the loan, itself and Barclays putting up 25 per cent each with a number of other banks sharing the remainder of the debt.

"But what if the Competition Commission rules against the acquisition", asked the worried lady from the Royal Bank of Scotland's syndication department? "What do we do then?"

The champagne was put on ice as first Chiappelli and then Bowdler stressed that the likelihood of a negative ruling, due within days, was remote. An hour later, and after a flurry of telephone calls and consultations, the bank recovered from its 11th hour jitters and sanctioned the £180 million that was needed to complete the deal.

Portsmouth and Sunderland shareholders had every reason to be pleased with the outcome – not only were they to receive a substantial bounty on their shares, but they had also benefitted already from the sale of P&SN's chain of 220 One Stop convenience stores – one of the UK's largest of its kind – for £68 million.

The buyer was the T and S chain, controlled by Kevin Thelfall, a former primary school classmate of Bowdler in Wolverhampton. The two had met up again some months earlier when Thelfall, unaware of goings on behind the scenes, had jokingly suggested that Bowdler should buy P&SN and he would have the shops!

Johnston Press was firmly committed to newspaper publishing and had sold its own wholesale stationery division for £2.5 million to York-based J.A. Magson while P&SN negotiations were taking place. The group had made it clear from the outset that it was not interested in the P&SN retailing division and would be unlikely to retain it if its bid was successful. Indeed, it had gone one step further by agreeing in advance a price of £50 million with T and S – a price that horrified the P&SN board when they found out, thus prompting them to conclude their own sale of the shops for an additional £18 million. Later the shops were sold again to supermarket chain Tesco and were rebranded as Tesco Express stores.

Waley-Cohen had been somewhat perplexed that Johnstons were prepared to disregard such a profitable activity as the local corner shop. "Johnston does not understand the significant growth potential of the convenience store business," he told shareholders. Nevertheless, he concluded that their best interests would be served by seeking separate offers for the two parts of the business.

A large proportion of P&SN resources had been ploughed into developing its One Stop chain and it had been opening new stores at the rate of more than 40 a year, financed by the strong cash flow from its publishing business. By 1999 the geographical area had been expanded from Exeter in the west to Gillingham in the east, and from the Isle of Wight in the south to Newark in the north Midlands.

As well as opening new stores, additional facilities such as post offices, bakeries and pharmacies had been introduced to existing branches, all of which had seen operating profits rise in spectacular fashion – the 1998/99 profit of £4,600,000, for example, was 32 per cent up on the previous year.

The first newsagent's shop was opened in 1970 at a time when a number of newspaper companies were looking to control the retail end of their supply chain. But unlike the rest P&SN persevered and succeeded, using the shops, which were relatively resilient to economic changes, to counteract the cyclical nature of newspaper publishing.

The policy was in sharp contrast to that of Emap who, three years earlier, had regarded the cyclical unpredictability as a hindrance and among the reasons for selling its newspaper division. Emap, too, questioned the viability of substantial periodic capital expenditure, especially on presses, whereas P&SN were happy to do so and reap the rewards of a strong cash flow in the intervening period.

This in turn had enabled them to invest in local retailing. Indeed there were those who had begun to question whether P&SN was first and foremost a newspaper publisher or a shopkeeper – its six year business plan to 2003/4 showed that 84 per cent of total capital expenditure of £163 million was to be concentrated on the expansion of the retail business.

When asked to explain this during the Competition Commission inquiry the company said it had unused funds of up to £40 million for buying new titles and if need be could make more money available by slowing down its retail expansion.

In May Bowdler and Chiappelli were able to find out at first hand how P&SN managed its business when they visited both Portsmouth and Sunderland, where they were given a cordial reception by the management at each of the centres.

Waley-Cohen had been somewhat perplexed that Johnstons were prepared to disregard such a profitable activity as the local corner shop

Bowdler's report to his fellow directors raised eyebrows around the table. It was clear, he said, that the P&SN head office in Portsmouth had surprisingly limited knowledge about the detail of the two operating centres, nor were these dependent on it for any vital functions. Everyone agreed that the head office would be wound up immediately if the takeover was successful – it was seen as an unnecessary luxury, but not nearly so much as the previous head office in South Kensington, which had recently been closed.

The two centres, related Bowdler, were run more or less independently and very differently by their local management. Major decision making was very slow with a high overhead cost. But he concluded on a positive note that the businesses were both well equipped with excellent products.

Finance director Marco Chiappelli also was not impressed by the way P&SN had been run in the past. For one thing he could not make head or tail of the accounting system, each of the centres having different methods of reporting. He and Bowdler uncovered more surprises – and the opportunity for considerable savings.

On the top floor of The News building at Portsmouth was the executive suite, where the executive committee, like many committees, talked at length but achieved rather less. But they did so in style – seated at a round table that was said to have cost £22,000. Not surprisingly, the directors were dubbed the Knights of the Round Table.

The needs of the former chairman had been looked after by not one, but two secretaries – one to deal with correspondence and typing, the other to keep his diary up to date.

It also became very clear to what extent the executive committee had allowed P&SN to stagnate – 15 years previously it had been a larger company than Johnston Press, and the first of the two to become a quoted company, but during that time had been overtaken by its Scottish suitor. Further evidence of this was found in the management library, which contained a file on every other British newspaper company – and evidence of prospective purchases that had never been pursued.

But despite the perceived shortcomings in the way in which P&SN conducted its business, the company had nevertheless produced excellent results, and none more so than its last full year's trading as an independent company.

In his annual report for the period up to March, 1999, chairman Waley-Cohen reported a pre-tax profit of £17.1 million, an increase of 55 per cent. The operating profit from its newspaper publishing activities was up 41 per cent to £12.8 million on revenue up 13 per cent at £70.6 million. (In comparison, Johnston Press recorded a pre-tax profit of £45.9 million on a turnover of £201.7 million in its last complete financial year, 1998).

It had also been a good year for circulation with most titles achieving growth, Waley-Cohen said. The Sunderland Echo, for example, had increased sales by 2.4 per cent and won a Newspaper Society award for its achievement. Similarly, the Chichester Observer had been feted after driving up newspaper sales by 15 per cent.

Contract printing earned the company £14.5 million during the year, primarily from the North East, where new presses that had been commissioned at Sunderland and Hartlepool in 1997 were producing high quality colour results. Since 1998 400,000 copies of the north-east editions of The Sun and the News of the World had been printed under contract three nights a week at Sunderland. At Portsmouth there was a contract to print the national financial paper Sunday Business.

Once the takeover of P&SN had been completed Johnston Press wasted no time in implementing its plans to absorb the new acquisition into the "family" and effect the changes that were considered necessary to improve performance. Within 24 hours the managing directors at Portsmouth and Sunderland were replaced. Danny Cammiade moved south from Chesterfield and Anne Blood, the deputy managing director of Northeast Press Ltd, the Sunderland operating company, was promoted. Some time later the editor at Portsmouth, Geoff Elliott, also departed to be replaced by Mike Gilson, then editor of the Peterborough Evening Telegraph.

Changes were also made to the divisional structure of Johnston Press with the creation of a new North East division based in Sunderland and a new South division, based in Portsmouth, which included the interests of T.R. Beckett and West Sussex Newspapers.

The impact of the takeover was felt across both centres as the new owners proceeded to introduce the first of many cost savings totalling £3.4 million. As expected the head office in Portsmouth was closed and staffing reductions led to 40 redundancies at Portsmouth and 53 at Sunderland. The new media department at Portsmouth, which was operating as a separate activity to build, host and maintain a large number of websites for completely unrelated businesses, attracted close scrutiny and was scaled down substantially.

In addition three small and heavily loss-making free newspapers that had been launched by P&SN in the Scottish Borders just over a year earlier were closed. This did not go down well in the very parochial area involved. Several telephone calls were received from irate residents and Members of Parliament and the national press in Scotland also reported the protests, but the closures went ahead nevertheless.

The two halves of P&SN could not have been more different. Although the Johnston Press ethos was quickly accepted at Portsmouth the new owners encountered a more combative attitude at Sunderland, Hartlepool and South Shields.

"There was stiffer competition in the area, a less buoyant market place and an altogether more militant workforce, who gave us a cool reception," recalled Chiappelli.

"The economies of running the two centres were also very different, but they both had good products and modern presses."

At Sunderland the assets also included 90,000 shares in Sunderland Football Club, where Sir Richard Storey had been a non-executive director. Chiappelli never lived down his advice to hold on to the shares, which declined substantially in value from a high £6 as the club's fortunes also plummeted.

The full complement of titles acquired is shown opposite.

In 2002 – 2003 the Hartlepool Mail attracted unwelcome national attention involving its colourful editor, Harry Blackwood, and the town's controversial and high-profile Labour MP, Peter Mandelson.

The Mail was certainly not alone among local newspapers in having a mixed relationship with its MP, although Mandelson was frequently on the phone to complain about aspects of its reporting that did not meet with his approval.

In December, 2002, he took matters further and lodged a complaint about editorial bias and the role of the editor at Hartlepool in a letter to Johnston Press head office. Before then Johnston chief executive Bowdler had already been forced into apologising to the former Northern Ireland Secretary over a derogatory comment about his eating habits in an article that appeared in another group title following Mandelson's appearance as guest of honour at that year's editorial conference in Grantham.

Andrew Smith, editorial director at Northeast Press, was asked to investigate the latest complaint and in his report ruled out suggestions of the Mail's alleged involvement in a conspiracy against the MP. But he highlighted a lack of balance, evidence that stories had

Newly acquired titles from P&SN

Evenings
- The News, Portsmouth
- Sunderland Echo
- Hartlepool Mail
- Shields Gazette

Paid-for weeklies
- Chichester Observer
- Midhurst and
  Petworth Observer
- West Sussex Gazette
- Bognor Regis Observer
- Petersfield Post
- Bordon Post
- Northumberland Gazette
- Hawick News and Scottish
  Border Chronicle
- Morpeth Herald
- Selkirk Weekend Advertiser

Free distribution weeklies
- Fareham and Gosport Journal
- Portsmouth and
  Southsea Journal

- Havant and
  Waterlooville Journal
- Bognor Regis Guardian
- Chichester and Selsey Journal
- Hayling Islander
- Ems Valley Gazette
- Guardian Home Finder
- News Post Leader
  (Ashington, Blyth, New
  Biggin and Seaton Valley)
- News Guardian
  (North Shields, Wallsend
  and Whitley Bay)
- Sunderland Star
- South Tyne Star
- Hartlepool Star
- Peterlee Star
- Washington Star
- Houghton Star
- Seaham Star
- Borders Gazette
- Galashiels News
- Kelso News
- Jedburgh News

not been sufficiently well researched as well and placed a question mark over editorial standards at the paper.

Subsequent disciplinary action led to the resignation of Blackwood, but by then the problems at Hartlepool had attracted national attention. Over three weekends the Mail on Sunday highlighted Blackwood's case, with questions raised about editorial integrity in Johnston Press and implications that senior management had bowed to political pressure from Mandelson to dismiss an editor.

Morale at the Mail ebbed away and in March, 2003, the Johnston board was told that the mood in the newsroom was "grim" and that there had been several resignations. A worried Chairman Parry demanded to know if indeed Mandelson was influencing events behind the scenes.

"Absolutely not," replied chief executive Bowdler. "This is entirely about editortial standards."

Parry assured the meeting that neither he nor his own company, Clear Channel, had been pressurised by Mandelson and then complimented Bowdler on the way in which he had handled the delicate situation.

Following Blackwood's departure from Hartlepool, Paul Napier, the editor at Scarborough, was drafted into the hot seat and gradually restored confidence and morale at the newspaper. By 2005 his editorial team was cock-a-hoop when the Mail became the only Johnston evening title to record year-on-year newspaper sales increases. In 2006 Napier moved on to the Yorkshire Evening Post.

The Johnston board, meanwhile, devoted most of one of its meetings to group editorial policy and re-affirmed the importance of ethical integrity, editorial independence, fairness and family suitable content. It also agreed to maintain a discreet distance from front line journalism by not being directly involved in specific editorial matters.

The effect of acquiring the Portsmouth and Sunderland "family" – itself the 12th largest regional newspaper business with about 2.7 percent or UK paid-for circulation and free distribution – was to propel Johnston Press from fifth to fourth nationally and increase its overall market share above 9 per cent. The most significant growth in market share was in the weekly paper arena.

In climbing the ladder, Johnston, now with a combined total weekly circulation of nearly six million, overtook Mirror Regional Newspapers' circulation of 4.3 million.

But no one believed that this would be the end of further changes of ownership, and in January, 1999, there were at least 126 smaller publishers throughout the country. The Johnston view was that there would be greater concentration in future towards an industry with four or five major enterprises, fewer middle ranking ones and a good many small businesses owning one or two titles.

In a snapshot of the newspaper publishing scene at the end of the 20th century the group had expressed the same opinion to the Competition Commission, stressing that the day of the great, all-embracing county newspaper (did it have the Derbyshire Times in mind?), real or imagined, had given way to more locally targeted titles.

The picture was one of regional and local newspapers with smaller circulation areas but more closely focussed on their reader-ship, of papers retreating to their citadels and possibly doing a better job within them. The exceptions were the metropolitan evening newspapers that were seeking to extend their presence well beyond their main centres of publishing.

Observers have often puzzled how Portsmouth and Sunderland Newspapers was created for, on the face of things, it appeared to be an illogical pairing. And while the name trips smoothly off the tongue, it might more accurately have been Sunderland and Portsmouth, for it was in the North East where the story began.

It was in 1873 that Samuel Storey, a former building society manager and savings bank actuary, founded The Echo in Sunderland with six partners and an investment of £3,500. The aim was to create a mouthpiece for his own radical views – and it succeeded, for in 1880 "Radical Sam" was elected as Liberal MP for the town.

Shortly afterwards he was introduced to Andrew Carnegie, the Scottish-born millionaire, and with others they formed a syndicate to create a chain of newspapers to promote their political influence, especially among working class readers. But the arrangement was short lived and dissolved in 1885 – hardly surprising since all the partners were men of strong opinions and used to getting their own way.

The syndicate was always on the lookout for buying or starting new titles and did so in rapid succession in Birmingham, Walsall, Wolverhampton, London and Middlesbrough. They tried but failed to buy the Northern Echo, at Darlington, and the Shields Gazette, at South Shields.

> " In climbing the ladder, Johnston Press, now with a combined total weekly circulation of nearly six million, overtook Mirror Regional Newspapers' circulation of 4.3 million "

Storey, Carnegie and another partner, Passmore Edwards, arrived in Portsmouth in 1883 and after surveying the newspaper scene bought the weekly Hampshire Telegraph (177 years old when it was absorbed into the East Hampshire Post in 1976). They also started a new evening paper, the Southern Standard, to rival the Evening News, at Portsmouth, which had been founded in 1877.

The Standard survived for eight issues, by which time Storey had persuaded the owner of the News that there wasn't room for both of them and bought him out.

A year later the Carnegie-Storey syndicate bought the evening paper in Hartlepool, the Northern Daily Mail, a title that was used until 1959 when it became simply The Mail. This, too, had been founded in 1877 from weekly paper parentage, the South Durham Herald. In a typical show of political partisanship the new proprietors changed its stance from mild Conservatism to advanced Liberalism.

When the syndicate collapsed Storey retained his controlling interest in all three evening titles and they ran as separate companies until 1934, when Portsmouth and Sunderland Newspapers Ltd, was formed. The company was floated on the Stock Exchange the same year.

At various times, weekly papers were added to the company's portfolio of titles. The oldest of these was the West Sussex Gazette, which was founded in 1853 and joined P&SN in 1969. The Mitchell family owned and ran the paper from Arundel for all those years, a record that was commemorated with a blue plaque outside the original premises when the paper celebrated its 150th anniversary.

Longevity remained a feature of the paper – one of its columnists, a Mrs Paddick, had been writing about Sussex ways and dialects for years and although she died in 1974 her articles from the past were reprinted each week.

Significant additions to the group occurred in 1950, with the purchase of the Chichester Observer series in West Sussex, and in 1983 when the Croydon Advertiser group was acquired, although this was subsequently sold in 1995.

The highly successful Observer series were all launched in Victorian times – the Bognor Regis Observer in 1872, the Midhurst and Petworth Observer in 1882 and the Chichester Observer in 1887.

In 1987 P&SN was reorganised with the formation of northern and southern subsidiaries – Northeast Press, based in Sunderland,

and Portsmouth Publishing and Printing, based in Portsmouth.

The acquisition of the Northern Press titles four years later added four weekly papers – the paid-fors Northumberland Gazette and Morpeth Herald, and frees News Post Leader and News Guardian – and a fourth evening title, the Shields Gazette, at South Shields, to the P&SN portfolio.

The Northumberland Gazette first appeared in 1883 as the Alnwick and County Gazette, and was bought by Northern Press in 1922. This in turn was acquired in 1934 by Westminster Press, who changed the Gazette's title to the Northumberland and Alnwick Gazette in 1943.

In the late 1980s Northern Press, which by then included the Morpeth Herald, which had been bought from the fifth generation of the MacKay family in 1983, was sold to Peter Fowler's Peter Press, who owned it for four years before it was purchased by P&SN.

The Shields Gazette has the distinction of being Britain's first provincial evening paper. It was founded as the weekly North and South Shields Gazette in 1849, and was joined by a daily edition on

Samuel Storey, founder of the Sunderland Echo

Monday, July 2, 1855, two days after the abolition of Stamp Duty had removed a restrictive and highly unpopular tax on newspapers. On the same day the Manchester Guardian became the first daily provincial morning paper in the country.

The Gazette has had a succession of owners over the years – for more than 50 years it and Northern Press were part of the Westminster Press empire. Even when the Germans scored a direct hit on the Chapter Row offices during an air raid in 1941 it continued publication and came back smelling of roses, or minted peas to be precise! (After the war the paper was one of the first to carry an early version of the "scratch 'n' sniff" advertisements).

Equally as interesting as the business history of Portsmouth and Sunderland Newspapers is the Storey family itself – five generations of newspapermen, ending with Sir Richard Storey and his son Kenelm. Of these the most famous was another Samuel Storey, grandson of the founder, who was chairman for 49 years and guided the company through the post-war technical advances that helped to revolutionise newspaper production.

Storey, like his grandfather, was an astute politician – a Sunderland councillor and Conservative MP for the town for 14 years. Later he served as MP for Stretford and in 1960 was created a baronet for public and political services. In 1965 he became Deputy Speaker of the House of Commons and was created a life peer in 1966, when he entered the House of Lords as Baron Buckton of Settrington in the East Riding, County of York, where he had lived since 1938.

In his distinguished newspaper career Lord Buckton was chairman of both the Press Association and Reuters and president of the Newspaper Society.

Set against such a family background it is easier to understand Sir Richard Storey's black mood when, after upholding his father's proud record since becoming chairman in 1973, he was not only left with little choice other than to stand down but also saw his son Kenelm denied the opportunity to succeed him.

The balance sheets provide their own verdict on Sir Richard's tenure, for they tell a tale of a company that continued to invest heavily in new plant and equipment and reaped the reward through increased efficiency and higher profits. Bricks and mortar add another dimension – in 1969 The News had moved to new premises at Hilsea, Portsmouth, but under Sir Richard a further multi-million pound plan to expand and develop the site saw the

Samuel Storey, grandson of the founder, later Lord Buckton, was chairman of P&SN for 49 years

creation of the present-day News Centre; the Sunderland Echo relocated to a new site at Pennywell and became a major print centre; at Hartlepool a modernisation and redevelopment project brought with it significant techological advances.

The aftermath of the bombing of the South Shields Gazette's offices in World War II

Although no members of the Storey family had an executive role at the time of the group's sale they still controlled about 36 per cent of the issued share capital. Outside the family the only holders of more than 3 per cent of shares were Johnston Press, Prudential Corporation (3.73 per cent), Legal and General Investment Management (3.43 per cent) and Phillips and Drew Fund Managers, on behalf of clients (5.2 per cent).

The sale made the principal family shareholders into overnight multi-millionaires – Sir Richard Storey's 18 per cent stake was worth £47.9 million, nearly 90 per cent more than before bidding began, and his sister Jacquetta Cator received £42.6 million for her 16 per cent holding. Other family members shared about £3 million between them. Kenelm Storey lives on his father's estate from where he manages the family investments from the sale of P&SN.

Chief executive Charles Brims, who left the company, received about £250,000 for the remainder of his two-year contract and more than £500,000 for his share options. He became chairman of two breweries and continued his newspaper involvement as a non-executive director of three publishing companies. Under his guidance he had the satisfaction of seeing P&SN expand in all directions, profits rise from £1.3 million to £17.1 million and the share price soar from £1.20 to more than £20.

They were not the only ones to benefit from the acquisition – advisors on both sides were well paid for their efforts and in the case of Johnston Press this amounted to costs of about £5 million.

Storey had been forced to watch the sale of his family business from the sidelines and took no part in the negotiations. But even after the sale he followed the progress of the P&SN titles with interest, even sending Bowdler a barely decipherable "get well" card several years after the deal – a reference to the apparent sharp decline in circulation of The News at Portsmouth. He was, of course, unaware that this had been caused by the removal of bulk copies from the sales figures, including those supplied to schools as part of the Newspapers in Education project.

News of Johnston's latest acquisition was reported widely on the financial pages of the national news media. The Times quoted media analyst Angela Maxwell as saying the deal would "give Johnston sufficient size to survive in a shrinking industry."

The Glasgow Herald commented: "Few Scottish companies have taken the high road to England so successfully and there is little reason to expect any slowdown.

"Accepting that geographic diversity lowers risk, the Edinburgh-based group has a huge potential for moving into new areas, particularly down the M4 from London to Bristol in a corridor of high prosperity.

"There appears little prospect of Johnston itself becoming a bid target."

Investors Chronicle said: "Shareholders in Portsmouth and Sunderland Newspapers should congratulate the board on its skilful negotiating." It spoke of the group's "sparkling" performance from publishing.

And the Financial Times remarked: "The news allows Johnston to establish itself as one of the country's big four regional publishers."

The enthusiasm of the financial media was matched by City analysts, who were briefed at a series of meetings by Bowdler and Chiappelli. In a subsequent report one firm of analysts, Salomon Smith Barney, said the price paid for P&SN was not excessive given the scope for cost synergies and operational improvements.

In an upbeat assessment of the regional newspaper industry in general, following a dramatic upturn in advertising revenues, the analysts sent a clear message from the City to Johnstons.

"We expect P&SN to add £16.5 million to operating profits in 2000 . . . we are confident that management will deliver its promise."

It did.

Johnston Press in pictures...

The first edition of the North & South Shields Gazette – later to become Britain's first provincial evening paper

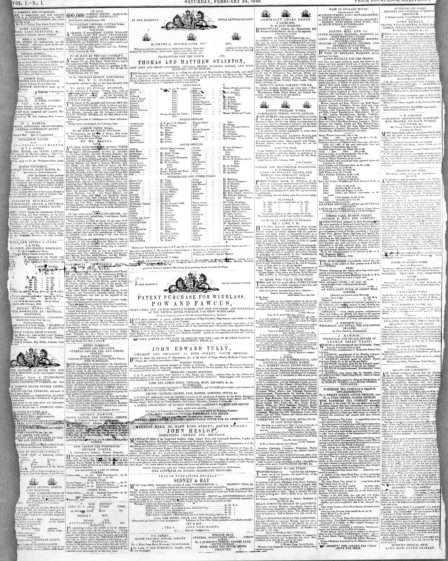

Michael Johnston (left) in 2004 as divisional managing director in the South of England, against a backdrop of Nelson's *Victory* in Portsmouth; Marco Chiappelli (below left), former group finance director; Freddy Johnston, on his retirement as chairman, with his wife Ann and sons Michael and Robert

Wellington Street in Leeds, home of the Yorkshire Post and the Yorkshire Evening Post

Sir Gordon Linacre, President of Yorkshire Post Newspapers (left); the first edition of the amalgamated Yorkshire Post & Leeds Mercury from 1939 – later to become the Yorkshire Post (background)

Staff outside the Lancashire Evening Post's Fulwood offices in Preston (right)

Life is Local: The History of Johnston Press plc

Putting the paper together. Then...

Clockwise from top left: On the streets selling the Yorkshire Evening Post; sub editors at work on the Sheffield Star; the Lancashire Evening Post's original offices in Fishergate (top right); the composing room at the Sheffield Star; the entrance to the Yorkshire Post's old premises on Albion Street; the pigeon loft at the Sheffield Star

215

...and newspaper production today

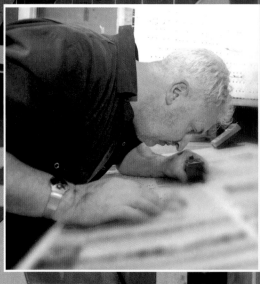

Checking registration
at the Yorkshire Post; papers
hot off the press at Hartlepool
and (main picture) the
Milton Keynes Citizen being
printed at Northampton

New media, new direction

Examples of websites from around the group, and (below right) the Johnston digital publishing team, 2005: (left to right) John Bradshaw, head of digital publishing; Andy Prior, group internet development manager; Dom Bradshaw, team operations manager; Kevin Pease, technical lead; Dave Martin, group internet technical development manager

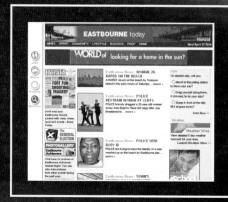

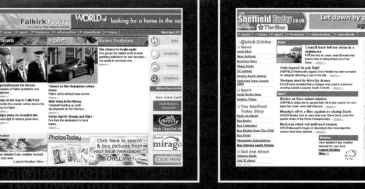

Building for the future

The old and the new: outside the Portsmouth offices on the outbreak of World War II, 1939 (far left) and (below) the Portsmouth offices today; the Sunderland Daily Echo's original offices, and (below) a bird's eye view of the present premises

Progressive outlook: architects' plans for the new print centre at Dinnington, and (below) work in progress on the complex, 2005

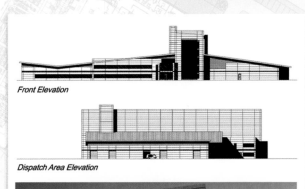

Front Elevation

Dispatch Area Elevation

Chief executive officer Tim Bowdler in 2004, and (opposite) the group management board: (left to right) Simon Kennedy, business development manager; Danny Cammiade, chief operating officer; Tim Bowdler; Stuart Paterson, chief financial officer; Malcolm Vickers, director of human resources; Richard Cooper, company secretary

The board of directors, 2004 (first row from left): R.G. Parry, non-executive chairman; P.E.B. Cawdron, non-executive; Lord Gordon of Strathblane, CBE, non-executive; S.R. Paterson, MA, CA, chief financial officer; D Cammiade, chief operating officer; (second row, from left) M.A. King, non-executive; S.J. Waugh, non-executive; L.F. Hinton, non-executive; H.C.M. Johnston, non-executive; P.R. Cooper, ACA, company secretary; (opposite) T.J. Bowdler, chief executive officer; (right) F.P.M. Johnston, CBE, non-executive

223

Pictures: Chris Close

Johnston Press: local news across the British Isles

Divisional managing directors

Margaret Hilton
Northwest

Michael Johnston
Scotland

Henry Faure Walker
JP Ventures

Chris Green
North

Jean Long
Northern Ireland

Nick Mills
Midlands

Edinburgh

Belfast

Dublin

Preston

Leeds

Northampton

Portsmouth

Barry Brennan
Republic of Ireland

Gary Fearon
South

224

Chapter Seven

The end of an era

Johnston Press completed a hat-trick of acquisitions in 1999 with the purchase in December of the family-owned Tweeddale Press, based in Berwick on Tweed.

For several generations the group of six somewhat old fashioned weekly titles, most of them established in the 19th century, had been owned by the Smail family and circulated widely in the Scottish Borders. At the time the chairman was Derek Smail – former president of the Scottish Newspaper Publishers' Association and a member of the Newspaper Society.

This was a typical Johnston deal, just the kind of purchase on which the strength of the company had been developed – newspapers that were leaders in their respective market places and shareholders who were prepared to sell to realise the true capital value of their shares.

What was somewhat unusual was that the initial approach came from Tweeddale Press and no other potential buyers were involved. Everyone seemed satisfied at the negotiated sale price of £7.7 million, although during Johnston discussions Chiappelli had gone on record as saying the price was too high – by £1 million, in his opinion.

But he also saw the potential of making an already profitable business – £400,000 on an annual turnover of £3 million – more so and consolidating the Johnston position in north east England and southern Scotland. The Department of Trade and Industry raised no objections when asked for its approval and for ease of administration the Tweeddale Press was placed in Stuart McPherson's Scotland Division.

Bowdler and Smail brokered the deal – codenamed Clive – while both were attending a meeting of the Newspaper Society in London. After a particularly heavy session of discussion and debate the two stepped outside into Bloomsbury Square to clear their heads.

As they sat together on a bench in the pleasant tree-shaded gardens that distinguish this part of London it was Smail who broke the silence. "Now that you've just bought Portsmouth and Sunderland are there any titles you'd like to sell?" he asked.

But what he really meant was "Would you like to buy my

Jim Smail, who bought the Berwick Advertiser in 1950 and Derek Smail (far right) who expanded the business

business?" Bowdler, having deciphered the code, jumped at the opportunity, realising that the Tweeddale titles would make a perfect fit with others in the north east.

There was only one witness to the agreement reached that day – a silent witness in the form of the Romanesque statue of the famous Whig statesman Charles James Fox (1749-1806), Britain's first foreign secretary, whose presence dominates the green oasis at Bloomsbury Square Gardens.

Bowdler later reflected that a key factor in the acquisition was the investment in strong personal relationships that was a hallmark of Johnston Press, and which had led to the exclusive sale offered by Smail.

Of the newly-acquired titles the Southern Reporter, based in Selkirk and with a sale of about 18,000 in the central Borders, was the largest and the undisputed paper of record for the region. It was established in 1855 and also incorporated the Kelso Chronicle, founded in 1789. In 2005 the paper was judged the best paid-for weekly paper in Scotland for the fourth year in succession.

The paper would never have been launched but for the discovery of gold in Australia. The prospect of getting rich quick so appealed to local printer Tom Brown that he sold his business to grocer and provision merchant George Lewis for £40 before heading Down Under to seek his fortune.

Lewis soon realised there was more money to be made from news than flour and butter. From being a monthly selling 500 copies the "Southern" progressed to weekly publication. Through a network of local correspondents it could soon measure its sales in thousands and became something of a Borders institution.

The paper was bought in 1950 by Col Jim Smail, a New Zealander who had been persuaded to return home to run the small Berwick-based newspaper company that had been in his family since 1885.

Under Derek Smail's stewardship there was further expansion, including the purchase of the Ponteland Observer and Morpeth Herald and the launch of the Alnwick Advertiser. But a business downturn in the late 1990s and spreading of resources too thinly within the enlarged group resulted in the sale of some titles and concentration on the Borders and Berwick. Although the measures worked the disposal of the business was in its best long-term interest, with Johnston Press a willing and welcome purchaser.

England's most northerly newspaper, the Berwick Advertiser, established in 1808 and occupying antediluvian premises redolent of that era, was also included in the package along with the county mouthpiece the Berwickshire News (1869) and the weekly free Berwick Gazette (1990).

The attractive border towns of Hawick and Selkirk were covered by papers acquired as part of the earlier P&SN deal, the Hawick News (1882) and the Selkirk Weekend Advertiser. The latter is a paid-for title established in 1992 and affectionately known in the area as "The Wee Paper."

The two important acquisitions during 1999 had an immediate impact on Johnston Press profitability. The company had started the year fearing that the economy might slow down but instead the favourable trading conditions throughout the United Kingdom continued unabated.

P&SN and Tweeddale – the former exceeding expectations – contributed £9.2 million to group operating profits, which rose to £65.9 million compared to £51.1 million in 1998, an increase of 29 per cent.

Johnston Press barely had time to pause for breath before it was on the acquisition trail yet again. But such was the tit for tat competition between the major provincial newspaper companies that Newsquest, publisher of 179 local titles, had the last word when Southampton-based News Communications and Media plc (Newscom) – also an initial bidder for P&SN – came on the market at the end of the year.

Bowdler, having been alerted that the group was probably available, broke the news to the directors in a round of telephone calls and gave a more detailed report at their meeting in December.

Newscom, he said, published almost 100 newspapers, including four daily titles, several magazines and also had a contract print division, with a combined turnover of £140 million. Its main centres were in Southampton, Bournemouth, the West County, South Wales and Gloucestershire.

The Department of Trade and Industry had already decided that the sale of the group should be looked at by the Competition Commission, with a decision expected the following April – but the prospect of another inquiry was not relished by Johnston Press so soon after its P&SN experience.

Newscom had become a takeover target in February, 1999 – further evidence of the moves towards industry consolidation – when Newsquest had held informal discussions about the possibility of a merger. But these came to nothing and as far as

The offices of England's most northerly newspaper, the Berwick Advertiser, dressed up for a visit to the town by the Queen and the Duke of Edinburgh in 1956

Newscom was concerned that was the end of the matter.

That October Newsquest again declared an interest, only to be rebuffed a second time. By then, however, the management of Newsquest were not acting alone for in the meantime that company, too, had been sold for £904 million – to the American publishing giant Gannett, who fully supported the bid by its subsidiary. With an annual turnover of $5 billion and profits of $1 billion it certainly had the financial muscle to succeed. It was the publisher of 75 daily newspapers in 45 US states, and owner of USA Today, North America's largest selling daily newspaper.

Gannett was not prepared to take no for an answer, and in a move that surprised the industry made a direct approach through Newsquest for the Newscom business and sought the consent of the Secretary of State for Trade and Industry.

From being interested bystanders Johnston Press, and also the Trinity Mirror group, now threw their hats into the ring and said they, too, would like to be considered as possible buyers. The scene was set for an epic battle for Britain's seventh largest publisher of local newspapers.

It was a prize worth having. Newscom – better known as Southern Newspapers until its full official Stock Exchange listing – had long been admired for its South Coast titles, including the Southern Daily Echo, at Southampton, the Daily Echo, at Bournemouth and the Dorset Echo, at Weymouth. The acquisition of the South Wales Argus, at Newport, Gwent, in 1966, and the Bailey Newspaper Group of weekly titles in 1997, had further boosted the business, which in 1999 recorded a pre-tax profit of £20.6 million on a turnover of £139.1 million.

Of the British-owned bidders, Trinity Mirror, formed in September, 1999, by a merger between Trinity plc and Mirror Group plc, was ranked first in the pecking order of newspaper publishers, with Johnston Press in fourth place.

The Competition Commission spent the early part of 2000 looking into the merits of the respective contenders, including a local hearing at the Angel Hotel, Cardiff, and concluded that none of the proposed transfers would operate against the public interest, thus opening the way for serious bidding by the interested parties.

Johnston Press, who had identified possible savings of between £6 million and £7 million if it acquired Newscom, were concerned about over-paying for the business and the effect this might have on its own share price. But such misgivings were not even hinted at when Bowdler met Newscom chief executive John Dux in March, 2000, to explore the way forward.

The battle was all over by June with Newsquest, bankrolled by its American owners, emerging victorious in a deal worth around £500 million.

The Johnston directors had agreed that an offer of £17.25 per share was "fair and appropriate" although they were prepared to increase this to £17.50 if bidding went to a second round. When it did Newsquest twice increased its own offer to £18 per share, a price that the Newscom shareholders were more than happy to accept and which was 26 per cent higher than the company's share price at the start of the year.

"The additional titles would have fitted in ideally with our other south coast interests," said Freddy Johnston. "But Newsquest weighed in with an offer that simple blew us out of the water."

It was to be another two years before Johnston Press completed its next major acquisition – the titles published by Regional Independent Media, including the prestigious regional morning, the Yorkshire Post. Nevertheless the company completed a number

> Johnstons waited patiently until the two weeks elapsed and confirmation was received that its offer to buy the Standard series and Four Counties had been successful

of smaller purchases during 2000 and 2001 which further helped to consolidate its position in the North Midlands and Lincolnshire.

Of these, the first came hot on the heels of the Newscom debacle when Johnstons paid £16.5 million for a raft of paid-for and free weekly titles published by the Lincolnshire Standard Group and Four Counties Newspapers, some of which overlapped with existing titles in Grantham, Worksop and Retford.

The deal was codenamed "Harry" – a thinly disguised reference to Harry Lambert, founder of the Adscene Group, which now owned the newspapers. But in a complex business structure Adscene was a subsidiary of Denitz Investments, which in turn had been a subsidiary of Southnews plc since 2000.

There was a further complication to any sale because of an agreement between Southnews and the Northcliffe group, which already had a strong presence in Lincolnshire, giving the latter the right to be approached about any potential disposal and two weeks in which to take up an option to buy.

Johnstons waited patiently until the two weeks elapsed and confirmation was received that its offer to buy the 12-title Standard series and the four titles which formed Four Counties had been successful. They were projected to enhance group earnings by £1.77 million in the first year and by £2.17 million in subsequent years. Among the savings anticipated were printing the titles at Johnston centres when a contract to print them in Hull expired.

The new titles acquired from LSG	
● Gainsborough Trader News	● Mablethorpe and
● Lincoln Chronicle	Sutton Standard
● Boston Standard	● Louth and Mid Lincs
● Sleaford Standard	Standard
● Skegness Standard	● Gainsborough Standard
● Spilsby Standard	● Epworth Bells and
● Alford Standard	Crowle Advertiser

Titles purchased from Four Counties	
● Dinnington and Maltby	● Newark Trader
Trader News	● Retford and Bawtry
● Grantham and Melton	Trader News
Trader News	● Worksop Trader News

A review of the new acquisitions was completed within two months and followed a visit by Bowdler and the recently appointed group managing director (publishing), Nicholas Rudd-Jones, to the main centres.

Rudd-Jones reported that while the businesses were generally in good shape staff morale was low because of the number of changes in ownership. There had also been a lack of investment and some markets were severely underdeveloped.

Titles in Nottinghamshire joined the North Midlands Division and those in Lincolnshire the East Midlands Division. In the north, the Worksop Trader was merged into the midweek Worksop Guardian to produce one strong free newspaper and a similar merger was planned for Grantham. The Newark Trader was sold later in millennium year.

The completion of Operation Harry was followed quickly by Operation Henry in February, 2001, which saw Mortons Media Ltd, of Horncastle, and its Lincolnshire Independent Newspapers join Johnston Press in a takeover worth £5.5 million in cash.

The additional titles bought were the Louth Leader, Horncastle News, Skegness News, Market Rasen Mail, Classified Gold, Mablethorpe, Sutton and Alford Leader and the Coningsby and Tattershall News.

At about the same time Johnsons also made another return to Scotland with the £100,000 acquisition of the Glasgow East News, a free title that had been started in 1995 and distributed in one of the most deprived areas of the city. The small operation had an annual turnover of £164,000.

Towards the end of the year a further £275,000 was paid for Days Out UK, a small travel database and guidebook publishing company based in Northampton. Among its many and diverse clients were the Museum of Hatting, the Cutty Sark clipper, Coventry Cathedral and visitor centre, and Painswick Rococo Garden in Gloucestershire.

In 2005 Days Out UK was transferred to a new division, JP Ventures, which was created to nurture and develop a number of non-local publishing activities. These included the Outbound magazines acquired via T.R. Beckett at Eastbourne, Letterbox Direct, a leaflet distribution business formerly operated by Regional Independent Media in Harrogate, and the off-road magazines Dirt Bike Rider and Trials and Motocross News, also former RIM subsidiaries.

> Operation Harry was followed quickly by Operation Henry, which saw Mortons Media Ltd and Lincolnshire Independent Newspapers join Johnston Press in a £5.5 million takeover

Although the influx of the additional weekly titles in England and Scotland was important to the continuing growth of Johnston Press the broader, long-term picture was less clear. The satisfaction of buying P&SN had been tempered by the failure to acquire Newscom and prompted the board to question the direction in which the company should be moving.

Clearly, the time had arrived to take stock of the business and plot its further development.

The directors were also concerned about the massive on-going investment in new technology, and especially the vast sums that were needed to upgrade and replace its printing presses.

The divisional managing director of the print division, David Crow, was invited to Edinburgh, to review current activity and point the way forward.

Since 1998 major refurbishments had been commissioned to the double width presses in Peterborough and Northampton, together with work at Falkirk, the Isle of Man, Wakefield and Scarborough. The presses in Kirkcaldy, Chesterfield and Eastbourne had been closed.

Crow's immediate need was to buy two new presses – one in Peterborough to replace the 34-year-old Goss Urbanite press, and the second in Portsmouth, at a combined cost of £16.5 million. The latter would also make possible the closure of Southern Web Offset, at Burgess Hill, which had been included in the Emap deal, where the presses were not meeting colour demands – but even that came at a price with £1.6 million earmarked for the shutdown.

The investment, together with ongoing work at Scarborough and the Isle of Man, would meet publishers' projected demand for capacity and colour over the next three to five years, assured Crow.

He left the meeting a happy man, with board approval for the capital expenditure he had recommended. But it was a salutory reminder to the Johnston directors that in order to remain competitive and abreast of technology they would have to continue spending heavily on presses in future years – the very scenario that had lead Emap to quit regional newspapers rather than pour money into what they seemed to regard as a bottomless black hole.

The Johnston decision was not taken lightly and there was a lively discussion before Crow's shopping list was approved. What, asked directors, was the payback period? What would be the effect of not proceeding? Why was external printing under contract not considered a good idea? And would the traditional printing process continue long term?

Spending on new pressroom machinery was crucial if Johnston Press was to continue printing its existing titles efficiently and economically, but the group also needed the capacity to accommodate new titles in the future. But what was that future . . . ?

The likely shape of the business in the years ahead was less easy to define, but it was a situation that needed addressing without delay. Expert help was summonsed in the shape of Schroders, the company's chief financial advisers, who prepared a summary of strategic options that identified opportunities and selective targets. These were discussed at the annual strategy meeting of directors held at the Seaham Hall Hotel, Seaham, Co. Durham, in June, 2001.

Minds were focussed by the announcement only days before that Gannett UK Ltd was looking to expand on its Newscom success and was seeking consent from the Department of Trade and Industry to acquire the titles owned by Regional Independent Media Holdings (RIM).

Schroders outlined four options, although their report had been prepared before the Gannett announcement, which now gave added importance to the meeting.

One scenario was for continued organic growth with smaller bolt-on acquisitions, of which the Lincolnshire Standard Group and the Horncastle business were good examples. But the advisers warned that such a low-key policy was unlikely to produce annual growth above 15 per cent, would miss the benefits of industry consolidation and leave Johnston Press as a potential take-over target.

Significant growth by acquisition was another option and one with which the company was already familiar, for this was the route that had placed it in such a lofty position within the British newspaper industry. Schroders identified several potential targets, some well-known names among them.

Diversification was also considered as a way forward with expansion abroad, radio, television, outdoor advertising and magazines as possibilities. But there was little enthusiasm for this option, which was regarded as a high-risk strategy in areas in which the company lacked expertise. There would also be less opportunity for group-wide cost savings as, for example, newspapers afforded in the buying of newsprint and other raw materials.

The fourth option was even more unpalatable, but one that had to be considered. Johnston Press, said the advisers, could arrange a managed exit from the business of publishing newspapers – after all it had been done before, Emap being a classic example.

The directors spent several hours chewing over the key points raised in the report and all were agreed that failure to make a major acquisition would leave Johnston Press vulnerable. Furthermore, simply relying on small bolt-on acquisitions would give the impression of a business running out of steam.

But how could expansion be achieved, since opportunities for large acquisitions were limited and had become less so after recent industry consolidation? A joint venture with another group – informal talks had already been held with one publisher to explore just such a possibility – was considered but did not generate much interest around the table. The general feeling was that this could shackle the company unless the Johnston Press management was clearly in control.

"We should always be masters of our own destiny and not junior partners in a venture," declared Freddy Johnston in an impassioned dismissal of the notion.

Johnston had a more enlightened solution. The Johnston family, he said, would allow their own shareholding to be diluted by new rights issues if a suitable acquisition came along. This significant offer was widely welcomed, for with this commitment and other funding available the company could now contemplate and be able to finance a deal worth £1 billion.

On their return to Edinburgh the directors who gathered around the highly polished board room table at Manor Place, overlooked by portraits and photographs of generations of Johnstons, knew exactly what their next target should be: Project Pacific was about to begin.

With the RIM titles clearly in sight advisers were briefed immediately to start work on the figures – what would be the likely cost if the whole business was purchased, or what were the financial implications of buying the whole and then selling RIM's considerable interests in Lancashire?

Before this ambitious venture was brought to a conclusion two significant changes occurred in the management structure of Johnston Press, two retirements that signalled the break-up of a team that for more than 20 years had shared much of the responsibility for the company's growth in size and prosperity.

First to stand down, in April, 2001, was chairman Freddy Johnston, who had made no secret of his intention to relinquish the position when he reached the age of 65.

But the retirement of finance director Marco Chiappelli, in July that year, at the age of 57 had not been foreseen, and his announcement that he intended to leave the company took his colleagues by surprise.

Johnston retained his seat on the board as a non-executive director and continued to play an influential part in the running of the company, but nevertheless his decision to take a back seat marked the end of an era. He had, after all, been the Johnston figurehead since succeeding his father as chairman and managing director in 1973, but now the group faced the future for the first time in its history without a Johnston at the tiller.

Freddy Johnston took immense pride in the father-to-son succession that had piloted the family firm from humble beginnings in Falkirk to become the country's fourth largest provincial newspaper business, but the idea of a self-perpetuating dynasty never appealed to him. Nor did the prospect of remaining chairman until he became too old or infirm to fulfil the role effectively.

"People who try to carry on after their sell-by date actually damage their reputation and diminish the good things they may have done. I am determined not to fall into that trap," he told colleagues.

The winding-down process had started four years earlier, in 1997, when Johnston ceased to be executive chairman of the company and handed over most of the day-to-day responsibility to his group managing director Tim Bowdler, who became chief executive. Both events had been planned well in advance and widely proclaimed so as to avert any loss of confidence in a public company such as can often result from unexpected boardroom reshuffles.

Bowdler had learned a great deal from Johnston in their short time together and especially admired his boldness, his vision, his integrity and his unswerving loyalty to colleagues and employees, many of whom regarded him as a father figure.

There was unanimity among the other directors that Johnston should be invited to stay on as a member of the board. They could ill afford to lose a colleague of such vast experience and knowledge and who still had a consuming interest in the company and the wider world of newspapers, where he was a popular and highly respected figure.

Johnston would have been deeply hurt by any other course of action. "After all, I was sort of wedded to the company and I still felt I had something to offer," he said. The gregarious Scot proved the

> *The retirement of Marco Chiappelli at the age of 57 had not been foreseen, and took his colleagues by surprise*

point by continuing in the ambassadorial role that had become his trademark, maintaining his many industry connections and always looking out for new business opportunities.

"The newspaper world is a bit like a village and by living in a village you become fascinated by the other inhabitants. Some you want to know better," he said.

Johnston cleared out his desk at Manor Place in the days before he was due to stand down but showed little signs of sentiment until it came to saying farewell to his efficient and loyal personal assistant, Jayne Cameron, who for nine years had planned and organised his working life. Johnston reflected that in 40 years with the company only three secretaries had assisted him – firstly Betty McInnes, then Norma Forbes and latterly Cameron.

Cameron was handed the task of organising the special events that marked the end of Johnston's chairmanship, culminating in a gala dinner at Edinburgh's swish Balmoral Hotel attended by more than 200 close friends and representatives from all the Johnston Press divisional companies.

Those invited to the black tie gathering dined in style in the hotel's Sir Walter Scott Suite – salad of lobster and Oban scallops followed by Highland venison, washed down by a 1998 Chablis and a fine 1966 St Emilion Grand Cru. Grace said by the Rev Colin Mailer, a former editor of the Linlithgow Gazette, the second title in the original Johnston company.

Then the speeches and presentations began. And the laughter, for this was no maudlin wake but a happy celebration. Tim Bowdler was allocated a 10-minute slot to welcome guests and set the scene before the microphone was handed over to Johnston's long-time friend Dougal Nisbet-Smith, a former director of the Newspaper Society, to propose the main toast of the evening.

Then it was Johnston's turn to take centre stage before a loyal, warm and receptive audience that included several former adversaries from past takeover battles. The urbane and articulate retiring chairman put on a bravura performance, recounting many of his famous anecdotes that most of those present had heard several times before, but which now sound more amusing than ever.

It was also an opportunity to single out for special praise some of the colleagues who over the years had shared in the growth and success of Johnston Press – the late Tom McGowran, Iain Bell, Marco Chiappelli, Scotland divisional managing director Stuart

McPherson, and his three indispensible secretaries/PAs. Johnston also offered a glowing endorsement of his successor as chairman, Roger Parry – "a man of huge ability".

Johnston's son Michael, South divisional managing director at Portsmouth, thanked the speakers and all those present before the presentations began. The first of these was an emotionally-charged gift of the late Tom McGowran's favourite watch from his widow Iris and son Tom Jnr, who were still mourning his death a month earlier. The gold Omega timepiece had originally belonged to Johnston's father and following his death had been given to McGowran as a keepsake.

The next presentation was a top of the range home computer system subscribed to by senior managers throughout the company. And finally, a large painting in caricature style by the acclaimed Scottish artist and cartoonist Hugh Dodd depicting people, places and events that had figured prominently in Johnston's career since 1962 was handed over.

Johnston formally stood down as chairman at the company's annual meeting the following day. Those present found it a much more poignant occasion than the previous evening's dinner, the line of succession now confirmed as Roger Parry assumed his exalted position – and wielding a brand new chairman's gavel to stand alongside a miniature gavel that Johnston has cherished, but rarely used.

No one doubted his suitability for the job and he had impressed his colleagues since being invited to become a Johnston Press director four years earlier. Parry had been highly recommended as a "people person" with sound judgement and wide media experience, and also enjoyed considerable support within the City, a crucial attribute now he had become chairman.

Parry was a popular choice from among the other Johnston Press non-executive directors, who had preferred to appoint within their own ranks, but as only the fourth chairman in 119 years and the first outside the Johnston family, much was expected of him. And he had to live up to the qualities outlined so eloquently by his predecessor less than 12 hours before – "a fine strategic mind . . . crystal clear vision . . . an innate grasp of our corporate life and activity."

His recruitment to the Johnston board was brokered by his long-standing friend and business associate Sir Harry Roche – both had been directors of the radio station Jazz FM and Roche was already a

Johnston director. Although Parry had spent much of his working life as a journalist this had been in radio and television. The chance to learn more about regional newspapers appealed to him as did the Edinburgh base of Johnston Press – his mother originated from the city, although he had never lived or worked there.

Freddy Johnston and Parry met each other for the first time over lunch of smoked salmon and Dover sole at Johnston's favourite London restaurant, Wiltons. He was vetted again by Bowdler and Chiappelli before being formally appointed as a non-executive director.

The invitation to become chairman was discreetly raised by Johnston during a board dinner being held at the Scotch Whisky Association in Edinburgh, but such was Parry's surprise that he initially turned down the offer. Johnston was persistent as usual, for he was looking well ahead and in Parry saw the opportunity to jump a generation, to be succeeded by someone in his late forties rather than an older man, someone who could remain at the helm for another 10 or 15 years. Johnston finally received the answer he was looking for over another meal at Wiltons.

"It was a great honour but not at all daunting," Parry said later. "The company was so well run and the double act at the time of Bowdler and Chiappelli was just so extraordinarily self-assured.

"I knew I was not inheriting any problems – more a question of picking up the golden chalice."

Parry was indeed well qualified for the mantle he had now inherited. Although he had no previous newspaper experience he had spent many years in the media, including seven years as a reporter and producer, working for the BBC and commercial television and radio. He was also a founder of London Radio, which operated the two London news-talk stations.

Forty-eight-year-old Parry combined his role as non-executive chairman with that of chairman and, until 2005, chief executive of Texas-based Clear Channel International, the world's leading out-of-home media company and the largest operator in radio, outdoor advertising and live entertainment.

Between 1995 and 1998 Parry was chief executive of the UK media company, More Group plc, until it was acquired by Clear Channel. He then became directly responsible for Clear Channel's operations in Europe, Asia and the Pacific and Africa, which spans 58 countries with 5,000 staff and annual sales of $1 billion.

Parry was able to repay the compliments paid to him by Johnston when he presented his first annual report as chairman. He reminded shareholders that under Johnston's 28-year leadership the company had grown from a small family business based in Falkirk with a turnover of £100,000 and four titles to a highly profitable publicly quoted company with a turnover of £301 million and almost 200 titles.

"His years at the helm of Johnston Press represent an exceptional achievement," extolled Parry.

The new chairman made an immediate impact and it quickly became apparent that there was no room for complacency about past successes. Challenges to the business model, his mental agility and searching questions aimed at his executive team had everyone on their toes.

But Parry's honeymoon period at Johnston Press was short lived, for almost immediately he was called upon to make the crucial appointment of a new finance director to replace the departing Chiappelli. It was not only the Italian-Scot's charm that made him a hard act to follow but also his considerable commercial acumen that he had displayed over the last 27 years.

"He played a vital and central role in the growth of what was a small family business into a substantial public company," Parry reminded shareholders in his annual report.

Chiappelli's decision to take early retirement had been kept a closely guarded secret and was not announced until after Johnston's move to the boardroom backbenches. But those in the know had been aware of his impending departure for several months.

Picture: Sam Sloan

Successful double act – Marco Chiappelli and Tim Bowdler

The first to be told was Chiappelli's close friend and colleague Tim Bowdler who was alerted to something important in the offing, although he could not guess what, by a surprise Sunday afternoon telephone call from the excitable Italian.

Chiappelli had been taking stock of his life for weeks, agonising over whether to continue in office for the foreseeable future or make a break from the job he loved and the people he admired. The impending acquisition of Regional Independent Media (RIM), on which he had been working flat out for months, was a key factor.

Chiappelli knew that once the deal was completed he could not simply walk away with so much reorganisation and restructuring to be done. Probably the next convenient window for retirement would be when he was 60 at the earliest.

"It's time to take the stress out of life and have control of my own time, our time," he told his wife, Jane. "I know Johnstons will go from strength to strength, but they'll do that just as well without me."

It was three o'clock when Chiappelli summonsed the courage to telephone Bowdler and then drove to his house. It was clear to Bowdler that something was amiss when he opened the door to find his friend shaking like a leaf and close to tears.

For the next emotional hour and a half Chiappelli poured out his reasons for retiring while Bowdler, inwardly wishing he would change his mind, listened patiently and kindly, saying all the right things at the right time.

That night Chiappelli enjoyed his best sleep for weeks, but Bowdler was alarmed when he failed to turn up the following morning to catch the six o'clock train from Edinburgh Waverely to Peterborough. As the doors closed and the GNER express moved out Bowdler's telephone rang.

"It's me – sorry, but I've overslept."

"Christ, Marco, I know you're retiring, but did you have to start today?" retorted Bowdler.

A few days later Chiappelli told Freddy Johnston he was leaving, although by then he was much calmer and felt like a great weight had been removed from his shoulders.

As the the wheels were set in motion to find a new finance director Chiappelli began organising his farewell dinner – not one, but two. A small party for family, close friends and business associates was held at Edinburgh's five-star Prestonfield House, one of the city's most prestigious hotels.

Company colleagues – all the managing directors and finance directors were invited – had their opportunity to give Chiappelli a send-off to remember at the Marriott Hotel, Peterborough. A champagne reception preceded a dinner with a strong Italian influence – Tuscan roasted pork loin and bottles of Chianti Classico Ricasoli.

Among the retirement gifts was a golf-themed caricature that had been commissioned by the company from Hugh Dodd, the artist who had impressed with his retirement painting for Freddy Johnston.

The next day, as his guests settled down to a group briefing and planning meeting, Chiappelli flew to Italy for a holiday – "a wonderful feeling to leave them behind, working away!"

His successor as group finance director was 43-year-old Stuart Paterson, who joined the company officially in July, 2001, although he had already spent a month as a director to allow him to familiarise himself with the financial complexities of Johnston Press. And to make sure that the transition was as smooth as possibly Chiappelli's services were retained as a consultant during the bedding-in period.

Paterson, who was born in Edinburgh, graduated from the University of Edinburgh with an MA honours degree in economics in 1979 He was personable, ambitious and experienced at a senior management level with several blue chip companies – his previous employers had included accountants Price Waterhouse, Hewlett Packard UK, and Motorola, where he became European manufacturing controller in 1995.

His career had also taken him to the world-wide rental power, temperature control and compressed air systems company Aggreko plc as finance director and later managing director, Europe. Paterson's next career move in 2000 saw him join the high-tech start-up optoelectronics company, Intense Phononics, in Edinburgh, as chief financial officer. The company was conceived in September, 2000 and was planned to be one of the largest venture capital fundings in British history with a potential value of £100 million.

Optoelectronics, which in Scotland had been developed by two former Glasgow University academics, uses integrated circuitry based on light beams and was widely regarded at the time as the next growth industry – a dream that evaporated as the technology sector collapsed along with scores of dotcom companies in the early years of the 21st Century.

But every cloud has a silver lining – and in Paterson's case it was the opportunity for a complete career change into the world of provincial newspaper publishing. But it took a helping hand from the retiring Chiappelli.

The two had known each other for five years as members of the Group of Scottish Finance Directors; indeed it had been the paternalistic Chiappelli who, as group chairman, had taken Paterson under his wing when he first joined.

When they met again over lunch at the Glasgow Hilton hotel to honour the new Scottish Finance Director ot the Year – an accolade subsequently bestowed on Paterson in 2004 – the conversation drifted from their shared love of golf and football to a series of abstruse and enigmatic questions from Chiappelli intended to establish whether his younger companion was aware of his impending retirement. He wasn't.

Back at his office in Edinburgh, Chiappelli wasted no time in telephoning headhunters Heidrick and Struggles, who had earlier been responsible for locating Tim Bowdler and had now been appointed to search out potential candidates as finance director.

"Add Paterson to your list," he suggested. They did, and when Paterson received a phone call several days later asking if he was interested in "an opportunity in the Scottish media sector" he knew immediately that the clients were Johnston Press.

Events moved swiftly after that as the shortlist was whittled down to four candidates – a meeting with chief headhunter Peter Breen, discussions with Bowdler, a tough session of psychometric testing, an interview with Freddy Johnston and finally a face-to-face session with the full board of directors.

Paterson, who had impeccable City credentials, did not need much convincing that the move to Johnston Press, a company he had long admired, was the right one for him. But what impressed him most was new chairman Parry's positive outlook and desire to continue the group's steady growth by acquisition.

"We're still looking at the menu – but we are the diner and not the dinner," assured Parry.

The next course was even more appetising than anything that had gone before – the £560 million deal to buy Regional Independent Media (RIM) and its mouth-watering mix of top-drawer titles.

Chapter Eight

Operation Pacific

In simple business terms the acquisition of Regional Independent Media Holdings was another stepping stone in the continuing growth of Johnston Press. In reality it symbolised much more, another defining moment in the history of the company.

At £560 million this was by far the largest deal in which it had been involved. It confirmed Johnston's ranking as the fourth largest provincial newspaper group in the United Kingdom by circulation and propelled it to the top of the league of titles owned – 244 dailies and weeklies.

But the real significance of the deal lay behind RIM's somewhat amorphous title, the kind so much beloved in corporate circles. RIM itself was a concoction that came into being only in 1998 when the Yorkshire and Lancashire titles of one of Britain's most famous and successful newspaper groups, United Provincial Newspapers, were sold to venture capitalists Candover Investments for around £350 million.

And now the former UPN and its dazzling array of 53 daily and weekly newspapers had another new owner; once again it belonged to people who were focused on its value as the publisher of quality titles and not simply as an asset to be sold on when the price was right.

A possible bid for United's northern interests had been discussed by Johnston directors when UPN first came on the market, but at the time they nervously agreed that the time was not right and interest lapsed. An acquisition on such a scale would have over-stretched the company's financial and management resources – a step too far, as Bowdler later reflected.

Much had changed in the intervening years – Johnston Press itself had grown with the acquisition of Portsmouth and Sunderland Newspapers, its financial base was more secure than before and the company felt it could afford a purchase of this magnitude without taking any unnecessary risks. Furthermore, its standing in the City was high, and in turn a bid now was more likely to receive a broad level of support from key investors.

Owners Candover had never regarded RIM as a long-term operation, but in the true spirit of venture capitalism had seen its

Chris Oakley circa 1971:
"not an archetypal
YP man with my hair
and weird dress"

investment mature to the point where a sale would produce a healthy return for shareholders. This was in line with its stated ethos to "build strong businesses with excellent prospects . . . to determine a fair and full price and create a productive environment for a buyout."

Candover was established in 1980 and listed on the London Stock Exchange in 1984. Since then almost 90 per cent of the companies it has backed have achieved successful exits via stock market listings or trade sales. It had previously made a successful foray into regional press ownership in 1991 with an investment of £190 million in Birmingham-based Midland Independent Newspapers, before selling the company to the Mirror Group for £305 million in 1997.

The acquisition of United Provincial Newspapers in 1998 took the industry by surprise, not least the price Candover was prepared to pay. While other potential bidders melted away, back to the safety of their boardrooms, Candover not only committed its own substantial funds but also received support from investment affiliates the Goldman Sachs Group and a Dutch venture capital company, Alpinvest.

The purchase led in turn to the formation of Regional Independent Media Holdings, which was incorporated in February, 1998, to manage Candover's investment. RIM's base was established within the Yorkshire Post building at Leeds, a welcome return to the city for journalist turned businessman Chris Oakley, who was appointed chief executive.

His homecoming was not without irony, and Oakley had good reason to reflect that he had come a long way since he joined the Evening Post as a long-haired sub editor with a love of rock music in 1971. His early months at the paper were unhappy times, a low point of his career, and were made even worse when editor Malcolm Barker told him that he was unlikely to make the grade and should look for another job.

Less than a week later Oakley was alone on the subs desk while his colleagues took their lunch break. The out-of-favour sub found himself in the hot seat when news came in of an armed bank raid in Bradford. This was a typical breaking story, with frequent rewrites and additions, and it was up to Oakley, with Barker taking a keen interest in events, to deal with it.

That afternoon Barker summonsed him to his office again. "I've been wrongly advised, forget what I said about leaving," he told Oakley, who was also rewarded with a promotion within the subbing section.

Oakley went on to become a features sub editor with the Evening Post before being appointed deputy editor of the Yorkshire Post – "not an archetypal YP man with my hair and weird dress" – and then editor of the Liverpool Echo. From there he joined Ralph Ingersoll's Birmingham Post and Mail Ltd as editor-in-chief, and rapidly became managing director of the American-owned company.

Oakley and Candover knew each other well, for it was he who had led a management buyout of the Birmingham business when Ingersoll ran into financial problems and decided to sell his British interests. The deal – worth £125 million and the world's biggest management buy-out of a media group at that time – was funded by Candover. Critics who described the acquisition as "complete lunacy" were forced to eat their words when the company was floated as Midland Independent Newspapers in 1994.

In the merry-go-round of newspaper ownership during the Nineties, the Mirror Group bought Midland Independent and Oakley became a Mirror director. But when United Provincial Newspapers came on the market the Mirror board turned down his recommendation to buy, leaving the way open for Candover, who approached Oakley with an offer to invest in the business and become chief executive.

In line with Candover policy, RIM's management team was given a 9.2 per cent equity stake in the new company, of which Oakley owned about half, with the bulk of the shareholding held by Candover (45.4 per cent), Goldman Sachs (27.2 per cent) and Alpinvest (18.2 per cent).

While RIM was a creation of convenience its pedigree was almost aristocratic. It had a lineage stretching back to 1754 with the publication of the Leedes Intelligencer, forerunner of the group's flagship, the Yorkshire Post, which grew to become England's second biggest morning regional publication. The formation of the Yorkshire Conservative Newspaper Company in 1866 led to the publication of the sister titles the Yorkshire Post and Yorkshire Evening Post, and the business prospered through organic growth and some acquisitions until a merger with United Newspapers in

1969. This company was itself merged with MAI plc in 1996 to form United News and Media plc.

By 2002 RIM was the leading newspaper publisher in Yorkshire based on circulation – a mantle since assumed by Johnston Press – and operated from centres across Yorkshire, Lancashire and Scotland. Six of its titles were daily newspapers, 29 weekly paid-for papers and 18 free weekly papers, with an aggregate weekly circulation of about 3.3 million copies, attracting a total readership of around 7.3 million. More than 20 of its titles were at least a century old.

In addition to the Leeds titles the Yorkshire portfolio also included The Star and the Telegraph, at Sheffield, and the Dewsbury Reporter and the Harrogate Advertiser, while in the North West the titles included the Lancashire Evening Post and Wigan Evening Post, Evening Gazette, Blackpool, Lancaster Guardian and Burnley Express.

RIM had also harboured ambitions of expanding into Scotland – traditional Johnston territory – and as a first small strategic step had made two acquisitions north of the border during 2000 – five weekly titles from Scottish County Press in Bonnyrigg, a commuter area south of Edinburgh, and the Alloa and Hillfoots County News, a paid-for weekly to the north-east of Edinburgh. A further six titles, in Galloway and the Stornoway Gazette in the Outer Hebrides, were added in 2001.

Unlike Johnston Press, which had long since divested itself of its non-newspaper interests, RIM had been ambitious to become a mixed-media group. With this in mind it had set up a subsidiary company to pursue its new media strategy and also decided to acquire local radio interests within its geographic newspaper areas. It was the principal shareholder in a consortium that was awarded the FM radio licence for the Burnley and Pendle area of Lancashire and part of another consortium seeking the FM licence in Yorkshire.

The sheer size of the RIM operation was a challenge to the Johnston Press management, who faced the daunting task of incorporating Britain's fifth largest publisher of regional and local newspapers into the framework of the fourth largest.

The acquisition not only added a further 3,300 full and part-time employees to the Johnston payroll but also considerably increased the group's printing capacity, an area that would require rationalisation in the post-purchase months. While most of the Yorkshire titles were printed in-house at Leeds, Sheffield and Harrogate the majority of the north-west titles were printed under a 15-year agreement at Broughton Printers Ltd, near Preston, which had been set up some years earlier by the Daily Express to print its northern editions.

Although RIM was top of the list of Johnston takeover targets, the company was not the only potential buyer, not the only major group weighing up the odds and deciding the optimum moment to declare an interest. But all were agreed, given the track record of Candover, that RIM would come on to the market sooner or later. The predators watched and waited.

The all-important breakthrough came in June, 2000, when Gannett UK Limited, the American owners of the Newsquest group, publicly announced that they had approach RIM and expressed an interest in buying the company. It took most observers by surprise, for in the same month Gannett had already completed the acquisition of the Southampton-based Newscom group for £444 million, beating Johnstons to the deal. Clearly, its war chest had funds left for further, rapid expansion.

Usually such public announcements are made when a deal has been completed, but in the case of RIM it was clear that no such arrangement had been reached with Gannett. The Johnston directors had to decide what they should do, and quickly, even though at that stage they had not had the opportunity to consider the full implications of the statement.

Within days Johnston Press threw its hat into the ring, followed shortly afterwards by the Guardian Media Group (GMG). All three bidders then sought consent for the purchase of RIM from the Secretary of State for Trade and Industry, who in turn referred the applications to the Competition Commission for a formal inquiry into the public interest considerations.

This had been anticipated, for in areas of both Yorkshire and the North West the overlap between RIM titles and those published by the three bidders was considerable. In the North West, Gannett held 29.2 per cent of the market against GMG's 27.2 per cent and RIM's 13.9 per cent, while in Yorkshire RIM's 31.6 per cent market share was only marginally ahead of Johnston's 26.6 per cent, with Gannett trailing at 14.1 per cent.

Even though there were widely broadcast declarations of interest from each of the rival groups, none had gone so far as to open negotiations with RIM, whose board had also not reached any conclusions but was reviewing all its strategic options. Oakley was strongly in favour of a Stock Market flotation and some preparatory work towards this goal had already started. He knew, however, that it would not be easy to convince Candover who, in typical venture capitalist fashion, appeared more interested in a trade sale and a secure exit, cash in hand.

Further developments were held in abeyance until after the Competition Commission deliberated. It was a huge relief when they reported favourably in November, 2000, for approval was an essential hurdle to clear ahead of the long negotiating process that followed.

The examination of the credentials of three of the industry's big hitters took several months to complete and provided a valuable insight into the relative strengths of the competitors and the process of consolidation that was taking place among the major publishing groups.

Gannett's financial clout had been well documented since it first appeared on the British newspaper scene in 1999 with the £904 million purchase of Newsquest. With a turnover of £3.5 billion here and in the USA it was well placed to pursue an expansionist policy, already evident by comfortably out-bidding Johnston in the tussle for Newscom.

On the other hand, the Guardian Media Group, the seventh largest British newspaper group, was a less familiar name in major acquisition circles although it had built up sizeable interests in national, regional and local newspapers, magazines, radio and television. By 2000 this great upholder of press freedom and liberal journalism was publishing two national titles, the Guardian and the Observer, two dailies, the Manchester Evening News and Reading Evening Post, 45 weeklies, one monthly and had a 50 per cent stake in the Auto Trader motor magazine.

GMG was wholly owned by the Scott Trust, originally created in 1934 by the son of C.P. Scott, editor of the Manchester Guardian, to secure the financial and editorial independence of that paper in perpetuity. Since 1975, when the Manchester Evening News was the only regional title in the group, there had been on-going expansion in the North West and in Berkshire/Hampshire, especially with the launch of a series of free weekly newspapers. All this activity had seen GMG pre-tax profits more than double to £68 million in the period 1995-99, but at 12.7 per cent its operating profit on sales was well below Johnston's 27.2 per cent and Newsquest's 29.1.

The Competition Commission asked each of the interested

parties about their intentions if they were successful in their bid for their RIM titles. All spoke of their commitment to the regional and local press and of the efficiencies that could be achieved through an enlargement of their activities – "of benefit to both businesses, the circulations and the readers," said Johnston Press.

The opinions of outside interests were less effusive, with the National Union of Journalists in particular taking a pessimistic stance over the concentration of newspaper ownership in fewer and larger chains. The NUJ estimated that three quarters of the regional press had changed hands in the previous five years – "driven by the fact that it was possible to make a considerable amount of money from the media."

By its own admission, the NUJ's relations with RIM were poor (whereas Johnston Press had traditionally taken a more moderate and inclusive attitude towards the union). It alleged that when RIM was formed by Candover a document had been prepared outlining 90 points on how to destroy any resistance among the workforce to management plans, especially redundancies.

Nevertheless, the NUJ viewed with caution any further concentration of ownership and spelled out its reasons, among them cost-cutting and the lowering of journalistic and production standards, elimination of choice for readers and advertisers, sharp reductions in employment opportunities and reduction of diversity of the regional press.

These were considerations that were relevant to the Competition Commission inquiry team when looking at the public interest and commercial aspects of the RIM bidders. In its final report it, too, sounded a cautionary note.

The Commission foresaw the development of more clusters of geographically proximate titles in common ownership – "We do not see an obvious natural limit to the process if it is left to market forces."

While acknowledging the arguments put forward by the three companies under review, the Commission sent out a strong signal to the industry at large and warned of the "potential danger" if the growth in concentration was allowed to go too far. It said this might:

- enable multi-market operators in new areas to exploit their market position, damage independent local rivals and raise barriers to entry if they were so minded;

> " The NUJ estimated that three quarters of the regional press had changed hands in the previous five years "

- increase the market power of newspaper owners, enabling them to raise rates for at least some types of local advertisers for whom alternative media are not, or not yet, a realistic alternative; and

- reduce the drive to maintain and improve quality that comes from editorial competition and comparison between independently managed titles, and increase the potential for sharing of editorial and other resources, in ways that could lead to a less diverse and innovative local press.

Its views, while looking at the worst options possible, were nevertheless sincere and were prompted by the nine major transactions in the UK regional newspaper sector since 1999, with an aggregate value of more than £3 billion, in which Johnston Press had been an active participant. But despite this level of activity the market remained comparatively fragmented in relation to other media and still had more than 90 publishers and about 1,200 titles.

When the Commission sought the views of other newspaper groups both Northcliffe Newspapers and Trinity Mirror cast old rivalries aside to stress the positive credentials of Gannett, Johnston and GMG. Among the trade organisations contacted the Institute of Practitioners in Advertising said the general perception among advertising agencies was that some consolidation was inevitable and a good thing for the health of the regional media.

Two of the most unexpected and bizarre protests at Gannett's involvement in the battle for RIM came from Anne Cryer, the left-wing Labour MP for Keighley, West Yorkshire, whose constituency fell within the Newsquest orbit, and the Leicester Campaign for Nuclear Disarmament.

Mrs Cryer said she agreed with some of her constituents who had shown concern that an American firm, which was the publisher of Space News, the trade journal for the US space industries, was trying to buy into the Yorkshire press when the USA was developing two military bases in the county as part of the national missile defence programme.

The Leicester CND also expressed concern that Space News supported space projects in its editorials. It counselled that it would be dangerous for the future of British decision making on space issues to have the media in Yorkshire owned by a company with this background.

The only things that went into orbit were the expectations of Johnston, Gannett and GMG when the Competition Commission delivered its verdict – on all counts there was nothing in the proposed acquisition to threaten the public interest.

This came as a massive relief to the Johnston team, who had found the inquiry even more onerous and time consuming than those in which it had previously been involved. There had been considerable dialogue over advertising rates, and how these were established, and rate comparisons between different advertisers and business types. The Commission was also concerned about editorial freedom within Johnston Press, prompted by the sudden departure of the editor of The News at Portsmouth soon after the Johnston takeover.

Now the way ahead was clear, even if the final outcome was still uncertain. Privately, the Johnston board had concluded that they were unlikely to succeed in a bidding war if Gannett was determined to buy RIM. Johnstons had the disadvantage of not being able to finance a deal without issuing more equity whereas Gannett would be able to do so for cash – a far simpler route.

However, there was an unexpected turn of events after Johnston's chief executive, Tim Bowdler, met his Newsquest/ Gannett counterpart, Jim Brown, with an interesting proposal.

"Why not form a consortium to bid for RIM and then share the newspaper titles between us?" he suggested.

"That way it might be easier to do the deal and reach the price that Candover wants."

Brown took little persuading that this was a sensible thing to do and the two men also agreed that GMG's chief executive Bob Phillis should also be invited to join the consortium. Over the course of several meetings the three reached a broad consensus, and each expressed concern at the prospect of being drawn into an auction where the ultimate winner would pay too much – more especially when dealing with a venture capitalist who, they feared, might have stripped out costs to the long-term detriment of the business.

Bowdler, Brown and Phillis also agreed how the spoils of RIM would be divided between them if their bid succeeded – Johnston to take over the Sheffield centre, Gannett the Leeds operation and GMG the Lancashire titles – and how each segment would be valued.

Brown was given the task of leading negotiations, in recognition that Gannett would acquire the largest part of RIM and that his company had initiated the process.

But when he met with Oakley and Candover director Colin Buffin he unexpectedly found the way forward blocked as RIM insisted that it was unwilling to deal with a consortium, preferring instead to talk to individual bidders. Within weeks progress was stalled, although Bowdler reported to his directors that the stance of the triumvirate was "robust" and that there were no signs of backsliding among the partners.

There was still a high degree of confidence, almost bordering on arrogance, among the consortium that if Candover was really serious about selling it would have no choice but to negotiate with them, more especially when rumoured bids from abroad failed to materialise.

The three partners never met the RIM team as a group and the impasse continued, even when Bowdler attempted to use his long-standing friendship with Oakley to prise open the door. But he remained resolutely inflexible and unwilling to listen to the consortium.

There was even talk of finding ways to by-pass Oakley to keep the talks alive, although privately Johnstons conceded that it was difficult working with two other partners anyway.

Frustrated at the lack of progress, the consortium decided on different tactics. At a joint meeting in the early spring of 2001 the members agreed they would entrust discussions to another negotiator who was highly respected by all of them – David Wormsley, a senior official of merchant bankers Schroders, Johnston's chief corporate advisor, and who also knew Buffin well.

He was authorised to open new talks with Candover in the hope that this would break the deadlock and pave the way for a more formal meeting. Wormsley put his own reputation on the line as he attempted to convince Buffin, with whom he had concluded previous deals, and Oakley of the consortium's credibility.

When this approach, too, failed to make any headway the collapse of the consortium was an inevitable consequence, although this did not happen immediately.

Nevertheless, after Wormsley's best efforts had proved insufficient to break the deadlock, Bowdler had become increasingly frustrated and pessimistic about the partnership, which until now had appeared so rock solid, and began to ask himself questions. What are the real motives of the other two? Do they have the desire and the determination to conclude the deal? In the end he became convinced that success was highly unlikely.

"We tried for a significant period of time to make that consortium work and, frankly, reached the conclusion that it was not going to," said Bowdler. "The relationship was a very constructive exercise, but there were four of us and it only takes two to tango."

Bowdler was not the only one asking questions – RIM and Candover had been doing so ever since Gannett's unexpected interest in the business. Foremost was concern about the credibility of the approach, and whether this had the backing of the American paymasters or was simply an unapproved inquiry from Gannett's British subsidiary, Newsquest.

Oakley and Buffin had decided at an early stage not to deal with a consortium, Oakley especially still remembering an earlier experience when he had been part of a consortium, of which Johnston Press was a member, that had entered into an unworkable attempt to buy Reed Regional Newspapers. Buffin, too, had bitter experience of dealing with consortia that fell apart without concluding a deal.

But the two negotiators were more favourably inclined towards Johnston Press, who they regarded as a company of substance that was most likely to receive City support, just as it had done when buying Emap and Portsmouth and Sunderland Newspapers.

Unaware of this, a weary and downhearted Bowdler was only too happy to take a break from the RIM impasse when he and his wife flew to Hong Kong to join several hundred other international delegates at the World Association of Newspapers conference. Although he did not know it at the time, this was to be the springboard, the breakthrough that had until now eluded him.

As luck would have it, sharing the same hotel as the Bowdlers was Chris Oakley and his partner, Lisa. It was inevitable that the four would get together, and they did so while walking on the Hong Kong waterfront to board a ferry to take the delegates to a distant restaurant.

As the two women discussed their most recent shopping expedition, Bowdler and Oakley, some way ahead, turned the conversation to the RIM situation.

"Why aren't we making any progress?" prompted Bowdler.

"The consortium, that's why. But if you want to have a direct conversation then perhaps we should talk."

Bowdler and Oakley met again the following day at a Chinese tailor's shop, where both were being measured for cut-price suits.

The location offered them total privacy and Oakley reiterated his view that the consortium would not work. Candover, he said, was not desperate to sell and would rather float the company when market conditions were right.

On his return home Bowdler briefed his fellow directors on the conversations he had had with Oakley. The strategy group was convened to consider all the options and again reaffirmed its belief that the purchase of RIM should remain the priority target.

When Candover confirmed officially that it was about to close all discussions with the consortium, the Johnston board gave the green light for a detailed bid to be prepared without delay.

A month later Bowdler interrupted his holiday at the family summerhouse in Sweden to fly back from Stockholm to join chairman Parry for a make or break meeting with Candover's Buffin. The talks went so well that the Johnston pair decided there and then to proceed with their bid and even persuaded Buffin to grant them exclusivity for eight weeks – a critical concession that enabled Johnstons to commit time, money and effort to the acquisition without fear of being gazzumped.

Anxious to avoid charges of duplicity and abusing the trust of his consortium partners, Bowdler telephoned both Brown and Phillis immediately after the meeting. Although he did not reveal the talks that had just taken place he obtained agreement to disband the consortium, thus removing any moral constraints towards reaching a private deal with RIM.

Brown, however, appeared suspicious and fired a warning shot across the Johnston bows that Gannett would simply blow them out of the water should an auction develop. It never did, thanks to the exclusive rights that Johnston had obtained.

Although industry speculation had valued RIM as high as £650 million the indicative offer of £555 million tabled during the talks between Bowdler, Parry, Buffin and Oakley remained the benchmark throughout negotiations. A broad agreement on price had been one of the greatest concerns voiced by Buffin when deciding to deal only with Johnston, and before doing so he had extracted assurances that finance was available and that there would be no attempts to chisel away at the figure unless serious flaws in the business were discovered.

RIM made it clear that it did not consider its valuation excessive and, indeed, was at the bottom end of the range. It argued the price had risen over the years partly because of consolidation, which meant there were now fewer regional newspaper groups available, and thanks to its own improved service to readers and advertisers.

There had, it was claimed, been a sea change in performance during RIM's stewardship and an increase in both profits and margins since 1998. Furthermore, costs had been stripped out, new investment made in presses, staff and IT and its new media strategy was set to derive additional revenue from the internet.

Roger Parry's enthusiasm for the acquisition was matched by his analytical and questioning approach to his role as chairman, and when the directors next met he was demanding answers to a number of key issues on which, he said, all the board should feel comfortable.

The state of the economy, the possibility of a downturn and the effect this would have on group revenues, was his most serious concern, but Parry also sought reassurance on the group's management resources and whether they had sufficient expertise and depth to handle such a large purchase.

He asked, too, about the legal, operational and financial due diligence work that had been carried out so far. Finance director Stuart Paterson, who had picked up on the research already carried out by his predecessor before his retirement, confidently replied that nothing had been discovered that would cause the deal to be reconsidered.

Paterson also reported on the complex financial arrangements that were being put in place, including a rights issue of shares to generate £200 million, a bank facility of £680 million and an overdraft of £30 million.

Bowdler, meanwhile, was called on to outline the post-management structure of a RIM acquisition and told his chairman that three new divisions would be created, two incorporating existing divisions.

Satisfied with the responses he had received, Parry authorised negotiations, which by now were at an advanced stage, to continue. But he was under no illusions about the task ahead, with Bowdler warning of hard bargaining from Buffin.

There was now a sense of urgency in the Johnston camp, fuelled to some extent by persistent rumours of a counter bid being made, possibly from overseas. Oakley and Buffin had privately discounted tentative inquiries they had received from European publishers and had also had a brief flirtation with Trinity Mirror, who never followed through their initial interest. Never categorically denying

> Parry was under no illusions about the task ahead, with Bowdler warning of hard bargaining from Buffin

the rumours was a negotiating tool they used sparingly but effectively to keep Johnston Press focussed and committed.

Paterson, meanwhile, concentrated on the financial structure of the deal, which was by far the largest in which he had been involved. There were several major considerations, among them the current profitability of the business and how this would be affected, and the impact on earnings per share from higher debt charges and the increased number of shares resulting from a rights issue.

These calculations were not only important to Johnston Press but also to the City, which was looking for added value from the deal – a higher rate of return as a result of the investment, which also included an additional £20 million in costs and fees paid to professional advisors. A key factor was the level of synergies that could be achieved – the £9 milllion savings that had previously been identified – and raising RIM's profit margin of about 22 per cent closer to the Johnston average at the time of 30 per cent.

Paterson convinced his fellow directors to increase the company's borrowings to the maximum level the banks would support. This, he argued, would be a cheaper way of financing the deal than relying on the funds raised through a rights issue of shares, since bank interest charges would be lower than the amount paid in dividends to shareholders.

Another series of calculations by Paterson, company secretary and group financial controller Richard Cooper and accountants Andersens, looked at a series of business situations, including a worst case scenario of revenue from recruitment advertising falling substancially and how this would affect Johnston's ability to service its debt. The number crunching confirmed the maximum debt the group could support was £600 million, with the balance being found from the rights issue.

Another consideration was the effect the issue of new shares on a two-for-five basis would have on the company's major shareholders, the Johnston family, by placing them in the impossible situation of having to find about £90 million in cash to take up their rights. Although it meant diluting their stake in the business from 28 per cent to 20 per cent, the Johnstons agreed to take part in a procedure known as "tail swallowing", in which they sold most of their rights on the open market and used the money generated to take up as many of the remaining option shares as possible.

The due diligence process began in earnest in August during which the bones of RIM were laid bare – every nook and cranny of the business explored to establish authenticity and any possible irregularities. Until then Johnston research had been confined to published reports and financial accounts, but now a data room was set up at RIM's London solicitors, McFarlanes.

The volume of documents to be examined and analysed was overwhelming – boxes stacked from floor to ceiling, shelves creaking under the weight of papers, piles of ring binders and files – with records stretching back even before the formation of RIM.

It took between four and five weeks for the investigation team of Johnston specialists, lawyers, accountants, property advisors, insurers and others to peruse leases, employment contracts, legal contracts, commercial information and management accounts.

After such critical examination RIM was given a clean bill of health. Only minor adjustments of around £5 million were taken back to the negotiating table, with the aim of announcing the deal at the same time as the Johnston Press interim results at the end of August.

This deadline proved impossible to meet and Oakley, accompanied by his former right hand man from his MIN days, Ernest Petrie, and Johnston Press directors Bowdler and Paterson shook hands on the purchase in Leeds late in the evening on Friday, September 7, 2001. Then Oakley went to an ante-room to telephone Buffin to seek the Candover seal of approval and returned to sign, along with Bowdler, a handwritten slip of paper detailing the few outstanding points that had yet to be agreed.

A veil of secrecy had been drawn over the final stages of the negotiations, but Bowdler and Paterson almost had their cover blown while waiting to board a train to Leeds from Peterborough, where they had been attending a group meeting of managing directors and finance directors to discuss the following year's budget outline.

To their horror they found the platform buzzing with Johnston executives also intent on catching the same train. Dodging behind the railway paraphernalia to avoid detection, the pair ended up at the very end of the platform with no option but to board Coach A, the smoker. Coughing and spluttering, they agreed that the Yorkshire air on arrival in Leeds had never been more welcome!

Late that night Bowdler and Paterson celebrated their success with a bottle of red wine on the rail journey north to Edinburgh.

But their joy at catapulting the group's share of the national circulation market from nine per cent to 14.3 per cent was short-lived.

Four days later on September 11 the world was stunned by the terrorist attack on the World Trade Center in New York. Around the globe money markets were thrown into panic, wiping millions of pounds off the value of stocks and precipitating a collapse in business confidence.

That day of mayhem and destruction will never be forgotten by those who lived through it. How often has the question been asked "Where were you on September 11?" in much the same way that people still inquire "What were you doing when Kennedy was shot?"

The dreadful news was broken to Paterson while he was in Wakefield conducting a business review of the old North division, when a reporter from the Express newsroom interrupted proceedings. Bowdler, meanwhile, had caught a glimpse on a tv set of smoke pouring from one of the twin towers while dashing for a train at Northampton, and did not learn the full truth until Paterson rang him on his mobile phone.

Both agreed there was little point in meeting in London to discuss financial details of the RIM deal with Deutsche Bank and were left wondering what the implications of 9/11 would be. Bowdler kept the appointment alone but no one was in the mood to do business.

The next day Bowdler rang Buffin to say that for the time being it would be impossible to proceed with the RIM deal. For Johnston Press the acquisition depended entirely on having a rights issue of new shares – but under the dramatically changed circumstances this had become untenable.

Johnston Press directors were despondent, but unchanged in their view that the acquisition was still the right strategic move for the company, although the issue of timing was now extremely delicate. Revenue from advertising, especially the recruitment sector, fell for a time, leading in turn to tighter margins and potential problems with the banks over the company's ability to finance such a large purchase.

The continuing support of the two principal backers, Royal Bank of Scotland and Deutsche Bank, was crucial, and up to that point they never waivered – later Bowdler was to describe their response as "exceptional" and singled out the Royal Bank's syndication manger Lois Salter for special praise. Furthermore, the Secretary of

State's consent for the deal had expired on October 30, but this was later extended for a further 12 months to include titles acquired by RIM since the negotiations had begun.

In the dark months of September to December RIM and Johnston Press maintained contacts, mainly through Oakley and Bowdler. Meanwhile, advertising revenue statistics surprisingly showed year-on-year growth in some classifications.

It was January the following year before the two sides resumed an informal dialogue, by which time Johnston's financial models for 2002 had been revised, although the post 9/11 effects had not been as severe as at first feared. Indeed, the year started brightly, and as share prices returned towards their pre-September levels directors authorised completion of the deal that had previously been agreed.

They were mindful, too, that further delay could result in a rival bid for RIM being made from competitors prepared to exploit any signs of indecision. Gannett and Guardian Media Group could not be ruled out, and both Jim Brown and Bob Phillis kept a watchful eye from the sidelines. Indeed, Gannett would probably already have been knocking on the door but for the damage to the American psyche and loss of confidence after the terrorist attacks – Gannett had been more scarred than many, for with offices overlooking the Pentagon the carnage there had been witnessed by most of the staff.

"For us it was a simple case of dusting down the previous process, running our eyes over the figures again and updating the due diligence," said Bowdler, who had met Oakley in London to reopen negotiations. "We had built up a great deal of trust and I think in the end Candover liked working with us because they saw us as straight people."

Candover never flinched about honouring the agreement they had reached the previous September, but in the period that had elapsed had drawn up contingency plans for their business. Only that month a decision had been taken to seek a Stock Market listing in the spring, or at the latest September, and work had begun to prepare a prospectus for the City.

Paterson's task was to ensure that the financial arrangements set up with such precision the previous autumn still stood. How, he wondered, would jittery investors react when invited to take up their rights issue? He need not have worried, and after a concerted marketing effort all the new shares were taken up in full.

Of greater concern was the attitude of the Royal Bank of Scotland, who had been happy to lead the entire deal and cover initial exposure for all the debt until parts of it could be shared out in a syndication with other banks. Now they were being asked to reaffirm their support – and reluctantly declined to do so.

Bank chiefs took a cautious view of the deal in the wake of 9/11. It was, they said, the first significant acquisition to come to the market since then and they were uncomfortable about taking the lead. The decision was taken at the highest level and flabbergasted senior managers who were closely involved in piecing together the financial package, among them Lois Salter, who was on a skiing holiday with her family when she was telephoned with the news.

Fortunately, Deutsche Bank, who had already been acting as Johnston's brokers and were familiar with arrangements, agreed to share the responsibility of underwriting the borrowing, and the crisis passed.

Other, smaller banks also showed a positive approach to the acquisition when syndicate partners were sought. At best, Johnston Press expected about eight or ten banks to accept a share of the risk, but after making presentations to 20 were delighted when 18 said they would join. Eventually 22 banks shared in the overall loan – a massive vote of confidence in Johnston's track record and the ability of its management team. They could also see a good return for their investment in a market where little business was taking place.

But the reluctance of the Royal Bank of Scotland to make the major commitment was a big disappointment to Johnston Press, who had received unerring support from the bank since the earliest days of the company in Falkirk.

Paterson now had a final hurdle to jump before the RIM deal could be concluded – a crucial piece of the jigsaw was that RIM should come debt free, which meant that some of the £560 million it received would be used in part to pay off its liabilities. These included bank debt of £292 million and £183 million invested by a small number of bond holders in America, who had helped to raise a slice of the capital when Candover took over the business of UPN in 1998.

Conditions and covenants attached to the interest-paying bonds, a relatively high risk form of investment, had limited RIM's activities by restricting levels of capital expenditure and blocking new acquisitions or sale of parts of the company without the bondholders' permission. As a result RIM's expansion had been limited to organic or self-funded growth in peripheral media activities, such as the internet and local radio and minor newspaper acquisitions.

They were terms under which Johnston Press could not operate – so critical that unless the bonds which, like shares, could be traded, were bought back by RIM the whole deal would flounder. But first it would take 75 per cent of the bondholders to agree on a price . . . and most of them did, leaving only bonds worth £450,000 unaccounted for.

Negotiations with the bondholders weighed heavily with RIM, and Oakley and Buffin faced the tricky task of appeasing two opposing interests – those investors who were demanding a high price for selling their lucrative bonds, and Candover's desire to purchase them as cheaply as possible to avoid eating into the profits from the RIM sale. The discussions went ahead in parallel with the main dealing with Johnston Press, but it took several flying visits to America by Oakley and Buffin to clinch agreement.

The long-awaited acquisition of Regional Independent Media was made public on March 12 and was formally signed a month later. The timing of the announcement had been planned to coincide with the release of Johnston's 2001 trading results, which heaped more good news on investors. Profit before tax was up 4.6 per cent on 2000 at £68.5 million, with turnover of £300.6 million up from £292.1 million.

Bowdler and his team were ecstatic and exhausted, for it had taken until 2.30 in the morning to complete all the formalities at the group's London lawyers, Ashurst Morris Crisp, in Appold Street, near Liverpool Street Station. The two parties had been accommodated in adjoining rooms with their advisors – in Johnston's case up to 20 of them – who scoured the fine print of the sale contract. Minor problem after problem was identified, breakout meetings were hastily convened, Bowdler and Oakley got their heads together, Paterson and RIM's finance director Sue Laverick crunched more numbers, brinksmanship seemed to take over from reality.

When at last the ink had dried on the final piece of paper the champagne corks were popped, and for the next hour the celebrations continued unabated. No one seemed in a hurry to go home and newcomers swelled the ranks, among them RIM's chairman, Lord Fowler, the group's managing director at Leeds, Mike Hutchby and the Sheffield managing director David Edmondson.

Oakley reflected on another segment of his career that had come to a close, but he relished the exciting prospect of moving to Brussels to pursue Candover's interests in Europe. The deal with Johnston Press, he told colleagues, had been a happy one, conducted in an atmosphere of trust and without the tantrums and staged walkouts that sometimes occur in the pressure cooker atmosphere of tough negotiations.

Bowdler managed less then three hours' sleep after the party, and as the City awoke, and with the adrenaline flowing, the chief executive launched into a hectic round of interviews and presentations. The addition of the Yorkshire Post to the portfolio was a crowning moment for the group and Bowdler personally – the highly respected paper had been essential breakfast reading when he lived in Ilkley before joining Johnston.

"Owning a regional daily, a major regional brand, might be a new experience for us, but then we didn't have an evening newspaper until 1994 when we bought the Halifax Courier. Now we have nine," he enthusiastically told anyone who was prepared to listen.

Bowdler also had another reason for feeling pleased. The accomplished skier, who had met his future wife on a cable car in Verbier, could at last head for the piste having twice been forced to postpone his skiing trip because of the protracted negotiations.

Among outside observers, no one was too surprised when the latest acquisition was confirmed, for the RIM deal had been the talk of the industry. Even so Johnston directors were slightly taken aback by the warmth of the reception the purchase received. Analysts and institutions provided positive feedback and in the City the rights issue of shares and bank syndication of borrowings had both been oversubscribed.

The market showed its approval as Johnston's share price leapt by 24p to 367$\frac{1}{2}$p – especially good news for those who had signed up to the two-for-five rights issue at the discounted price of 280p per share.

The financial Press, too, gave a thumbs up to the deal, although it did not meet with universal approval. Brian MacArthur, a respected media commentator with The Times, who had started his journalistic career at the Yorkshire Post, found little to cheer him.

"Perhaps unfairly, my heart sinks at the news, especially reading that Johnston expects to make annual savings of £9 million and to move RIM's operating margins of 23 per cent towards Johnston's 30 per cent – statements that are usually bad news for journalism," he bemoaned.

"Among its rivals Johnston has a reputation as a management machine driven by City expectations . . . Until now its flagship has been The News in Portsmouth. The Yorkshire Post is a much bigger fish and journalists will hope that Johnston will cherish it and prove the cynics wrong."

His colleague on The Times, Martin Barrow, warned investors that Johnston Press would struggle if the economic climate took a turn for the worse. Nevertheless, he thought the shares worth buying – "RIM is the sort of acquisition opportunity that rarely comes up and the benefits that can accrue could more than offset the raised risk profile."

Scotland on Sunday declared: "To pull off a half-billion pound buy at a time when most firms worldwide are reigning back costs following the slump in advertising revenues was described as 'brave' by one industry watcher. Brave, yes. Ambitious, undoubtedly."

Business a.m., which described the takeover as "audacious", wondered who else would be in Johnston's sights, while the Glasgow Herald branded the deal as a "blockbuster".

The Yorkshire Post wisely declined to comment about its new owners, but in a sentimental reference to RIM said it was "one of the last remaining jewels in a rapidly consolidating regional newspaper market."

Citywire had no inhibitions about Johnston Press. "There's a lot to like about Johnston – some of the best margins in the business, no national publications, no dotcom black holes and a good track record in integrating big acquisitions.

"This is another giant leap forward . . . but assuming Johnston keeps the same formula with RIM under its belt, this should be another winner."

But it was left to the Financial Times to give a definitive verdict. "Venture capital companies are not in the business of offering bargains," it wrote. "Candover has extracted a healthy price from Johnston for the privilege of a leading part in the consolidation of regional publishing. It looks a price worth paying."

The financial media were not the only interested spectators wondering how RIM would be tailored to fit the Johnston formula. In the corridors and canteens of all the newly acquired newspapers staff who had endured months of uncertainty speculated on what changes were about to be made and how they would be affected.

In City parlance, the low hanging fruit was not difficult to reach, but nevertheless Johnston Press monitored the planned savings with military precision

Also watching enviously from the sidelines was former finance director Marco Chiappelli who, while not involved in the final stages of negotiations, had undertaken a vast amount of preparatory work before his retirement. Possible synergies had been identified, valuations carried out, individual titles analysed and evidence prepared for the Competition Commission hearing. The task had been made more difficult because access to detailed RIM statistics and management accounts was withheld; instead Johnston Press was forced to rely on published reports that were already in the public domain.

"It was quickly evident that substantial cost savings, eventually amounting to £9 million, were possible by integrating RIM's huge printing capacity into the Johnston print division, on newsprint and by cutting central costs where duplication would be created," recalled Chiappelli.

"But there was concern about the state of the Lancashire economy, on which a large number of RIM titles depended, which was perceived as not being as strong or buoyant as that in neighbouring Yorkshire."

Johnston Press wasted no time in starting to deliver the cost savings it had promised shareholders and City investors. It already had a clear idea of where the bulk of the £9 million cuts could be made and within two months of the acquisition Bowdler was able to report that integration was going well with savings above expectations. By the time Johnstons "signed off" to the City and ceased to report RIM as a separate part of the business, when it was considered totally integrated, synergies of more than £11 million had been achieved.

The immediate concentration fell on the head office functions such as marketing, human resources and IT in Leeds, which had been centralised by RIM and were now decentralised by Johnston Press, with consequent job losses in all departments. Further redundancies – there were 250 in total – occurred when accounting, payroll, training and new media – once described by Oakley as "a sprinkling of stardust" on the operation, but which was losing £2 million a year – were incorporated within the group's existing structure. RIM's national sales force was disbanded, this activity being handed to Mediaforce, which already looked after Johnston's interests at national level.

All corporate contracts and advisory agreements were terminated and a review started into pensions, insurance, printing and newsprint costs, the latter leading to substantial savings. Excess printing capacity within the group led to the closure of the obsolete press at Harrogate, which had been used to print the Ackrills weekly series, with a further saving of £800,000.

Several non-core activities were disposed of, including Writers News, a specialist publication for aspiring authors, and the Rugby Leaguer weekly sports paper. In addition four of RIM's Scottish newspaper titles were sold at a price below that which had originally been paid for them. The Stornoway, Galloway and Carrick Gazettes were bought by Scottish Radio Holdings plc and the loss-making Wee County News, in Alloa, was sold to its management.

As expected, steps were taken to withdraw from all RIM's local radio initiatives, leaving a 33 per cent holding in Two Boroughs Radio, in Burnley, which was sold later.

Chris Oakley held key posts at United, RIM and Candover throughout the 1990s

In City parlance, the low hanging fruit was not difficult to reach, but nevertheless Johnston Press monitored the planned savings with military precision. Group business development manager Henry Faure Walker was handed the role of project co-ordinator, working from a sheath of spreadsheets containing almost 300 cost-saving items down to the finest detail. The list was monitored at weekly meetings as part of the most organised and professional integration that Johnstons had ever undertaken.

THE JOB losses associated with rationalising the enlarged business were the most sensitive and unpopular aspect of merging the activities of RIM and Johnstons. When it became clear that a sale was

The Sheffield Star newsroom more than half a century ago, and (above right) the current editor Alan Powell (seated) with deputy editor Paul License

likely Oakley called together his senior managers and editors from across the group, revealed the identity of the buyer for the first time and warned them that Johnston Press would be looking for cost savings that included redundancies. Those most vulnerable, he explained, were staff at head office in Leeds and those with group responsibilities.

Later, when Bowdler and Paterson met most of the same managers again, the message from the new owners appeared more optimistic, leading to a situation where some threatened employees felt their jobs were safe after all. This led to even greater dismay and disappointment when the full scale of the redundancies was announced.

A key to the rapid integration of RIM was the organisational structure of the larger business. Two enlarged publishing divisions were formed, one based in Leeds to create an expanded North division, and the other in Sheffield to include the South Yorkshire and North Midlands companies. A new North West division, at Preston, was created to manage RIM's former Lancashire operation.

In each case appointments to run the new divisions were made to ensure that either the managing director (d.m.d) or the finance director (d.f.d) were existing Johnston Press employees. The line-up was: Leeds – d.m.d Chris Green (from JP Northeast), d.f.d Kathryn Armitage (RIM); Sheffield – d.m.d David Edmondson (RIM), d.f.d Adrian Wetton (from JP Wilfred Edmunds); Preston – d.m.d Margaret Hilton (RIM), d.f.d James Reneghan (from JP Northeast). Graham Gould, who had previously been North divisional managing director in Halifax, was appointed to a new role as group head of IT, a reflection of the importance the group attached to a co-ordinated approach to new technology.

RIM's spread of titles across the North of England ranged from newspapers in small communities such as Garstang, in Lancashire, and Bedale, in North Yorkshire, to the big cities of Leeds and Sheffield and Britain's most popular holiday resort, Blackpool.

The new titles acquired from RIM

- Doncaster Star
- Lancashire Evening Post
- West Lancashire
  Evening Gazette
- Sheffield Star
- Wigan Evening Post
- Yorkshire Evening Post
- Yorkshire Post
- Galloway Gazette
- Herald and Champion
  Shopper
- Leeds Weekly News
- The Yeller
- Midlothian Advertiser
- Wee County News
- East Lothian News
- Midlothian Times
- Stornoway Gazette
- Peebles Times
- Pudsey Times
- Wharfe Valley Times
- Harrogate Advertiser
- Knaresborough Post
- Northallerton Times
- Pateley Bridge Times
- Ripon Gazette
- Wetherby News
- North Yorkshire News
- Dewsbury Reporter

- Batley News
- Morley Observer
- Spenborough Guardian
- Weekly Advertiser
- Sheffield Telegraph
- Sheffield Weekly Gazette
- Sheffield Journal
- Chorley Guardian
- Garstang Courier
- Preston and Leyland Reporter
- Longridge News
- Lancaster Guardian
- Morecambe Visitor
- Lakeland Echo
- Lancaster and
  Morecambe Starbuys
- Wigan Observer
- St Helens and
  Prescot Reporter
- Wigan Reporter
- Ashton News
- Standish Village News
- Lytham St Annes Express
- Blackpool Reporter
- Fleetwood Weekly News
- Burnley Express
- Clitheroe Advertiser
- Nelson Leader

But in a crown of many jewels it was the Yorkshire Post, published in Leeds, that dazzled the most. The self-styled "Yorkshire's national newspaper" had long been regarded as a mouthpiece for the county, widely respected for its views as well as for the quality of its journalism.

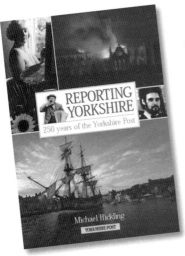

Sadly, space does not allow any more than a brief summary of the YP's history, but it was told in greater depth in Guy Schofield's "The men that carry the news", the story of United Newspapers, and in "Reporting Yorkshire", a splendid book published in 2004 to mark the paper's 250th anniversary.

Ten monarchs have worn the crown of state since the Leedes Intelligencer was founded on July 2, 1754, the brainchild of pharmacist Griffith Wright, who also unashamedly used the columns to advertise his own pills and potions. Starting a new newspaper was a brave move, for Leeds already had an established paper in the Mercury, although it was not until 57 years later when both publications were under new ownership that rivalries became most intense.

For a time the Mercury, riding high on a current of Liberal support, appeared to be winning the battle, until in 1848 the Tory-inclined Intelligencer changed hands once again. During the next quarter-century its new owner, Christopher Kemplay, led it from being a local weekly into a daily for the county and "a paper fit for a gentleman's table".

On July 2, 1866, exactly 112 years since its creation, Kemplay made the historic move to launch the Yorkshire Post and Leeds Intelligencer – a title that continued until 1883 when, in response to common usage, it became more simply the Yorkshire Post. Kemplay made no attempt to conceal his paper's political affiliation and at the time of the change from weekly to daily also set up the Yorkshire Conservative Newspaper Co. Ltd, in due course modified to Yorkshire Post Newspapers Ltd.

Successive editors of the Yorkshire Post have kept the newspaper at the cutting edge of regional and national current affairs and none more so than Arthur Mann who, in the period before the Second World War, was an outspoken critic of the Government's policy of disarmament and appeasement with Germany. This defiant and unfashionable stance caused consternation at Westminster and anger among Conservatives, who wrongly assumed that the Yorkshire Post would meekly toe the party line.

Mann was proved right, of course, but his unpopular stance saw sales haemorrhage to a low of about 30,000 a day. This, coupled with the outbreak of war in 1939, brought chaos to the paper's finances. By then the rival Leeds Mercury had already been bought out, but it became obvious that in wartime conditions the two papers could not remain viable. Economics demanded that the two would have to be merged.

The shotgun wedding of the bright and breezy Mercury and the quality Yorkshire Post saw Mann resign in protest, to be replaced by his Mercury counterpart Linton Andrews. He was destined to take his place in a line of distinguished Yorkshire Post editors and, as Sir Linton, held the post until 1960, when he was well into his seventies. Thanks to his skill the fundamentally different styles of the two newspapers were successfully welded together and, due in part to an insatiable appetite for war news, sales soared to 120,000 copies daily.

At the time of the paper's acquisition by Johnston Press the editor was Tony Watson. When he left to join the Press Association his successor, in 2003, was Rachel Campey, formerly of The Times, who became the first woman editor in the paper's history. She in turn

Yorkshire Post editor Peter Charlton at the paper's 250th anniversary dinner in 2004

was replaced a year later by Peter Charlton, who transferred from the Sheffield Star.

Since its conversion to a daily the Yorkshire Post had occupied premises at Albion Street, Leeds, which it shared with its sister paper the Yorkshire Evening Post after its foundation in 1890. But despite alterations and extensions it became increasingly obvious that the cramped and rambling building could not keep pace with modern requirements.

The result was the erection of a new newspaper complex at Wellington Street, Leeds, at a cost of £5 million. When the Prince of Wales opened it in 1970 it was the most striking building of its generation in the city and attracted industry visitors from all over the world.

Most of the credit for the move to state-of-the-art premises belonged to the Yorkshire Post's managing director Gordon Linacre (later Sir Gordon), who had been enticed to Leeds from Sheffield in 1965. The wartime Bomber Command veteran was intent on propelling the company and its newspapers into the second half of the 20th century – a task in which he succeeded admirably.

Prince Charles attends the opening of the new premises of the Yorkshire Post and Yorkshire Evening Post, in Wellington Street, Leeds, in 1970

Linacre's private opinion on moving to Leeds was that the directors were good people but relatively clueless about publishing newspapers. And they had not spotted signs of the technical revolution that was about to happen with the advent of photo-composition and web offset printing.

Linacre made it his priority to take full advantage of the latest technology and in premises suited to the new production needs. The result was the concrete citadel at Wellington Street, which under Johnston Press is not only home to the two city newspapers but also a major print centre within the group.

The official opening of the new building led to a change of name for the company. Such was the significance of the development that only a royal personage was considered good enough to perform the honours – but with the word Conservative in the title a refusal was more or less guaranteed.

The solution was simple: Yorkshire Conservative Newspapers became Yorkshire Post Newspapers, and in due course Prince Charles arrived in Leeds to cut the ribbon with all the pomp and ceremony that such an occasion demanded.

Linacre went on to become deputy chairman of United Newspapers, as well as numerous other industry positions, and in 1990 was created President of Yorkshire Post Newspapers Ltd, a fitting honour to a man who had done so much to progress the company.

The Evening Post was born on a puff of water vapour – printed for the first time on September 1, 1890, using a steam press at Albion Street. Compare that with today's press in Leeds with full colour capability and an output of thousands of copies an hour.

Although the Evening Post, too, had county pretensions its strength has always been in Leeds and the thriving towns that surround it. For a great part of its life the Evening Post faced unrelenting competition from its city rival the Yorkshire Evening News, which was eventually acquired and closed in 1963.

A steady stream of industry awards has matched the commercial success of the morning and evening papers. Between 1999 and 2004 the titles and individual employees collected more than 200 awards, in many cases as outright winners of prestigious accolades.

The bulging silverware cabinet at Leeds is testament to the quality of the whole team, with everyone basking in the reflected glory of such tributes as Regional Newspaper of the Year and Daily Newspaper of the Year, both won on several occasions by the

> " Between 1999 and 2004 the Leeds titles and individual employees collected more than 200 awards, in many cases as outright winners of prestigious accolades "

Yorkshire Post at various award ceremonies, and the Daily Newspaper of the Year titles similarly bestowed on the Evening Post.

The historic rivalry between newspapers in Leeds was matched only by an even greater competition between Leeds and Sheffield to be Yorkshire's principal city. The aspirations of the one-time steel capital of the world were championed by its local newspapers, which have served the Sheffield community and the wider area of South Yorkshire since 1855.

The flagship is The Star, which started life as the Evening Telegraph in 1887 as the sister paper of the Morning Telegraph, founded in 1855. After 70 years of family control the papers were acquired in 1925 by Allied Newspapers Ltd, which later became Kemsley Newspapers.

A succession of owners saw the titles pass to the Thomson Organisation in 1959, to United Newspapers in 1964 and eventually to RIM. The Morning Telegraph ceased printing in 1986, only to be reborn in 1989 – now as a weekly paper and one of the most successful paid-for weekly launches of that decade.

The newspapers have gained widespread industry recognition over the years but the most satisfying award was that of Provincial Newspaper of the Year bestowed on The Star in 1990. This was given for the newspaper's sensitively prepared special edition, without advertising, following the Hillsborough disaster in April, 1989 – a special that remains the only Sunday edition of The Star ever published.

But the strength of the Yorkshire portfolio bought from RIM was vested in equal measure in the numerous weekly titles that joined Johnston Press, principally those belonging to the Reporter series, based at Dewsbury, and Ackrill Newspapers, of Harrogate.

The addition of the Ackrill titles extended the group's interests to the broad acres of North Yorkshire for the first time, an area of picturesque countryside and bustling market towns where the local weeklies were cornerstones of the community.

They owed their ancestry to the Victorian love of spa towns, of which Harrogate became one of the most fashionable. Anybody who was anybody was to be found there taking the waters during the summer months, something that did not go

Harrogate newspaper proprietor Robert Ackrill

unnoticed to an enterprising printer and stationer named Pickersgill Palliser, who launched his List of Visitors in 1834 to record the people staying at the hotels and guest houses in the town. Two years later this developed into the Harrogate Advertiser and Weekly List of Visitors, which included one blank page so that spa folk could write a letter on it and post the paper and message to a friend or relative.

When the rival Harrogate Herald was started in 1847 its first editor was Robert Ackrill. In 1871 he bought the Advertiser, and so Ackrill Newspapers began. Eventually control passed to his son-in-law William Breare, the first of three generations of that family to run the company until it was bought by United Provincial Newspapers in 1983.

Ackrills' Victorian-era letterhead (top), and an early copy of the Harrogate Herald

We have already seen how the last of the Breares – Robert – used his share of the £3.4 million sale money to buy the Sussex Express in 1984, before selling out to Emap three years later.

Under the stewardship of the Breare family the Ackrill group expanded its coverage with such papers as the Nidderdale Herald, Northallerton, Thirsk and Bedale Times, Knaresborough Post, the Ripon Gazette, and the Wetherby News.

In 1990 Ackrill's moved from Harrogate centre to a purpose-built, multi-million pound print centre on the outskirts of the town, complete with a Rockwell Goss Super Gazette press as part of the investment – the same press that was decommissioned by Johnston Press as part of its RIM rationalisation.

Just as the Ackrills established their own newspaper dynasty in Yorkshire, so two other families dominated the publishing map in

West Lancashire and laid down the foundations for Johnston's first serious foray into the Red Rose county after the short-lived ownership of the Bury Times.

In Blackpool it was the Grimes and in Preston the Toulmins, although such is the nature of newspaper ownership that there are several links between the two. Indeed, it was from Preston that John Grime, the founder of The Gazette, moved to the coastal town so that the sea air could clear his bronchitis.

Not only did he start the weekly Blackpool Gazette in 1873, but as alderman on the local council helped to plan the resort's most famous landmark – its tower.

Over the years generations of the Grime family ran the newspaper and its successor, the West Lancashire Evening Gazette, which first appeared in 1929. Fathers, sons, uncles and nephews held key positions one after the other – editor, general manager, managing director. Even after the company had been taken over by Provincial Newspapers in 1964 the family influence remained as strong as ever with, at one time, four Grimes in the business – brothers Alan and John Frederic Grime as joint general managers, John Favell Grime as editor and Sir Herbert Grime as chairman of the Blackpool Gazette and Herald Ltd and editor in chief.

What is surprising is that Blackpool had to wait so long for its own evening paper. By 1929 the resort had grown dramatically and was the destination for thousands of holidaymakers, mainly from the northern factory towns on either side of the Pennines. After much family deliberation the Grimes decided the time was right to take advantage of such a flourishing economy. But they almost got it wrong. Not only did the paper appear on the 13th of May, but to the superstitious this appeared even more ominous when, a short while after, a great depression hit Lancashire and the paper's fortunes, a setback from which it took years to recover.

The Gazette is unusual among evening newspapers in having changed its format no less than four times. It started life as a 10-page broadsheet, converted to a tabloid in 1941 because of newsprint rationing, reverted to a broadsheet in 1967 and became a tabloid again in 1999. It also holds the distinction of winning a top national award in both formats – Best Designed Provincial Evening Newspaper in 1990 and UK Newspaper of the Year in 2003.

In Preston, the name of Toulmin is synonymous with the town's newspaper history that began in 1844 with the founding of the Preston Guardian by Joseph Livesey and the equally zealous George Toulmin. Livesey also achieved nationwide celebrity as the "father" of the total abstinence movement.

In 1886, and with the Toulmins now in control, the first copy of the Lancashire Evening Post appeared. The paper contained morning news and also published early morning editions, something that seemed so lacking in integrity to the honest and

Outside Blackpool's offices in the early 20th century

sensitive Toulmins that they changed the title to Lancashire Daily
Post. And so it remained until 1949 when the word 'Evening' was
used again.

Although the company passed out of family control in the 1920s
the Toulmin association continued for many years. When the
Evening Post and the Evening Gazette were both owned by
Provincial Newspapers a Grime – Alan Grime – moved to Preston as
general manager in 1968, and in 1970 Michael Toulmin, great
grandson of the founder, made the reverse journey to become
assistant general manager at Blackpool. This was to be the first step
on a successful business career – Toulmin became general manager
in 1976, general manager at Sheffield Newspapers in 1978 and by
1989 had risen to become chairman of United Provincial
Newspapers.

In addition to its evening titles, Lancashire is well served by
numerous quality weekly newspapers, the best of which joined
Johnston Press as part of the RIM acquisition.

These included the bi-weekly Burnley Express, and the Nelson
Leader and Colne Times, to the east of the county, the Wigan, St
Helens and Leigh Reporter series to the south west and the Chorley
Guardian in central Lancashire.

In the north west the Lancaster Guardian has been serving the
former county town since 1837. There have been lots of dramas
and crises in the decades that have followed. There was consternation when the front of the premises collapsed in 1898 and
pandemonium when a compositor found a three-foot snake in his
quoin drawer.

It was surmised that "some bird of prey, flying over with the
reptile in its claws" had dropped it through a
skylight. As commotion reigned, the
Guardian's management called in an
expert, but unsure of their sciences
summonsed a geologist to remove the
slippery visitor. Then the real culprit
owned up – an apprentice who had
found the snake while walking the fells
and taken it to work to await events. His
practical joke over, he was ordered to
return it to the wild and office life returned
to normal.

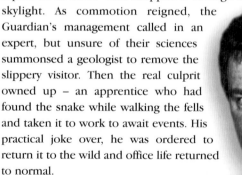

FOR JOHNSTON Press the satisfaction of acquiring the RIM titles was short lived, for less than a month later the Secretary of State for Trade and Industry brought to an end the longest running takeover saga in the company's history – Project Pernod – when she ruled that only part of the intended acquisition should be allowed.

Optimism was running high in October, 1997, when Bowdler met the chief executive of Midland Independent Newspapers, Ernest Petrie, to discuss the purchase of eight free newspapers circulating in Peterborough, Northampton and Derby – hence the acronym Pernod. The meeting was initiated by Petrie who had reached the conclusion that, try as he might, it was unlikely that the papers would ever produce the financial returns required by MIN. Bowdler, he suggested might be able to achieve better results.

Given the sizeable Johnston Press presence in the north and south Midlands the addition of more titles made a great deal of sense. Not only were they a good geographical fit, but by printing them in-house at existing centres, and with other efficiencies, it should be possible to reduce overheads and increase margins.

Bowdler convinced his fellow directors that the Pernod titles would be a useful acquisition, with a potential £2 million contribution to profits, and very soon after his meeting with Petrie a formal offer was tabled. About to join the Johnston portfolio, or so it seemed, were the Peterborough Herald and Post, Derby Trader, The Trader, Harborough Herald and Post, Stamford Herald and Post (including the Spalding edition), Northampton Herald and Post, the East Northants Herald and Post series (comprising the Wellingborough and Rushden Herald and Post, the Kettering Herald and Post and the Corby Herald and Post), and the Brackley and Towcester Post series (comprising the Brackley Post and Towcester Post).

During their brief history they had endured a chequered existence. Most of the titles were founded by entrepreneur Keith Barwell in the late 1970s and early 1980s and sold by him to Thomson Regional Newspapers (TRN). The only exception was the Peterborough Herald and Post, which had been founded as the paid-for Peterborough Standard in 1872. Johnstons could never understand why the Standard, which had been a well-respected city newspaper, had been discarded and would have considered reviving the title if its bid had been successful.

TRN included the titles in a batch of newspapers sold to Midland Independent Newspapers in 1993. Four years later MIN was acquired by the Mirror Group, which itself merged with Trinity Newspapers in 1999 to form Trinity Mirror.

At each twist and turn the sale of the Pernod titles was revived, put into cold storage and then revived again by three successive owners, each of them prepared to accept essentially the same deal.

Serious discussions began between Johnston Press and Trinity Mirror in 2000 and an agreement for a cash sale worth £16.1 million was signed in July the following year. It was a deal that suited both parties.

Trinity Mirror regarded the titles as being financially weak, even after attempts to resuscitate them, and rather than allocate more resources to a lost cause decided they should be sold. Chief executive Philip Graf put the proposal to Bowdler and also invited an offer from Northcliffe Newspapers, who already published other newspapers in the Derby area.

Graf's belief was that these were the only two companies which had the potential to achieve synergies by publishing the titles from existing centres. What's more, they would be able to offer a higher price than anyone else. He was probably right, but Northcliffe threw a spanner in the works by making it clear they were only interested in the two Derby titles. The last thing Trinity Mirror wanted was to be left with the remaining six struggling titles, and quickly closed the deal for all eight newspapers with Johnston Press.

It seemed like a mere formality when Johnstons and Trinity Mirror sought approval from the Department of Trade and Industry, fully expecting the minister to rubber-stamp the sale under the Fair Trading Act 1973, especially as all the titles were distributed free. Instead she promptly referred the application to the Competition Commission.

Months later, and after one of the most detailed inquiries ever conducted by the Commission, its five members reached the majority decision that the acquisition by Johnston of four of the eight titles would be against the public interest. They were the East Northants Herald and Post series, the Peterborough Herald and Post, the Northampton Herald and Post and the Stamford Herald and Post – all areas where a substantial overlap would arise with existing group titles.

The refusal to sanction the whole deal took everyone by surprise – Johnstons had argued that the proposed sale was much less significant than a number of other transactions that had been approved by the Commission in recent years, among them the RIM, Newscom

Staff outside the Avroe House offices of The Blackpool Gazette in 2005, with managing director Philip Welsh (front right)

and Portsmouth and Sunderland deals.

How, they wondered, was it possible to turn down the sale of eight free weekly titles with a turnover of £8 million and yet approve the sale of RIM, with 53 titles and a turnover of £156 million? It just didn't make sense, although the Commission was clearly signalling that in its view the consolidation within the industry had gone far enough, at least for now.

The Commission inquiry, led by Professor Paul Geroski, who had earlier conducted the RIM hearing, was thorough in the extreme and even its report ran to 244 pages. Not only had it looked at the public interest of the proposed deal but also examined the broader issues of newspaper ownership, the economics of newspapers in general and free newspapers in particular.

Not everyone had been pleased about the proposed acquisition. A significant number of objectors who expressed concern were advertisers, who suggested that the transfer would allow Johnston to raise advertising rates in some categories – a view that prevailed, especially, said the Commission, if Johnston Press felt unconstrained by the threat of competition from other titles.

Bowdler led the Johnston team at the numerous Commission hearings and spelt out the synergies that could be achieved to make the ailing titles profitable. These ranged from savings on premises, staff costs, newsprint and outside printing to improved advertising revenue. The allegations of higher advertising charges were hotly denied.

Trinity Mirror presented a far gloomier scenario and its attitude towards the eight titles was wholly negative. Their performance, it was stated, had deteriorated further, therefore requiring increases in income to achieve profitability. But there was no realistic way of doing this other than by reducing costs in editorial and distribution – both of which might affect the quality of the titles and their attractiveness to advertisers.

If performance continued to decline it might mean the closure of some or all of the titles, warned Trinity Mirror. It was a threat that was never carried out, and the group continued to publish all the newspapers involved.

Unusually for an inquiry looking only at free distribution titles, the editorial content and the freedom granted to editors within Johnston Press became a major issue. Bowdler was quizzed at length about group policy, which, he said, allowed editors to edit without interference from general management.

The Commission also conducted its own survey among other newspaper publishers, which revealed that the dismissal of editors was a relatively rare occurrence. So why, Bowdler was asked, had Johnston Press dismissed four of its editors in the last six years, three of them following acquisitions? The details of each case were examined by the inquiry and made for uncomfortable hours on the witness stand as the dismissals were carefully dissected.

Bowdler dealt with the issue confidently and openly. "Johnston Press is renowned for giving its editors full independence," he declared – words that he was later forced to justify as the inquiry, by now in its closing stages, took a sudden and dramatic turn.

Over the years the Commission had become increasingly sceptical about the protestations of total editorial freedom at this and other inquiries and commented in its final report on Pernod: "We take the view that the situation in practice is often not as absolute and clear-cut as publishers sometimes imply."

But it was unprepared for the bombshell that propelled the issue to the top of the Pernod inquiry agenda when, on February 11, 2002, an article appeared in the New Statesman magazine under the heading "The hero they tried to muzzle."

This concerned Don Hale, the former editor of the Matlock Mercury, who had conducted a long and ultimately successful campaign to secure the release of a local man, Stephen Downing, following his conviction for murder. It was a victory that had attracted international attention.

The article alleged, among other things, that Johnston management had put pressure on Hale to drop the story – a claim that, if true, would have cast serious doubts over the company's commitment to editorial freedom. "The corporation (ie Johnston) worked as hard as the other vested interests to kill the story," said the New Statesman.

The Commission felt obliged to investigate. Both Johnstons and Hale were asked to submit written submissions and supporting evidence, and both parties were quizzed at specially convened hearings. It quickly became obvious that the magazine article was at best an inaccurate piece of journalism, and Hale himself said that although he had other complaints of interference and general meddling in editorial matters at local level these did not concern the Downing case, where there had been little interference.

If it was not careful the Commission ran the risk of becoming too deeply involved in a domestic squabble between the company and one of its former employees. Wisely, it decided not to investigate Hale's allegations further. Although they were "not unimportant" they were considered less serious than the Downing claims and, said the Commission, even if proved would fall short of casting material doubt on the way in which the policy of editorial freedom was exercised.

Meanwhile, Johnston Press lawyers had been asked for an opinion on the New Statesman article and they concluded that it was potentially libellous. But, rather than increase the profile of the article and give Hale another publicity platform, the company decided not to issue proceedings, although it did write to the publishers of Hale's forthcoming book and the New Statesman with a carefully worded warning.

> The New Statesman article alleged that Johnston management had put pressure on Hale to drop the Stephen Downing story... The Commission felt obliged to investigate

The effect of the Hale diversion was to delay publication of the Commission's verdict on the Pernod deal until after the announcement of the RIM acquisition – a very unfortunate anti-climax following such a pivotal event in the Johnston Press history.

Johnstons never actually quantified the full cost of the abortive Pernod operation, but it absorbed thousands of working hours, scores of meetings and diverted many staff from other duties. The legal costs alone approached £500,000 and the whole sorry affair was neatly summed up in the company minutes as "tortuous".

Now all that energy could be put to better use – the massive task of integrating the RIM titles into the Johnston business culture and achieving savings of £9 million that had been identified as part of the financial structure of the deal.

But it was not all cuts. As well as looking for logical economies the company also identified areas of new investment in equipment and people to improve the efficiency of the business. The numbers employed in editorial and advertising, for example, increased while at Sheffield plans were drawn up for a massive new print centre that would be the largest single investment of its kind ever undertaken by Johnston Press.

Chapter Nine

The age of technology

One of Freddy Johnston's earliest and most vivid childhood memories is of the times when his father took him along to the offices and print works of the Falkirk Herald. It was an exciting outing for the proprietor's son, and at first a little daunting, and it left an indelible impression on the youngster's receptive mind.

In those days, in the 1930s, the Herald occupied a prime position on Falkirk's High Street, its Edwardian design with a distinctive arched frontage setting it apart from neighbouring properties. The two ground floor shop units were tenanted and visitors to the newspaper office were forced to climb a flight of steps to the floor above in order to place an advertisement or hand in a news report.

Little Freddy didn't find that very interesting, but behind the shops and offices it was a different story. The print works, in a dilapidated old building, were full of strange looking machinery, men in long aprons and a distinctive smell . . . aah, that smell of ink and oil on the creaking wooden floors and the aroma of hot metal from the typesetting machines. And as a party trick those kind compositors would set Freddy's name in type and present him with the hot slug, or light their cigarettes by dipping a folded sheet of paper into the pot of molten metal pot so that it burst into flames.

What small boy could resist this busy, noisy, dirty world that was typical of scores of small newspapers at the time? There on the ground floor was the small rotary printing press, built in the 19th century, bought second hand and still giving sterling service. A flight of narrow, dingy stairs led to the composing room, dominated by seven or eight clanking and snorting Linotype machines, also mostly second hand and of Victorian vintage.

But what an event it must have been when the Falkirk Herald took delivery of this "new technology", when the old flatbed press was consigned to the scrapheap, when the Linotypes revolutionised typesetting – a whole line at a time instead of painstaking hand setting, letter by letter.

New technology? In those days little changed, and then only slowly. So when Freddy Johnston, by now a young man, married with children of his own, joined the family business in 1962 the equipment and the printing process at the Falkirk Herald were

> " The offices and print works of the Falkirk Herald left an indelible impression on young Freddy Johnston's receptive mind "

instantly recognisable, still at the same technological level as in his childhood. But the newspaper had a new second-hand press, a much improved Foster rotary letterpress machine, one of several that had been ordered by The Times as a stand-by in case its London works were bombed during the Second World War.

Johnstons could never claim to be at the cutting edge of technology, but such was the lack of development in the first half of the 20th Century that they were also never far behind. But a revolution was about to happen, spurred on once post-war newsprint restrictions had been lifted and the economy began to recover – web-offset printing, widespread use of colour images, photocomposition, digital typesetting and on-screen page make-up would soon change the face of newspapers everywhere.

But progress came at a price, capital investment that was almost beyond the means of many small, unenlightened family-run businesses. But, for those able or prepared to invest, the rewards of increased productivity, lower costs, higher circulations and greater profitability were powerful incentives.

The Johnston directors took a decision long ago to espouse new technology in all areas of the business and reap the benefits that this would bring. It is a policy that holds good today – for example, £5 million was spent on computer systems alone in 2004 and £100 million was allocated for new print facilities at Sheffield and Portsmouth in 2005–2006.

The company's first investment in the new generation of equipment that began flooding the market, mostly from America, was at Ardrossan in 1968, a few years after the acquisition of Guthrie's Ayrshire newspapers. There the antiquated and obsolete Swiss Duplex flatbed press was replaced by a new Goss Suburban web offset machine printing 15,000 copies an hour, coupled with typesetting using IBM selectric typewriters – one of the first examples of in-built computers for this function.

Two years later Johnstons repeated the exercise at Falkirk, but already press technology had moved ahead and the Goss Super Suburban, which Freddy Johnston had first seen in operation at a newspaper in Sweden, had a capacity of 30,000 copies an hour – sufficient to print a medium sized evening newspaper if the need ever arose.

When the company took over the Strachan and Livingston business at Kirkcaldy in 1970 it also inherited typesetting and printing equipment that was hopelessly outdated – the Hoe press was installed in the late 1880s – and eventually this was replaced, thus helping to confirm a sequence of development that has been repeated many times since.

Almost every acquisition, every newspaper, brought with it a technical challenge of obsolete equipment from the mechanical age through to computer systems that were either outdated or unsuitable, or were simply not compatible with anything else being used in Johnston Press at the time.

There were good reasons for standardising IT – information technology, as old-fashioned "modernisation" had become – across the group, even if it was likely to take some years to achieve. Harmonising production, editorial, advertising and accounts systems would lead to greater productivity, improved efficiency, a better service to customers and ultimately higher profitability.

Tim Bowdler recognised the opportunities when he became chief executive in 1994 and soon afterwards formed the group Technical Committee to look at ways of integrating the ageing and disparate systems within Johnston Press – a task not made any easier by the substantial number of new acquisitions in the eight years that followed.

The man charged with chairing the committee was computer enthusiast Graham Gould, who had introduced new technology to Wakefield when he was managing director there, and was now asked to combine the technical function with that of North divisional managing director and managing director at Halifax.

Gould worked tirelessly on IT, often late into the evening or early morning – long after he had waved goodbye to the night watchman and the last departing journalist or photographer.

The Johnston Press style of management utilised Gould and his committee in an advisory role on many issues, with most of the decision making and purchasing made at divisional and local level, but that policy changed in 2002 following the acquisition of the 53 RIM titles. In the reshuffle that resulted from this sudden growth in the size of the company it was decided that IT should be more co-ordinated and Gould was appointed to the newly-created position of Group Head of IT.

As we have seen, technology in one form or another had always been an integral part of producing newspapers, but here at last was recognition that in its 21st century guise information technology was core to Johnston Press's very existence – the indispensable enabler to improving all-round performance.

It was a far cry from the period only 20 or so years before, when computerisation was feared by many and baffled and bewildered managements who were coming to terms with a whole new vocabulary, new working practices and spiralling capital costs. Gould recalls the horror on the faces of Johnston directors when he suggested upgrading an 80 megabytes production system hard drive to 300 megabytes at a cost of £300,000. Today's generation of 300 gigabyte disk drives can store a thousand times more data and cost less than £150.

Although composing rooms were the first to feel the wind of change through systems such as Hastech, PCS and Atex, the next major step forward in the mid-1980s was the direct inputting of copy by journalists, instead of having their typed stories input by printers. Single keystroking, as it became known, and other technology issues ignited the flames of trade union resistance that had been brewing for years.

Nationally, things reached a climax in 1986 when Australian media tycoon, Rupert Murdoch – who had bought the Times and the Sunday Times in 1981 – moved his publications and staff from

Grays Inn Road and Fleet Street to Wapping in East London.

New technology introduced at Wapping resulted in 4,000 print workers losing their jobs, but in spite of months of vociferous picketing of the Wapping plant by print unions Murdoch was able to produce and distribute his papers at a vastly reduced cost.

Murdoch's success not only encouraged other newspapers to adopt new technology and leave Fleet Street for cheaper premises in East London, but also opened the doors for regional publishers to make similar investments.

Johnston Press chose the Wakefield Express as the guinea pig site for introducing single keystroking, but, unlike some companies who attempted to ride roughshod over union sensibilities, set out to make the change with a negotiated union agreement – one of the first of its kind in the industry.

Discussions, much of which centered around extra payments in return for giving up a traditional working practice, were led by Gould, but behind the scenes group managing director Iain Bell orchestrated developments, making frequent telephone calls to Gould and demanding to be informed of every detail.

Satisfied with the outcome, Bell allowed Gould greater freedom when, two years later, Wakefield was again chosen as the first Johnston centre to introduce full page make-up on screen – another significant step forward that this time was achieved without extra payments.

Negotiations were conducted jointly with the National Union of Journalists and the National Graphical Association. NUJ national organiser Colin Bourne lead the union team, accompanied by the fathers and deputy fathers of the respective chapels.

The initial meeting coincided with one of the first Red Nose charity days, although there seemed to be little goodwill about as the abrasive Bourne sat opposite Gould, put his head down to shuffle through a pile of papers and prepared to speak. Gould stood up, turned away and placed an enormous plastic red nose on his face, then returned to his chair.

At last Bourne was ready to open his case, but the comic figure of the managing director across the table left him speechless. Bourne burst into laughter and everyone else laughed too. But the ice had been broken, and when negotiations eventually got underway the initial tensions had gone, although it was still weeks later before an agreement was reached.

The rapid spread of computerisation and improved communications meant that many small production units were closed and the work transferred to larger centres. One of the first examples was in 1988 when Johnston Press bought the small, loss-making Morley Advertiser and almost immediately moved operations to nearby Wakefield. The purchase of the South Yorkshire Times at Mexborough in 1989 resulted in a similar move, with news stories and advertisement bookings being transferred to Wakefield by dial-up modems, which were slow by modern standards.

With the benefit of high speed digital wide-area networks, the centralisation of production, accounting and printing is common-place, with consequent cost savings. Large central databases of advertising and editorial content are also possible, although staff can still be based locally to stay close to their customers and contacts.

As Johnston Press grew in size the Technical Committee had been working on a single IT strategy for the group. By the time of the RIM acquisition a blueprint was in place, but it took on additional importance with the need to integrate the IT activities of the new titles.

Fortunately this proved easier than at first expected as much common ground existed in the IT policies of both companies, although RIM had already agreed and implemented a well-documented strategy and had a centralised IT team mostly based in Leeds.

Both companies had established wide-area communication networks to enable the rapid digital transmission of data, including fully made-up pages, between sites and from production centres to print centres. At an early stage Johnstons had adopted the IP networking protocol, which became the widely accepted standard, and this was used throughout the group infrastructure, giving staff the ability to work in one place with access to data stored in another. Leeds, for example, holds all the editorial and photographic data for much of the North Division even though journalists are unaware of the computer link in their normal work. Similar arrangements for editorial and advertising data exist in most other divisions.

Johnstons have had a central accounting unit in Peterborough for several years, but the first truly national wide-area system supporting customer-facing operations was proposed in 2005 after trials in the South of England the previous year. This was the Matrix system from Atex, which uses a common database and will link all the group's newspaper sales, distribution and leaflet activities across the UK.

It will not only make information more easily accessible but also replace a confusing array of systems, some of them based on simple Excel spreadsheet, others home-made database concoctions, but none of which was linked to any other.

In line with the new group policy, all the negotiating and purchasing of the wide-area installations was handled centrally by Gould, who also turned his attention to the introduction of voice-over IP telephony – a new generation of computerised telephones. This involves the replacement of 7,500 handsets throughout the company over a two year period.

An essential ingredient of the integrated IT policy was compatible systems across Johnston Press that could not only support its traditional newspaper publishing activities but also feed content to its many websites, which continue to gain importance as revenue earners. For this to succeed it was essential to establish common platforms of hardware and software from carefully chosen suppliers – Dell for computers, Cisco for IP phones and networking equipment, Miles for editorial and advertising software, Atex for newspaper sales and PCS, which provided its PropertyNet application to help in the make-up of estate agents' advertising.

This was in sharp contrast to the situation that had existed only a few years before when the range of computers and software used throughout the group read like the pages from a who's who of manufacturers.

At the same time as Johnston Press was working to standardise its pre-press, editorial and advertising procedures, so too printing of the group's titles was refined and concentrated at several key centres throughout the country. Not only had press technology changed beyond recognition, but also the high-speed transmission of data made it possible for newspapers to be printed many miles away from where they were produced.

Gone were the days when every newspaper had its own press on which its ultimate survival depended. Gone was the gentle, reassuring hum from deep in the bowels of the building which told everyone that the next edition was about to hit the streets. No longer could most editors cry "Stop the press!" to insert another snippet of local news simply by dashing to another part of the premises.

But there are still many people around who remember the so-

Gone were the days...when editors could cry "Stop the press!" to insert another snippet of local news simply by dashing to another part of the premises

called good old days of the small-town weekly newspaper, run on a shoestring and with everyone expected to help out, especially on press day.

The Driffield Times in East Yorkshire was typical, and for newly appointed junior reporter David Wilson his introduction to the big wide world of newspapers in August, 1952, was to enter the dilapidated premises in Exchange Street and a scene that had probably not changed for decades.

Reporters – all two of them – wrote their copy by hand and passed it straight to the linotype operator. The "news room" was a bench in the print works alongside the press and next to the stitching machine, used to bind the Driffield Show catalogues and other important commercial jobs.

Press day was the highlight of the week, when the faithful Wharfedale flatbed was called into action to print its quota of 8,000 copies. It took two days – four pages per sheet, which were then put through the press again to be printed on the reverse side. Wilson's job on Tuesday and Wednesday mornings was to stand on a packing case at the end of the press to ensure that the pages were kept square, ready for when they were turned over.

Now the combined sale of Johnston paid-for titles in Driffield is more than 10,000 a week – the Times, published on Wednesday, with around 5,250 copies, and the Post, which was established in 1991 and published on Friday, with about 4,750 copies.

The Wigan Observer, which was acquired as part of the RIM deal and celebrated 150 years of continuous publication in 2003, is typical of the many weekly papers that successfully made the transition from hot metal to photo-composition and web-offset printing. It did so in 1966 to become only the third provincial paper in the country to use the revolutionary new process.

Until then little had changed at the Observer for decades, its elderly Victory Kidder rotary letterpress machine faithfully printing an equally elderly looking 10-column broadsheet paper that was 44 inches wide when fully opened out.

Credit for the transition to web-offset printing belonged to John Barrington Dakeyne, who started as a junior office boy and rose through the ranks to become managing director. Marrying the boss's daughter was also a wise move!

It was Dakeyne's foresight that helped to put the Observer well ahead of the field at the time. The prototype Crabtree Spearhead Mk2 printing press, built by Hoe-Crabtree in Gateshead, improved output and quality while the advent of photo composition prompted a long overdue redesign of the paper – the front page no longer filled with adverts and, for the first time, colour pictures.

The Observer was sold to Provincial Newspapers before the new press was commissioned, but there is no doubt that this single piece of equipment contributed greatly to the newspaper's subsequent success story. By the time Dakeyne retired in 1981 it had become the largest single edition weekly in the country selling almost 50,000 copies a week.

Newspapers that failed to invest in both typesetting and printing technology were doing both themselves and their readers and advertisers a great disservice, but keeping pace with change was an expensive business.

But it has always been so – ever since American Richard Hoe developed the first version of a rotary press in 1846. Using steam and later electricity, Hoe's presses offered publishers an increase in output from a few hundred copies per hour to many thousands.

The even faster web-offset presses with colour capability that rapidly replaced the mono-only letterpress machines from the 1970s proved attractive to newspaper publishers large and small. Within Johnston Press the most popular installations were the single width Goss Community and Goss Suburban presses that admirably suited the needs of weekly papers and smaller evenings – used at Halifax until 2005, when the Goss press was closed and printing transferred to Leeds, at Scarborough and Wakefield until 2006, and at Falkirk and the Isle of Man.

The way we were: a Linotype operator in mid-flow in the 1960s

Now even they have been rendered somewhat old-fashioned, due largely to the seemingly insatiable demand for colour for editorial and advertising use. This in turn had prompted further advances in press technology with such innovations as automatic registration, colour and ink settings and robots making fast and smooth reel changes.

The time when every regional newspaper had its own printing press is indeed a distant memory. For many years Johnston Press was content to operate a number of such community presses, although it did close those it had acquired that were clearly obsolete and ineffi-cient. But as the group increased in size the scattering of numerous presses throughout the country was itself deemed inefficient and uneconomic.

The acquisition of the Emap titles in 1996 added further presses to the list, and created the basis of a separate printing division. This was given greater impetus when David Crow, a widely experienced newspaper engineer, was recruited from Associated Newspapers as director and asked to draw up a five-year strategy of the group's printing needs.

Crow inherited presses at Kirkcaldy, Falkirk, Scarborough, Halifax, Wakefield, Chesterfield, Northampton, Peterborough, Horsham and Emap's former Southern Web, at Burgess Hill, Sussex.

Chief executive Tim Bowdler's brief was simple: What are the right jobs to put on the right presses? But in looking at the broader picture he was well aware that feathers would be ruffled among his printers and publishers who until now had been semi-autonomous in making their own print decisions. Bowdler was also keen to maximise the use of all the group presses instead of having many of its titles printed elsewhere, often by competitors. The need for additional colour printing capability was also apparent.

Crow talked at length with his fellow divisional managing directors and local managing directors to establish new ground rules that would enable their titles, with the exception of the time-critical evening newspapers, to be printed anywhere that fitted the technology and presses available across the group. It led, for example, to a title from Milton Keynes being printed 200 miles away in Sunderland, where it also slotted in with other titles from North Nottinghamshire.

The Johnston board was receptive to Crow's philosophy and agreed to invest heavily in presses that were necessary to implement the new strategy of achieving quality, adequate colour and self sufficiency. They also approved the closure of the Goss Urbanite press at Chesterfield which was considered too old, lacking colour capacity and too cramped to expand. Instead money was spent on the presses at Northampton and Peterborough to provide extra colour for titles printed at both centres. Another casualty was the press at Kirkcaldy, which was offset by investment at Falkirk, which then became the main centre for printing the group's Scottish titles at the time.

At both Northampton and Peterborough Web, the lack of investment by Emap was quickly apparent – the latter, for example, was still running a mono press that was more than 40 years old.

David Crow, head of the group's print division

"We have these newspaper printing operations in very good strategic positions, but they can't deliver what our publishers say they need – more colour and better quality," Crow told the Johnston directors as he prepared his plan.

The year 2000 saw major investments to close the gap. At Peterborough a new Goss Universal 70 single-width press was installed – up to 128 pages, every one in colour, printed at 70,000 copies an hour – and an ageing Koenig and Bauer press given a new lease of life with the installation of additional colour towers, increasing its colour capacity by 200 per cent. Northampton, meanwhile, benefitted from costly improvements to the Goss Metro double-width press to provide two press lines each with an output of 96 pages of back-to-back colour.

Crow returned to the drawing board in 1999 when the acquisition of Portsmouth and Sunderland Newspapers, including presses at Hartlepool, Sunderland and Portsmouth, forced a revision of the group's printing strategy to accommodate the additional capacity.

Sunderland could boast a three-year-old double-width Goss Colourliner press, although some of the units were only printing colour on one side of the web – but nevertheless far more colour than anywhere else in the group. Yet more colour capacity was available at Hartlepool with a single-width Univeral 45 press offering 32 pages of back-to-back colour.

Portsmouth presented an even greater challenge and the opportunity to print all the group's southern titles there, which led to the eventual closure of Southern Web. At Portsmouth the capacity was considerable – a heatset Goss Community press, and two double-width Goss Metro presses from the 1980s that had been extended with two colour towers shortly before the Johnston takeover. Later a fourth press, a single-width Universal 70, was added to the print factory as part of the 2000 investment programme.

There was a lengthy debate before the Southern Web v Portsmouth issue was resolved. Both centres required new capital investment but consolidation at one made more sense than spending large sums of money at two places. But which? What finally swung the decision in Portsmouth's favour was the need to print the evening paper, The News, on site or in close proximity, a criteria the Sussex plant could not fulfill. Most of the work from Burgess Hill – the group's Sussex titles and a high volume of contract printing – was transferred.

By 2002 most of Crow's strategic targets were being met, but just as he was able to reflect on a job well done the long-term future of printing in Johnston Press was again put under the spotlight following the acquisition of Regional Independent Media and its host of new titles.

Of these, the titles in Lancashire and the North West are still printed at Boughton Printers, near Preston, as part of a RIM contract that expires in 2013, but in Yorkshire three additional presses were inherited at Harrogate, Leeds and Sheffield.

The strategic position of both Leeds and Sheffield in West and South Yorkshire opened up new potential for absorbing the printing of Johnston's numerous titles in both areas, leading quickly to the closure of the press at Harrogate and putting an end to the practice at Leeds of always having the second press line on stand-by when the Evening Post was being printed.

Crow's immediate priority at Leeds was a new digital inking system and an additional colour tower, which he bought along with other pieces of equipment from the former Scottish Media Group plant in Glasgow.

The expenditure at Leeds had an immediate impact on quality and colour capacity, which was increased to 64 pages all in colour or 80 pages in a 96 page book. It meant that Sheffield's property pages could now be printed there, as well as meeting the contractual needs in order to print the daily Metro free newspaper for Associated Newspapers and a four-year extension to the arrangement for printing the Financial Times.

Simultaneously, the capacity at Sunderland was extended from a 64-page colour press to 128 pages all in colour – an enormous boost for titles in the North East. It also advanced the aim of commonality at every print site, when every paper would use a standard web width and work could be switched effortlessly from one site to another without loss of quality, which was achieved in 2005. In comparison, 12 different web widths were in use in 1998, which not only added to newsprint costs but also made flexibility a logistical nightmare.

But overcoming these problems was nothing compared with the situation that Bowdler and Crow faced at Sheffield, home to the daily Star and the weekly Telegraph. They had inherited confined city centre premises, with poor access and limited newsprint storage capacity and which were incapable of being extended. The elderly press in the basement of the building could only print 16 pages in colour out of 96, and there was no space to install additional units.

A joint report presented to the Johnston Press board in June, 2003, spelled out the difficulties, highlighting how the limitations were hampering the economic growth of the Sheffield newspapers and not giving advertisers, especially estate agents, the colour they required. By then Johnstons had gained sufficient experience in colour printing to quantify exactly the benefits it could bring – higher advertising volumes, better yields and improved profits.

After a tour of the Sheffield premises the directors did not need any further convincing of the need to replace the press and told Bowdler to look for a green field site on the outskirts of the city on which to build a new press centre. They also approved the specification for a double-width press on which to print the city titles and others in the region at a cost of more than £40 million.

David Crow was as pleased as Punch. He couldn't wait to tell the good news to his friend Ian McDonald, managing director of operations for News International, when the two met for dinner in London. But the reply he received not only took him by surprise but also led the Johnston board to revise its Sheffield plans and much of the group's print strategy.

News International, said McDonald, was looking to move out of its Wapping base to a new print centre where The Sun, The Times and the News of the World would be printed. "But it doesn't make sense, both of us spending a fortune on hardware," he declared. "Why can't we do something together?"

The idea of a joint venture made sense to Crow, but it also left him in a terrible dilemma. Not only would he have to return to his directors with a new plan, but also persuade them to amend the core principle of Johnston print strategy, that the group was self sufficient and would not invest in capacity for contract print purposes alone. With N.I. on board a commitment would be needed to allocate valuable press time in which to print their high volume titles.

Bowdler's initial reaction was cautious. He needed convincing that the additional costs could be justified by a guaranteed long-term return and that a secure agreement could be reached with News International.

His doubts were quickly removed when serious discussions began between the two companies. In the absence of a competitive element between them talks were conducted in an open, friendly

> Bowdler needed convincing that the additional costs could be justified by a guaranteed long-term return and that a secure agreement could be reached with News International

manner but it took the lawyers several more months to iron out the finer contractual points. The multi-national group's British team, headed by chief executive Les Hinton, who in 2005 was appointed a non-executive director of Johnston Press, conducted all the negotiations on behalf of N.I. The group's Australian supremo Rupert Murdoch was clearly involved as Bowdler discovered when he met him late in the negotiations.

The Johnston board was kept informed as talks progressed and readily gave their approval when Bowdler and Crow returned with a final blueprint of the Sheffield project. At the insistence of News International the original double-width press was replaced by a triple-width, high speed press printing 86,000 copies an hour, with full colour throughout and at the very cutting edge of press technology.

What's more, the cost of the Sheffield scheme increased from £40 million to around £60 million, although this was tempered by a lucrative 15-year contract with News International to print 3.3 million newspapers a week, which City analysts suggested would add £3 million annually to Johnston profits.

In addition to the guaranteed financial returns, the partnership with N.I. also promised a press that would provide high levels of quality, low levels of waste and the opportunity for numerous group titles to be printed on the best press available. But such was the insatiable demand for colour that Crow warned that even with the Sheffield press in full operation from 2006 the group's colour requirements were unlikely to be met beyond 2008.

The final hurdle was to ensure that the triple-width technology worked. At the time there were about only about 70 installations worldwide, all of them used for commercial printing, although the first triple-width newspaper press was being installed in Munich.

Johnston directors were uneasy at the thought of being used as guinea pigs in press development and sought assurances that they would not be leaving themselves exposed to unnecessary risks.

Trials were arranged at the Augsburg base of German manufacturers MAN Roland using pages flown over from the United Kingdom. Bowdler, Crow and his team were impressed with the results – they had never seen speed and quality like it before and spoke in superlatives at the prospect of much reduced costs per copy. It was one thing to print half a million copies of The Sun every night but also a giant leap forward for all the Johnston titles that would use the new press.

Bowdler also visited the German works of Koenig and Bauer, who were also developing triple-width technology, and returned home convinced that this was the direction the newspaper industry would eventually take.

But it was the efficiency and commitment shown by the MAN Roland team that impressed the most, especially the confidence and personal involvement of chief executive Gerd Finkbeiner.

The group's property consultants, Rapleys, were briefed to search for a suitable site near Sheffield, an agonising process that took a year to complete with the support of Sheffield and Rotherham councils, Yorkshire Forward, the regional development agency, and Sheffield First, the city's regeneration and inward investment group.

Access and distribution problems ruled out many of the sites earmarked by the helpful authorities. Other plots of land, once occupied by former steelworks or pits, were now owned by developers who were more interested in build and lease arrangements than selling to Johnston Press.

Only three sites were identified that met the criteria and of these the most suitable was a 10 acre plot close to the M1 at Dinnington that had been cleared for redevelopment.

For 87 years it had been occupied by the Dinnington Colliery, which closed in 1992 with the loss of a thousand jobs, dealing a body blow to the community that had grown up around the pit. Its former use presented special geological problems and numerous boreholes were sunk and contamination tests conducted before the site was given the all clear. Because of the risk of subsidence the new press sits on piles each more than 50ft deep.

Although the site had originally been chosen to meet Johnston Press requirements it was also equally suitable for the much larger triple-width press that was now top of the agenda.

Planning permission was granted by Rotherham Council on Christmas Eve, 2004, and work started on January 4 the following year. A tight timetable overseen by project manager Jon Roche – the son of former Johnston Press non-executive director Sir Harry Roche – saw the new press delivered in early 2006, with full production via the 14 units and three folders due to start in September. The entire printing process will be highly automated and computer controlled with only a handful of people managing the running of the press.

Superlatives are easy to apply to the Sheffield project, sending

A computer-generated impression of the Dinnington print centre, set to open in 2006

out a powerful message to those who doubt the future of the printed word in a world increasingly overshadowed by the internet. It is the biggest single investment of its kind ever made by Johnston Press – twice the value of the Halifax Courier Ltd in 1994 when £30 million bought an evening newspaper and a clutch of weeklies – and when completed the plant will be the most advanced newspaper production unit in Europe.

The group's commitment to newspaper publishing was further emphasised by the decision to undertake a similar venture costing approximately £50 million at Portsmouth, although a start was delayed because of planning issues that were not resolved until May, 2005. The project involved the closure of the heat-set press and demolition and extension of the existing building to develop a new print centre as technically advanced as that in Sheffield. The Sun was already printed under contract at Portsmouth and agreement was reached on a similar 15-year contract to print News International titles there when work is completed in 2007.

The Dinnington site when still in use as a colliery

298

If the newspapermen of yesteryear could see the pressrooms of the 21st century they would surely marvel at the progress that has been made – print speeds that were once unimaginable, colour on demand, plate making machines turning out 200 plates an hour, the "local" rag printed hundreds of miles away. Their minds would boggle at the 120,000 tonnes of newsprint costing more than £40 million consumed by Johnston Press in 2005 or the £6 million spent on ink. What they would make of news delivered online is anybody's guess.

Prophets of doom have written off newspapers on several occasions during the lifetime of Johnston Press – radio, especially local radio, television, and free distribution weeklies were all forecast to bring about the end of the paid-for titles on which the industry relied for its survival.

And every time the pessimists were proved wrong.

But as the 20th Century drew to a close another more potent threat emerged that, if some commentators were to be believed, sounded the death knell for traditional newspapers once and for all. The internet.

Here was a new medium that knew no boundaries, was ideally suited to the rapid and widespread dissemination of news and information, was easily accessible to anyone with a computer at home or work and was virtually cost free.

Suddenly the cherished and carefully nurtured markets that had been developed by newspaper publishers over many decades were about to be attacked by newcomers who did not play by the usual rules and were about to create exciting platforms for local news and advertising. Setting up websites was relatively simple and did not require massive capital investment or a large workforce.

And so the dotcom boom was born and took the business community by storm. According to those who were swept along by the tide, here at last was a virtual licence to print money, an opportunity to share in the new worldwide market that was being created. Soon, it was claimed, everyone would be living their lives online – and as for newspapers, well who needed newsprint and expensive presses when a simple click on a mouse button would give immediate access to local and global information?

History tells a different story, of how the boom turned to bust and how many of the companies that had been created as part of the internet hysteria collapsed and died when the promised returns failed to materialise.

Johnston Press could have afforded a smug "I told you so" as those who had criticised the company for not doing enough to jump on the new media bandwagon were forced to eat their words.

Chief executive Tim Bowdler was at the receiving end of most of the criticism that poured in from City analysts and investors and some of the company's influential shareholders, who all thought more resources should be directed towards creating a web-based business.

"They believed that print had a limited life and that we should be putting a huge amount of energy and investment into online activities," recalled Bowdler. "The feeling was that as a company we did not appreciate how quickly the print model would diminish and that competitors would soon be taking our business away from us."

Bowdler was surprised and disappointed that the City fraternity, who had hitherto been so supportive of Johnston Press, should now display such negative views as they were consumed by the dotcom euphoria. These came to a head in 1999 when the annual report and accounts for 1998 were published – a splendid set of figures that showed a 16 per cent increase in operating profit to £51.1 million, dividends up by 17 per cent and company debt down to a very respectable £69 million.

As Bowdler and finance director Marco Chiappelli did the rounds of analysts and City institutions to explain the good news in greater depth they were met with searching questions about internet strategy and suggestions that the company was not taking new media seriously.

This was far from the truth. The first Johnston Press website was created at the Mansfield Chad in 1997 and it was intended that all centres should be online before the end of 1999. Some websites,

Bowdler told his critics, were already generating useful revenues from a variety of online services including business directories, and classified and banner advertising.

But the pace, regarded as slow, was deliberate. "We didn't see the virtue of spending £100 million on developing an entirely new business. It would have been a huge gamble and we couldn't see the return on that scale of investment," said Bowdler.

Nevertheless action was called for to silence the critics. Consultants Arthur Andersen were invited to examine current strategy and advise on future policy. Building on the distinctly local theme that the company had adopted for its websites, they helped to clarify the group's approach to the internet and especially as far as the key classified advertising categories were concerned.

However, they warned: "Life is Local is unlikely to excite the analyst/investment community and the proliferation of websites that this creates might be perceived as lacking in focus."

The Johnston directors discussed their internet policy at length at a board meeting in September, 1999 and again the following month, and confirmed Bowdler's opinion that "the best way forward was to exploit the group's local strengths – its core competence and the foundation on which to build." This contrasted markedly with the route being taken by some other major newspaper publishing groups who were actively looking to market national brands for their websites.

By the time Johnston's report and accounts for 1999 were published in 2000 (again showing encouraging performance on all fronts) realisation was sinking in that the dotcom boom was slowing down and was not the immediate source of untapped new wealth or likely to bring about the rapid demise of local newspapers.

The critics who 12 months before had been so vocal remained strangely silent! But Johnstons were taking no chances and a large part of the annual report was devoted to the group's internet activity. Chairman Freddy Johnston gave an upbeat assessment and Bowdler introduced his comments with a picture of himself superimposed on the website home page of the Milton Keynes Citizen.

Bowdler told shareholders that more than 50 local websites were now active and that during the year the pace of investment had increased substantially with the launch of new sites at a rate of at least one every two weeks. For 2000 he promised further rapid expansion.

66

Johnstons were taking no chances and a large part of the annual report was devoted to the group's internet activity

99

"Local newspapers, the print medium, will continue to be the key information source of choice for many, but . . . the new media represents an exciting and rapidly growing opportunity for Johnston Press."

Bowdler went even further to confirm his commitment to the internet by registering himself as a domain name at www.bowdler.com with an email address of tim@bowdler.com – a clever public relations ploy that had unexpected consequences.

News of the website was picked up by The Scotsman and published as an amusing diary story, which in turn was read by one of Bowdler's former girlfriends from the dim and distant past.

"When she sent me an email I thought to myself, this is getting dangerous and de-registered," he confessed later.

The task of overseeing and developing the group's new media activity was entrusted to John Bradshaw, who had joined the company as part of the Emap acquisition in 1996 and who already had experience in creating websites for his former employers as their head of marketing.

At Johnston Press at the time there was no more than a passing interest in online publishing. The naivete that existed was unwittingly shown by finance director Chiappelli, who on their first meeting turned to Bradshaw and asked: "Tell me, who owns the internet? And can we make any money out of it?"

"I had to tell him that no one actually owned it but, yes, there was potential for making money," recalled Bradshaw.

The first experimental site was set up at Mansfield, where interest was being shown by Chad editor Jeremy Plews and the sales team – an enlightened attitude that was not repeated at many other print centres. The response elsewhere varied from indifference to downright resistance, especially when it was realised that in the main website maintenance would be absorbed alongside other duties.

"There was a genuine fear of the unknown," said Bradshaw. "We were asking traditional newspaper people to accept a new market that was fast moving and had to be learned at a pace they had never experienced before. It was little wonder that it was seen as a threat rather than an opportunity."

The lessons learned at Chad Online proved invaluable in breaking down the barriers of change. The model format attracted a stream of visitors to the Nottinghamshire newspaper offices who were anxious to discover the potential and the pitfalls and come to terms with a baffling array of unfamiliar technical terms.

The emphasis throughout was on community websites. Initially the content of most sites was editorially led with pages of local information and regular updates of news stories, usually lifted direct from the parent newspapers. This created an instant response from internet users but attention quickly switched to revenue earning content based on the core classified platforms of property, jobs and motors.

Although it was difficult to measure the impact of local newspaper websites on newspaper sales there was no evidence to support the doomsday theorists. But as internet usage figures increased it soon became clear that the mediums were as much complementary as competing, and together had the potential to fulfill the Johnston Press aim of providing a truly local service. Now, however, the internet gave access to niche and global information at the same time.

Statistics provide a clear picture of the growth of internet business. Although by 2005 advertising revenue accounted for only one per cent of the Johnston Press total this still amounted to a respectable £6.3 million, 17 per cent up on the previous year and the fifth successive annual rise.

By then the group could boast 185 websites across the eight publishing divisions, attracting two million unique users creating 23 million page impressions a month. Looked at another way, the annual number of page impressions increased from 64 million to 210 million between 2001 and 2004. These figures were further enhanced as a result of acquisitions in 2005 which, with related new launches, increased the number of websites to 262.

More sophisticated monitoring of usage also provided an accurate profile of the people turning to Johnston websites, more than 80 per cent originating from the area in which the site was located. Statistics showed a bias towards a younger audience than that attracted by newspapers and also a predominance of A, B and C surfers compared with the predominantly D and E readers of newspapers.

The increasing number of visitors to the company's websites was further boosted by the integration of sites operated by Regional Independent Media following the 2002 acquisition, although this provided a difficult and unexpected challenge.

John Bradshaw, head of digital publishing

By then all the Johnston local newspaper sites had been given the complementary "Today" branding with Bradshaw heading up an Electronic Publishing division within the group structure. RIM, on the other hand, had developed their "this is . . ." websites as a separate business enterprise with its own dedicated staff, centralised in Leeds. Less effort than at Johnston Press had been made to build on the local strengths of their newspapers and there was much less contact between the two activities and only limited revenue generation, mainly from developing websites for external clients.

As a first step, Johnstons dismantled the RIM development section and absorbed the work into its own new media unit at Peterborough. The next task was to integrate the 25 or so RIM sites into overall activities of the parent newspapers, with a local internet manager to develop sales and generate revenue and a web designer to maintain the sites and focus on online/newspaper packages for advertisers.

Within six months of the changes being implemented all the RIM sites were profitable and within 12 months an annual loss of £2 million had been reversed. The number of visitors to the sites increased dramatically.

As part of its emerging internet activity Johnston Press at one stage toyed with the idea of becoming an internet service provider in its own right as Go Free. When it tested the water at Halifax with a CD cover-mounted on the Evening Courier 6,000 people were attracted to sign up. But the concept never took off nationally.

In another venture, in 2000, the company bought a 17.5 per cent share in the Mirago internet search service at a cost of £3.5 million with the idea of providing a locally centric search engine based on the use of postcodes. Portsmouth was chosen as the centre to trial the new facility, but with limited success. Although Mirago never delivered the perceived benefits, Johnston Press retained its interest and finance director Stuart Paterson joined the Mirago board as the group's representative.

Another short-lived venture so far as Johnston Press was concerned was the nationally branded Fish 4 classified advertising platform which, more by accident than design, the company twice joined and then left.

Johnston's initial involvement was through the Adhunter venture, which was supported by all the main regional newspaper companies and of which Emap had been one of the founder members. Its aim was to bring classified groupings together across the UK on a shared basis, the theory being that each member would then have a strength that it did not possess individually or locally. Visitors to websites could thus broaden their search for, say, a house or a car throughout the country.

Adhunter, which had been largely constructed on a regional newspaper format, was redesigned and rebranded as Fish 4 to improve its internet image, but this did nothing to ease the concerns of Johnston Press, who were uneasy about the concept and unhappy with having to contribute to the substantial annual promotional and running costs with, in its view, little prospect of profits in return.

Soon after acquiring Emap the group gave notice that it was quitting Fish 4 to pursue its own online classified advertising strategy, eventually tailored to fit the Today branding as Motorstoday, Propertytoday and Jobstoday, each with its own distinctly local flavour.

Johnstons again became a member of Fish 4 through the RIM acquisition, but soon resigned, preferring instead to put additional resources into promoting "Today" and improved training for sales staff, all of whom now offer online advertising as part of a complete print/internet package.

The development of its classified "Today" brands, drawing on data from its newspaper titles, was a key element of electronic media strategy agreed by directors in October, 2003.

So too was the need to increase the profile and awareness of its online brands. Although directors firmly believed that many local advertisers would continue to rely significantly on local newspapers for classified advertising, they could not afford to ignore trends that were emerging elsewhere.

In the United States, for example, research indicated that a structural change was taking place with online recruitment advertising accounting for 15 per cent of the total market. If this was an early warning of similar changes about to take place in the United Kingdom, then Johnston Press was determined not to miss the opportunity across its main classified sections of motors, jobs and property. Cross-media development was, said chairman Roger Parry, a huge strategic issue.

But as the 21st century unfolded the group was again having to face up to yet further changes in the way it delivered its cherished mix of local information. Having established itself as a long-term internet player, it was confronted with the advent of so-called third generation (3G) mobile telephone technology which would enable users to access the same local content via their hand held phones from just about anywhere. Far from being a threat, 3G was seen as a potential addition to traditional newspaper advertising, property pages for example. It was now becoming possible for a buyer to see a house in his local paper and by dialing a number to have immediate access to further pictures and details.

"It's an ideal marriage between the printed word and online technology if we get it right," extolled Bradshaw. "It's going to be a very interesting time."

Getting it right . . . in retrospect Johnston Press could feel justified that its internet strategy, so heavily criticised at the time of the dotcom boom, was better conceived than many had thought. But by 2005 there were clear indications that the wider dotcom market – and with it stiffer competition – was beginning to emerge from the turmoil that followed the collapse five years earlier.

The internet's prospects were transformed by increasing consumer engagement, thanks largely to broadband connections that transformed home surfing, rapid advertising growth, the popularity of online retailer Amazon and the eBay auction site, and Google's initial public offering.

As Johnston Press usage figures confirmed, for many people using the internet for information and shopping had become part of their daily life – local life that for generations had been the exclusive territory of traditional newspapers.

But at its strategy meeting in June 2005 the board confirmed its absolute belief in the long term future of local newspapers as a central part of the ongoing media mix. It also commited the company to significantly greater investment in its digital publishing platforms in recognition of the need to meet and benefit from changing consumer behaviour.

Chapter Ten

Into Ireland

The rapid growth that propelled Johnston Press into the top four of British regional newspaper publishers in the late 20th century had slowed down by the early years of the new millennium

Following the RIM purchase in 2002 there were no significant acquisitions for three years, although organic growth and improved margins continued to increase profitability.

"It is a question of being patient. Bigger things will happen and key to this is being in a strong position to take advantage of any changes that occur," promised chief executive Tim Bowdler when shareholders, champing at the bit for another big deal, asked for his assessment of the company's prospects.

Their patience was rewarded with four deals in the second half of 2005 when Johnston Press not only expanded by a further 57 titles but for the first time acquired newspapers in Northern Ireland and the Irish Republic. Within three months a first, tentative toehold in the Emerald Isle had become a sizeable foot in the door thanks to significant acquisitions either side of the border. The year reached a climax with the purchase of The Scotsman Publications Ltd – a return to Scottish ownership of Scotland's most prestigious and influential newspaper.

A first move beyond the United Kingdom mainland since the purchase of newspapers on the Isle of Man in 1994 had been on the Johnston Press agenda for several years and acquisitions overseas were among the options presented to the directors' annual strategy meetings. As well as Ireland, investment in Australia, New Zealand, Canada and Europe was also discussed though never actively pursued beyond preliminary exploration.

The first of these strategically important developments was made possible by the acquisition of Score Press in a complex arrangement involving the Glasgow-based media group Scottish Radio Holdings and magazine and broadcasting group Emap.

Johnston Press was alerted to the expansion opportunity some 12 months earlier when Emap first showed an interest in SRH by buying the 27 per cent shareholding in the company owned by Scottish Media Group. Chairman Parry and Bowdler knew immediately that the real target was SRH's clutch of local radio stations, including Radio Clyde and Radio Forth in Scotland and Downtown Radio in Northern Ireland, and that Emap, who had sold its provincial newspaper interests to Johnstons in 1996, would not be interested in the associated weekly newspaper titles.

They were also well acquainted with SRH – that company's chairman and former chief executive was Lord Gordon of Strathblane, who was also on the Johnston board, while former finance director Marco Chiappelli was a SRH director too. The group had begun with the launch of Radio Clyde in 1974, supported by high-profile backers including actor Sean Connery and Grand Prix driver Jackie Stewart. The station merged with Edinburgh's Radio Forth in 1991 to form SRH and in 1995 expanded into weekly newspapers.

Bowdler made contact with Emap at a breakfast meeting, with chief executive Tom Moloney at the Grange Holborn Hotel, London, in June, 2004. This was conveniently close to his office and the Newspaper Society offices, where Bowdler had a later appointment. The discussions were polite and businesslike, as both men were strangers to each other, but Bowdler convinced his companion of the merits of selling SRH's newspapers to Johnston Press if the possibility arose.

The goodwill and trust between the two companies, stemming from the business deal eight years before, was a key factor – especially when a number of other newspaper groups later showed a similar interest. Moloney left after giving an assurance that he would keep in touch, but after six months had elapsed with no further news Bowdler decided it was time to re-establish contact.

This was done at finance director level at a meeting between Johnston's Stuart Paterson and Emap's Gary Hughes at which it became clear that an offer for the whole of SRH was being seriously considered. This in turn triggered a series of negotiations between Johnston and Emap culminating in an agreement to buy the Score Press group of newspapers when the SRH acquisition was completed.

The timing of these discussions allowed a back-to-back deal to be announced to the City and financial media simultaneously with the confirmation of the Emap transaction.

Johnston Press, accepting the same conditions as offered to Emap, was unable to carry out the usual due diligence investigations that accompany such acquisitions and had to rely entirely on published figures to get the initial measure of Score Press. They

were not even sure to what extent the newspaper operations were enmeshed with SRH's other media interests and precisely how these could be separated.

But such information as was available pointed to a company that was well managed and profitable. In the financial year to September, 2004, Score Press reported revenues and operating profit of £35.1 million and £11.2 million respectively and net assets of £55.5 million. When SRH released their interim trading results in March, 2005, they showed that in a six month period Score Press had revenues of £18.7 million and an operating profit of £6.1 million, up by 7 per cent and 15 per cent respectively on the previous year.

Agonisingly, it was more than a month after the public announcement before Johnston Press could finally lay claim to Score Press, a month in which SRH shareholders were given time to reflect on the Emap offer for the company and notify their acceptance.

Johnstons made good use of the breathing space by planning the integration of the Score Press titles – those in Scotland joining an enlarged Scottish division with the Irish businesses on both sides of the border reporting directly to Danny Cammiade in Edinburgh. There were obvious synergies in the purchasing of raw materials and services and other savings to be made, and these were included in a two-month action plan.

Two of the Northern Ireland titles added to the Johnston Press portfolio with the purchase of Score Press

309

The combined deal was one of the biggest in Scottish newspaper history with Emap agreeing to pay £391 million for Scottish Radio Holdings after having a bid for £374 million rejected. In turn Emap agreed to sell Score Press to Johnston Press for £155 million in a cash transaction.

The group was enlarged by the addition of 16 paid-for weekly titles in Scotland led by Score's Forfar-based Angus Press subsidiary, 24 paid-for and free weeklies in Northern Ireland operated by Morton Newspapers, and five paid-for weeklies in the Irish Republic.

New titles bought in the Score Press deal

Northern Ireland:
- Antrim Times
- Ballymena Times
- Ballymoney and Moyle Times
- Carrick and East Antrim Times
- East Antrim Advertiser
- Larne Times
- Lisburn Echo
- Newtonabbey Times
- Lurgan Mail
- Portadown Times
- Coleraine Times
- Londonderry Sentinel
- North West Echo
- Roe Valley Sentinel
- Banbridge Leader
- Craigavon Echo
- Dromore Leader
- Mid-Ulster Echo
- Mid-Ulster Mail
- Tyrone Times
- Farm Week

Republic of Ireland:
- Kilkenny People
- Nationalist and Munster Advertiser
- Tipperary Star
- Leitrim Observer
- Longford Leader

Scotland:
- Brechin Advertiser
- Donside Piper and Herald
- Deeside Piper and Herald
- Forfar Dispatch
- Inverurie Herald
- Montrose Review
- Mearns Leader
- Kincardinshire Observer
- The Buteman
- Cart Mart
- Holiday Passport
- Galloway Gazette
- Carrick Gazette
- Stornoway Gazette
- The Hebridean

Ironically, three of the Scottish titles – in Stornoway, Galloway and Carrick – had previously been owned briefly by Johnston Press after the Regional Independent Media acquisition in 2002 and had been sold to Scottish Radio Holdings as neither was considered a good fit within the structure in Scotland at the time.

The Stornoway Gazette has been serving the Western Isles and parts of western Scotland since 1917 and is the principal mouthpiece of this remote part of Britain as well as being Johnston's most northerly publication.

Its pages are packed with community news and vital information on the weather and tides, so essential to the inhabitants of the Outer Hebrides – a circulation area of thousands of square miles but sparsely populated. Healthy sales of 13,000 copies a week include 560 subscription copies posted to all parts of the world.

Printing of the Gazette and its weekly stablemate the Hebridean, founded in 2002, was transferred to Angus Press, in Forfar, when Score Press acquired the titles, giving rise to a situation similar to that when the Isle of Man titles were printed in mainland Halifax. It is not unusual for the papers to be a day late when the ferry bringing them to Stornoway has been held up by bad weather – a fact of life stoically accepted by the loyal readership.

Looking ahead, analysts were confident that the purchase of five newspapers in Eire would not be the end of Johnston's interest in the Irish Republic and that was certainly the impression given by a confident Bowdler. How right they were. As a first step the company appointed a firm of corporate advisers in Dublin to keep an eye on the Irish media activities.

For a country with a population of less than four million people the Republic has a surprisingly extensive media spread with 54 radio stations and 56 local and provincial newspapers. At the time of the Johnston acquisition the principal groups were Independent News and Media (12 titles), Thomas Crosbie Holdings (eight), Leinster Leader Group (seven), Alpha Newspapers (five), Dunfermline Press (three) and 3i Group (three), with 13 independent newspaper titles.

An article in the Irish Times that analysed the country's media sector highlighted the remarkably stable circulation figures and finances of all the publishers, singling out the Johnston-owned Kilkenny People with a circulation of about 18,000 that had changed little in the previous five years. It had been part of Score Press since 2000.

"The balance sheets of most local and regional newspaper groups are a study in consistency and good order – an accountant's dream," said the article.

However, there was some sadness at the departure of SRH from the Irish scene, where they had been regarded as good employers and good for the economy. "Of all the companies that have entered the Irish market over the past decade, SRH has probably contributed more to the high valuations put on Irish media assets, both radio and print," commented the Irish Times.

In Northern Ireland all the titles acquired by Johnstons formed part of Morton Newspapers, based in Portadown, a company with a successful track record for 70 years. Its titles covered about two-thirds of the province with a weekly circulation of 200,000 copies.

Mortons were formed in 1936 when businessman John Morton bought the Lurgan Mail, followed by a succession of other purchases and new launches to bring its portfolio to 25 titles, including the specialist Farmweek aimed at Northern Ireland's farming community.

The group was acquired by Scottish Radio Holdings in 1995 through its Score Press subsidiary. In the same year the company moved to new premises near Portadown. Its Rockwell Universal 35 press provided more full-colour capacity than any other weekly printer in Ireland.

The ink had barely had time to dry on the Score Press deal before Johnston Press was involved in two other Irish acquisitions that were announced simultaneously in September, 2005.

The first of these stemmed directly from Emap's disposal of Score Press, which attracted interest from a number of newspaper groups, including Local Press Ltd, in Belfast – formerly part of Trinity Mirror's newspaper division in Northern Ireland and the Republic. It was subsequently run by a management team led by Jean Long and backed by the 3i venture capital and investment company.

Since first acquiring its Irish interests in 2004, 3i had harboured ambitions to expand there and saw the Irish titles owned by Score

Press as an ideal opportunity to do so.

With Johnstons also rumoured to be interested in the Score Press newspapers, 3i came up with an interesting proposition for it to acquire those in Ireland, leaving the remainder in Scotland to join the Johnston stable.

But, as we have seen, the Johnston board had a very different agenda and politely declined the suggestion. This in turn left 3i asking itself searching questions about its future in Ireland – whether to sell its interests or look round for other opportunities to expand by acquisition.

Johnston's Bowdler had struck up a good working relationship with 3i's advisors, Longacres, and during subsequent meetings in London an agreement was reached to buy all of 3i's Irish operation in an exclusive deal worth £65 million on a cash and debt free basis.

It was a neat piece of business that suited both parties. For Johnstons it meant the acquisition of 12 main titles, eight in Northern Ireland, three in the Republic of Ireland and one that is published in both.

The Local Press group comprised three separate publishing companies – Derry Journal Ltd and Century Press and Publishing Ltd in Northern Ireland, and the Donegal Democrat Ltd in Eire. The total weekly circulation of its titles was 343,000.

Johnstons were in no doubt that they had bought a very successful and well-run organisation that would make an immediate contribution to group profits and also provide opportunities for operational and purchasing synergies. In the 12 month trading period to January, 2005 the Local Press group had reported total revenues of £18.5 million and an operating profit of £4.9 million before exceptional items, representing a 54 per cent increase over the previous year.

For 3i there was the satisfaction of a substantial return on the £46.3 million it paid Trinity Mirror for the Local Press group in 2003. Former Mirror group chief executive David Montgomery, who had been instrumental in setting up Local Press, held 5 per cent of the equity through his company, Mecom.

Nevertheless, the sale of Local Press was tinged with some regret, summed up in a comment by 3i's head of media, Crevan O'Grady, who admitted they had been frustrated in attempts to use the company as a springboard for further deals in Ireland.

"We struggled to deliver in consolidating the small newspaper businesses, " he said. "People like to own a newspaper, they like to

> " Johnstons were in no doubt that they had bought a very successful and well-run organisation that would make an immediate contribution to group profits "

have that local influence and often the newspaper has been in the family for more than 100 years. The titles have more of a political role in Ireland and that makes it more difficult to sell them off."

New titles bought in the Local Press deal

Northern Ireland:
- Derry on Monday
- The Derry Journal – Tuesday
- The Derry Journal – Friday
- The Journal (Coleraine)
- Sunday Journal (Derry)
- Foyle News (Derry)
- News Letter, including Farming Life on Saturday (Antrim)
- Belfast News (Antrim)
- City News (Derry)

Republic of Ireland:
- Donegal Democrat – published Tuesday and Thursday
- The Donegal People's Press – an edition of the Donegal Democrat
- Letterkenny Listener
- Donegal on Sunday

Of the newly acquired titles, the most interesting both historically and politically was the daily Belfast News Letter, which could lay claim to be the oldest continuously published daily newspaper in the English-speaking world.

The paper increasingly became the voice of the Unionist people, articulating the growing alienation of many within that community. This led to an increase in circulation as many Unionists felt the paper accurately reflected their position.

Within a city that became the centre of world attention since 1968, when the so-called "Troubles" began, the News Letter faces competition from the Belfast Telegraph, which is also Unionist in outlook, and the Irish News, which adopts a largely Irish Nationalist approach.

In the long and destructive period since the upsurge in sectarian violence the News Letter, along with other aspects of life in the province, contended with the destabilising effect this had while continuing to report on dramatic and tragic stories and publish pictures of the terrible destruction.

Twenty one of its staff were injured in an explosion near their premises but still the paper continued to appear as normal, making its unbroken history of publication stretch to almost 270 years by 2005.

The News Letter can lay claim to many dramatic headlines and sensational reports over the years. It covered the trial and execution of the infamous highwayman Dick Turpin in 1739 but reserved its greatest scoop for August 23, 1776, when it published the full text of the American Declaration of Independence.

Front pages of three of the titles published by Local Press

The Belfast News Letter's most celebrated exclusive: publication of the full text of the American Declaration of Independence, 1776

[Remainder of the laſt PACKETS.]

A M E R I C A.

In CONGRESS, JULY 4, 1776.

A DECLARATION *by the* REPRESENTATIVES *of the* UNITED STATES *of* AMERICA, *in* GENERAL CONGRESS *aſſembled.*

WHEN in the courſe of human events it becomes neceſſary for one people to diſſolve the political bands which have connected them with another, and to aſſume among the powers of the earth the ſeparate and equal ſtation to which the laws of nature and of nature's God entitle them, a decent reſpect to the opinions of mankind require that they ſhould declare the cauſes which imp'd them to the ſeparation.

We hold theſe truths to be ſelf-evident ; that all men are created equal ; that they are endowed by their Creator with certain unalienable rights ; that among theſe are life, liberty, and the purſuit of happineſs. That to ſecure theſe rights, governments are inſtituted among men, deriving their juſt powers from the conſent of the governed ; and whenever any form of government becomes deſtructive of theſe ends, it is the right of the peo...

66

> How the editor gained access to the text of the American Declaration of Independence has never been explained – and in true journalistic tradition he did not reveal his source

99

The boat carrying the first copy to leave the United States, and bound for London, ran into stormy waters off the north coast of Ireland and was forced to seek refuge in the port of Londonderry. There arrangements were made for the declaration to be sent by fast horse to Belfast, where it would be met by another ship for delivery to King George the Third.

Somehow the editor at the time gained access to this priceless document and duly printed the complete text on the front page of the News Letter. How this extraordinary feat was achieved has never been explained – and in true journalistic tradition the editor did not reveal the source of his world exclusive.

The paper was founded in 1737 by Francis Joy, a pioneer of paper making in Ballymena, where his twice-weekly news sheets were first produced. Subsequently the paper moved to Belfast and became daily in 1855. It is now located on the Boucher Road industrial estate, but in High Street, Belfast, the name "Joy's Entry" still commemorates the family name.

In 2005 the daily circulation was about 29,000, boosted to nearly 40,000 on Wednesdays and Saturdays with the inclusion of the Farming Life supplement, which is essential reading among the agricultural community right across the sectarian boundaries in Northern Ireland.

The longevity of the News Letter is matched only by the Derry Journal, the main title published in Londonderry, which was established in June, 1772 and claims to be one of the oldest newspapers still in circulation in Ireland.

It started life as a hand-set, hand-printed, four-page tabloid, published twice weekly and costing one penny. The Journal has appeared ever since without significant interruption although publication arrangements have varied considerably. It has been a weekly, a tri-weekly and, for a brief period, a daily – an experiment in 1877 that lasted only three months.

Throughout its early life the Journal was a Conservative, Protestant paper with allegiance to Queen and Constitution, a stance that was clearly indicated on its masthead for many years. When it did adopt a more liberal policy – in 1829 – by supporting Catholic emancipation the change so angered editor William Wallen that he left and helped to found the rival Londonderry Sentinel and General Advertiser. Since then, however, the ethos of the Journal has continued to support strong Constitutional Nationalist/Catholic interests.

Johnston's late summer spending spree totalled almost £160 million to add to the £155 million it had already paid for Score Press when it announced the acquisition of the thriving Leinster Leader group in the Republic of Ireland for €138.6 million (£93.9 million) in cash – a price tag that sent shockwaves around the newspaper world and was described as "irrational exuberance by naïve outsiders" by one commentator. Another writer said: "The massive price paid for the Leinster Leader has astonished the industry."

The cost of the purchase was seen as "sensational" and "inflated" by the Irish Times but it did concede that Johnston Press had demonstrated "an unstinting faith in the Irish economy."

Bowdler admitted that Johnston's had paid a "full price" in the blind auction bidding process that the Leinster Leader directors had used to sell the business. Nevertheless, the impressive performance of the six titles in the group and the potential for further growth were regarded as ample justification for this significant foray into Ireland and Bowdler confidently expected the acquisition to be immediately earnings enhancing.

Together with the Local Press titles, it meant that in less than three months since the acquisition of the Irish businesses from Score Press Johnston's had become the largest regional newspaper

> " When the Derry Journal supported Catholic emancipation in 1829, editor William Wallen was so angered that he left to found a rival paper "

publisher on the island of Ireland. Its share of the paid-for market in the Republic amounted to 20 per cent. "Johnston Press clearly does not set much store on messing around too long with toeholds," wrote a financial journalist in The Scotsman.

Such apparent haste was not on the agenda when Bowdler tied up the deal with Score Press, but it was always his intention to expand the group's Irish interests at an appropriate time. As we have already seen, the links with venture capitalists 3i brought sooner-than-expected results but when it was announced that the Leinster Leader titles in the Republic were for sale it was an opportunity that simply could not be ignored.

Bowdler, finance director Paterson and business development manager Simon Kennedy met in Edinburgh in July, 2005 to formulate their plans and, after initially proposing an offer of €80 million (£54 million), agreed to submit a modest indicative offer of €90 million (£60.8 million) in the first round of bidding – reported to be the lowest received. But it was enough to see the group through to the second round of the auction and provided a chance to carry out due diligence inquiries into the affairs of the Leader company at a data room set up at the Dublin offices of accountants PricewaterhouseCoopers.

Discussions were also held with the Leader's chairman John McStay, a prominent Dublin accountant and insolvency practitioner, and deputy chairman, solicitor Anthony Collins. The Johnston team was impressed, not only by the strength of the Irish economy but also by the company's overall performance, especially its newspaper in Limerick, and the potential for further growth. A study of the management accounts revealed that total revenues for the year to August 31 were about €21.1 million (£14,2 million), an increase of around 15 per cent on the previous year – and this at a time when Johnston Press advertising revenue in the UK had declined by 0.8 per cent in the first half of 2005. Earnings in the same period were €7.2 million (£4.8 million), representing an increase of more than 30 per cent.

Johnston's final sealed bid of €138.6 million was submitted on September 14. Such is the nature of a blind auction that not only was it unclear who the other bidders were, but there was no indication how much they were prepared to pay for the business. Bowdler, Paterson and Kennedy each wrote down on a piece of paper what they considered a fair price, added the figures together and then divided the total by three – "not a very scientific way of doing things," said Bowdler later.

An agonising three days followed during which the Leinster Leader directors and their advisors weighed up the bids they had received. Bowdler and Paterson were in Leeds meeting separately with divisional and local managing directors and finance directors when Bowdler took a telephone call to say the Johnston bid had been successful.

Overjoyed, he dashed to tell Paterson but mischievously put on a glum face before declaring, "We've got it! We've done it!" But the prank had unfortunate consequences for the unsuspecting Paterson as Bowdler shook him by the hand, squeezing it so hard that a tendon snapped in his little finger. After hospital treatment Paterson spent six weeks with his hand strapped up while Bowdler tried hard to live down the sobriquet of Bone Crusher.

There was every reason to feel pleased over the latest acquisition, for the opposition of six rival bidders had been formidable and included other Irish newspaper groups Independent News and Media, The Irish Times and Celtic Press, a subsidiary of the Scottish-owned Dunfermline Press. Unknown to Johnstons a second data room had been set up in Dublin during the bidding process and had been used by a UK private equity group Exponent, which later had more success when it bought the prestigious Times Educational Supplement and the Times Higher Educational Supplement from News International for £235 million.

Six paid-for weekly newspapers were included in the deal – the Leinster Leader, Leinster Express, Offaly Express, Dundalk Democrat, Limerick Leader/Chronicle and the Tallaght Echo. An unusual publishing arrangement saw the Limerick titles become quasi-evenings by publishing late morning editions three times a week. Total circulation amounted to about 92,000 copies, of which 72,000 were from weekly sales and 20,000 from the evenings.

Another attraction for Johnstons was the modern printing centre that the company had recently completed on a greenfield site in Limerick. This not only enabled the Leader group to print all its own titles and other newspapers on contract but substantially increased the colour content of all titles.

Many newspapers in Eire reflect

Leinster Leader chairman John McStay provided healthy performance figures for Johnston Press to consider

the country's political past with words such as "leader" and "nationalist" in their titles. The Leinster Leader first appeared in 1880 and was among numerous new provincial papers that were started at the time of the Land War and Home Rule agitation in Ireland and gave voice to the nationalist fervour. The first editor was Patrick Cahill, who began the less than glamorous tradition of Irish provincial editors and proprietors being jailed, either for their nationalist writings or libel.

A direct link with the turbulent times of the late 19th century was provided by two of the 27 shareholders of the 125-year-old Leinster Leader – octogenarian widows Elizabeth Kelly, of Kildare, and Heather Smallbone, living in England, who received €26.4 million (£17.8 million) and €25.7 million (£17.4 million) respectively from the sale of their shares. Both were believed to have inherited their holdings from descendants of James Laurence Carew, the Home Rule MP for Kildare, who took control of the Leader in 1886 to further his political career and also ended up in prison.

The Leader's shareholding beneficiaries shared a windfall of about €120 million (£81 million) after payment of outstanding debts but retained property interests of about €15 million (£10 million), which were then transferred to a new company.

Before they reaped the benefits of the sale and before Johnstons could begin to integrate all its newly-acquired Irish titles into the corporate structure there was an agonising wait of some weeks while the Local Press and Leinster Leader deals were scrutinised by the Republic authorities. Both required – and received – the approval of the Irish Competition Authority and the Irish Minister for Enterprise, Trade and Employment under legislation governing competition and the ownership of newspapers.

The delay provided a breathing space in which to create two new divisions to administer the company's Irish Interests.

Jean Long, the chief executive of Local Press, was appointed divisional managing director in Northern Ireland to look after the combined businesses of Morton Newspapers and Local Press. Barry Brennan joined the company from Independent News and Media, where he had been group marketing director, to become divisional managing director in the Republic of Ireland.

A further acquisition in 2005 saw JP Ventures add to its portfolio with the inclusion of Asian Media Ltd, a small publishing company based in Rochdale, Lancs, with three niche titles aimed primarily at the large Asian communities in Greater Manchester and West

Yorkshire. They were the Asian Leader, a fortnightly free pick-up English language newspaper with a 20,000 distribution, the twice-yearly glossy magazine Asian Life, and the annual Eid magazine published to coincide with one of the holiest events in the Muslim calendar, the end of Ramadan and the festival of Eid.

Asian Media was jointly owned by its founder and managing director Mohamed Parwaz and his business partner Amjad Ali. After the acquisition both remained with the company to help develop the three titles to reach a wider audience among the two million ethnic Asians in the United Kingdom.

IN DECEMBER, 2005, the group completed the purchase of Ashwell Associates Ltd for £3 million. The business comprised the Rutland Times, a weekly paid-for newspaper established in 1978 and distributed in and around Oakham, the Bourne Local (1989), a weekly paid-for title centered on the small Lincolnshire town, and three lifestyle magazines, Embrace, Your Perfect Day and Your County. The new acquisition, which was based in Oakham, was incorporated into Johnston's Welland Valley Newspapers at Stamford.

The deal took almost two years to come to fruition after a speculative telephone call to Bowdler from Ashwell's owner, Bob Featham, who had acquired the Rutland Times following Johnston's takeover of Emap's regional newspaper interests, where he had been joint managing director.

Not only had the two remained on friendly terms, but also they shared a passion for Wolverhampton Wanderers Football Club. The protracted, but amicable, negotiations also involved Featham's journalist daughter, Katie, who stayed on at Oakwell as general manager, and was quickly promoted to newspaper sales director at the nearby East Midlands Newspapers, Peterborough.

The Ashwell purchase raised no more than a flicker among City investors and analysts, or the media in general. After all, it was the month of festive fun when big business winds down for Christmas and, in any case, the attention of the newspaper industry was focused on a far more significant development.

"Stunned" was the most frequently used word when Daily Mail and General Trust (DMGT) announced that it intended to explore the possible disposal of its Northcliffe Newspapers subsidiary, at the time ranked third by circulation in the Newspaper Society league table of regional publishers with 113 titles.

Inevitably, this sparked off a wave of speculation about how the

> The attention of the newspaper industry was focused on a far more significant development

group would be sold and split up and who the new owners would be. Johnston Press was seen as a strong contender for at least part of the business.

Officially DMGT said little, other than it was looking for opportunities to diversify its business activities, but many observers concluded that in considering the sale of the family silver it had lost the appetite for the cut and thrust of regional newspapers. Others even questioned whether this was the beginning of the end for regional papers, although the same scenario had been raised years before – wrongly as it turned out – when Thomson Regional Newspapers and Emap reached similar decisions to DMGT.

Nevertheless, the anticipated demise of Northcliffe Newspapers, valued at £1.5 billion, was generally seen as a sad day for the industry, an unlikely victim of the ongoing process of consolidation. It would also have brought to an end almost 80 years of tradition in which the name of Northcliffe – the peer who co-founded the Daily Mail with the first Lord Rothermere in 1896 – had been synonymous with a patriarchal style of management less focussed on profit margins than its rivals.

However, in February 2006, DMGT again surprised onlookers and those more directly involved with an about-turn which resulted in the abrupt end of the sale process and a decision to retain the business. Blaming the difficult short term advertising climate for a failure to obtain a sufficiently attractive offer for Northcliffe, DMGT re-affirmed their long term belief in local newspaper publishing and committed to improved financial performance through their 'Aim Higher' restructuring programme.

News of the possible Northcliffe disposal prompted a flurry of activity among Johnston executives who, once they had recovered from the surprise, rapidly took stock of the situation and how it might be turned to the group's advantage. At the same time the kafuffle caused by the Northcliffe bombshell provided the ideal smokescreen for Johnston's Bowdler and Paterson to work uninterrupted and undetected on an equally surprising development of their own.

Thus when the directors held their December meeting at Manor Place, Edinburgh, they were handed two Christmas presents – confirmation that the Leinster Leader deal had been approved by the Irish authorities and news of perhaps the most prestigious acquisition in the company's history.

Chapter Eleven

The Scotsman and beyond

The Christmas dinner enjoyed by Johnston Press directors at the Scotch Malt Whisky Society, in Edinburgh, on December 15, 2005, had even more festive spirit than usual. Business discussions gave way to light-hearted banter as the formalities of the boardroom were set aside.

And why not?

That afternoon chief executive Bowdler had hand delivered his own Christmas cracker – the £160 million acquisition of The Scotsman Publications Ltd from the Press Holdings Group, a package that comprised Scotland's most famous newspaper, The Scotsman, the Edinburgh Evening News, Scotland on Sunday, and the Herald and Post weekly free series.

The importance of such a deal was not lost on that evening's diners – not only did it give Johnston Press ownership of a highly successful and profitable company, but it also meant that for the first time for more than 50 years The Scotsman had Scottish owners.

No one was more aware of this than former chairman Freddy Johnston, for whom the deal had personal as well as commercial significance. It was while working on The Scotsman as a senior reporter between 1929 and 1934 that his father, Fred, met and fell in love with Kathleen Macbeth, the attractive young secretary to editor Sir George Waters. The couple went on to marry and had three sons, Freddy and Harry, who joined the family business, and Jim, who worked as a journalist with The Scotsman for many years.

The Johnston family link was further renewed following the acquisition when Freddy's son, Michael, was transferred from his position as South division managing director in Portsmouth to become managing director of Scotsman Publications. He was subsequently put in charge of the entire Scottish operation when long-serving divisional managing director Stuart Macpherson retired.

The announcement of the deal to the London Stock Exchange was greeted with amazement and a slightly mixed reaction. No one had suspected that the owners of Scotsman Publications, the billionaire Barclay twins Sir David and Sir Frederick, were on the verge of selling one of their prized assets, although an astute financial journalist writing for The Guardian a week earlier had come close to guessing their intentions.

But when she hinted that " . . . the word is that they (the Barclays) are actively thinking of selling the country's proudest title" few people took the remark seriously. The City was more interested in where the next Christmas drinks party was being held or speculating who would buy the Northcliffe Newspapers group in the New Year.

Even so, Bowdler's heart missed a beat when he read the article – had there been a leak, were weeks of careful negotiations about to be exposed at a crucial stage, was there another potential buyer lurking in the wings?

It was the second minor scare during highly confidential sale discussions – weeks earlier a journalist from a national Sunday paper rang Bowdler asking if it was true that Johnston Press was interested in buying The Scotsman. But an evasive response was sufficient to put the reporter off the scent and the story was not followed-up.

The Scotsman and its sister titles had been part of the Barclays' enormous business empire since 1995 and operated as part of their Press Holdings Group, itself a subsidiary of Ellerman Investments, the brothers' main trading company. Even on such a significant and strategic disposal as the sale of their Scottish newspaper interests the 67-year-olds maintained their intensely guarded privacy, and all the discussions were fronted by Sir David's son, Aidan, from the Ellerman headquarters in St James's Street, London.

During a 40-year career the reclusive brothers gained a formidable reputation for big business deals that in turn had made them into two of Britain's wealthiest men. They were rarely seen in public – during the 1990s they were based in Monaco and also spent much of their time at a £60 million castle on the island of Brecqhou in the Channel Islands.

The twins hardly ever visited Edinburgh to check on their newspapers, but one such occasion was in 1999 when the Queen and Duke of Edinburgh opened The Scotsman's new offices, close to the royal residence at Holyrood House and the new Scottish Parliament building.

Former editor Magnus Linklater was among the guests and found himself standing alongside the Barclays as they listened to the Queen's speech. This, he decided, was the ideal opportunity to meet the men who owned the newspaper where he spent six years at the helm.

"The moment the Queen finished, I turned to my right, thinking that here was my chance, but – puff! – they had disappeared," he recalled later.

Media speculation moved into overdrive when news of The Scotsman sale was announced. Why had the Barclays decided to sell at this time? Was it a lack of confidence in the Edinburgh titles? Or simply that the £160 million received from Johnstons could be better used elsewhere, such as an injection of cash into the Telegraph group that had been bought from Chicago-based Hollinger International Inc in 2004 for £665 million? None of these was accurate.

It was left to Press Holdings Group publisher Andrew Neil to explain the Barclays' first sale of a major media asset. In a prepared statement he said the company was delighted to have reached an agreement with Johnston Press "which not only recognises the value and improvements we have added to the titles but secures their long-term future."

However, in subsequent comments he was less upbeat, describing Scotsman Publications as a "mature business in a mature industry" and suggesting that prospects for further growth were limited because the titles lacked scale – a credible assessment under Press Holdings, but not so under Johnston Press, which could offer both scale and considerable synergies within the group.

One observer suggested that the Barclays had simply lost heart in running newspapers in Scotland after their failed £200 million bid to buy the Glasgow Herald and Evening Times when they were auctioned by Scottish Media Group. Neil conceded that this had been a factor in the sale of Scotsman Publications – "Our politics did not fit into the left-wing collectivist consensus in Scotland," he said.

Although the Barclays did not appreciate it at the time, the Herald disappointment proved to be a turning point in their Scottish newspaper activities but the decision to sell Scotsman Publications was not made until much later. However, the setback left them with limited options in Scotland and an even harder task in dealing with stiff competition and changes in the market place.

In a prepared statement Andrew Neil said the company was delighted to have reached an agreement with Johnston Press

The Barclay brothers with Andrew Neil

325

The first copy of The Scotsman from 1817, and (far right) the paper in 2006

Had things worked out differently, acquisition of the Herald would have given them a powerful presence across the central belt of Scotland and produced synergies and savings worth as much as £10 million. Plans to build a new printing centre midway between Glasgow and Edinburgh would, for example, have made economic and geographic sense on top of other savings in sales, marketing and distribution.

Instead, the Barclays found themselves facing fierce business and political opposition from the Scottish lobby opposed to the sale to them and quickly realised that it would take a minor miracle to achieve a deal. Among those believed to be involved in the campaign was former Foreign Secretary Robin Cook, who had been a racing tipster with The Herald for seven years in the 1990s, but negative innuendos and rumours were received from numerous sources – among them the Scottish Media Group itself, which was looking for a quick, clean sale instead of a protracted competition inquiry that a Barclay purchase would have involved.

The Herald group was eventually sold to the American-owned Gannett, parent company of the Newsquest newspaper conglomerate.

Johnston Press interest in The Scotsman could, loosely, be traced back to the acquisition of Regional Independent Media in 2002, which proved to be a watershed in the company's development – a quantum step in the size of the group and the addition of a very different kind of newspaper, a regional morning, in the Yorkshire Post. Not only had Johnston Press proved itself more than capable of running the much-enlarged business but had also gained sufficient confidence to consider adding another prominent quasi-national/regional title to its portfolio.

In the summer of 2004 the directors identified Scotsman Publications as a potential target. It would, they believed, make a comfortable geographic fit with other activities in Scotland and, as a stand-alone, privately-owned business would probably become available at some time in the future.

At the board's behest, Bowdler rang Aidan Barclay to request a meeting and expressed his interest in buying The Scotsman when the pair met at the Ellerman offices. Barclay, sharply dressed in an immaculate pinstripe suit and smoking his first cigar of the day, gave a forthright reply. "It's not for sale, we're not even thinking of selling."

Bowdler's interest was not entirely unexpected, for the Barclays had already concluded that there were only three likely buyers for Scotsman Publications – Northcliffe Newspapers, who already owned the Aberdeen Press and Journal, the new owners of the Glasgow Herald, and Johnston Press.

And of these Johnston seemed best placed to achieve the synergies and savings that would ensure a bright future for the flagship titles. It was simply that the approach was mis-timed.

Another 12 months elapsed before the seeds that Bowdler had sown took root, by which time Johnston Press was heavily involved in absorbing its newly-acquired Score Press titles and looking to expand in Ireland. But a phone call from Barclay, during which he suggested another meeting, set his pulse racing. There could only be one reason for this surprise development.

The two men had already developed a healthy respect for each other, and Barclay seemed impressed that at their previous meeting Bowdler had shown the confidence to attend alone and without the phalanx of advisers who are often present on such occasions.

Barclay did not beat about the bush. An inquiry – one of many, mainly from private equity companies – about the business had been received, he said, but he was not interested in an auction; if Johnston Press still wanted to buy The Scotsman he would listen to sensible proposals.

"You bet we are," said Bowdler.

It was the response Barclay had anticipated. A shrewd businessman and good judge of character, he believed that the Johnston approach was motivated for all the right reasons and that a deal would be relatively uncomplicated – factors that appealed to him.

Within a few days he provided essential financial information about Scotsman Publications and by late September, 2005, Bowdler presented the Johnston offer. After amicable and surprisingly straightforward negotiations the figure of £160 million was agreed for Johnston to acquire the business debt-free, and to lease The Scotsman's ultra-modern offices. In a helter-skelter of activity the deal was tied up by December, and with it access to the titles' core circulation area of Edinburgh and the Lothians, both of which were strong economically.

In the last complete financial year Scotsman Publications had reported a profit before interest and tax of £7.7 million on a turnover of £63.5 million. Significantly, the company had an operating margin only about a third of that of Johnston Press, but this was partly because of the quasi-national character of The Scotsman, which had incurred costs that were well above those of a purely regional newspaper of similar size.

"We were never in doubt that we had bought some brilliant brands and a very successful company," said Bowdler.

Once he and Barclay had shook hands on a deal they handed over the detailed negotiations to Johnston finance director Stuart Paterson and Ellerman director Michael Seal, who dealt swiftly and effortlessly with the numerous points that arose, often talking five or six times a day on the telephone. Seal's involvement had an added advantage; he was also a director of Holyrood Holdings, a company that had been formed to manage Scotsman Publications, the premises and subsidiary activities, and knew the business thoroughly.

Paterson also had personal responsibility for dealing with the complex banking arrangements, although these were much simpler than when, for example, the RIM acquisition was being considered. Then the company's borrowings had been shared by a syndicate of banks, but this method had been abandoned in favour of bi-lateral facilities with individual banks, of which there were numerous anxious to obtain the Johnston business.

Royal Bank of Scotland and Lloyds TSB agreed to share The Scotsman funding by lending £80 million each, confident in Johnston's record of investing in companies, improving their profitability, generating cash flow and repaying debts with interest.

Scores of column inches were given over to The Scotsman acquisition on the financial pages of the principal national newspapers, but not all the comments were helpful and some took a somewhat unenthusiastic view. But there was also criticism of Andrew Neil, who was accused of failing to deliver the new golden age he had promised when taking on the role of publisher 10 years previously. During his tenure the former editor of the Sunday Times had seen seven editors of The Scotsman come and go and circulation, briefly boosted by price-cutting, fall by 13 per cent.

The most scathing verdict on his time in charge came from the National Union of Journalists. "We're glad to see the back of him," declared Paul Holleran, the NUJ's Scottish organiser, who also welcomed the new ownership as "a great opportunity for long-term sustainability."

Campaign, the advertising, marketing, media and PR magazine, described the sale as a "surprising retreat" by the Barclay brothers but applauded Bowdler's optimism for the future of the British newspaper industry.

"Bowdler sees opportunity where others see none, and is prepared to pay handsomely. And it has worked. His track record as a successful manager of regional newspapers is sound, and under his guidance Johnston has become one of the giants of the regional newspaper market," said the magazine.

"It will deliver sharper, leaner management but the real test is whether Bowdler can discover a coherent editorial and marketing strategy for national, rather than regional, newspapers. If he can, then Bowdler will have spent his £160 million wisely and his optimism will have been rewarded."

The Independent conceded that while the price obtained by the

> "
> Paul Holleran, the NUJ's Scottish organiser, welcomed the new ownership as 'a great opportunity for long-term sustainability'
> "

Barclays looked a decent one, the deal also seemed to work for Johnston Press. "Bowdler only needs to improve the profitability of Scotsman Publications by £1 million a year for the acquisition to be earnings enhancing, which should be a stroll in the park."

The Times had some useful words of advice for the Johnston management. "The Scotsman remains a remarkably profitable publication," wrote former editor Magnus Linklater. "But its new owners must resist the temptation to strip out costs and push up margins when it needs nurturing and a commitment to the home market."

Meanwhile, the Daily Telegraph refrained from commenting directly on the deal and simply published quotes from Bowdler and Neil. As a Barclay-owned title it would perhaps have been seen as inappropriate to do otherwise.

Thanks to the internet and international media agencies, news of The Scotsman acquisition was transmitted worldwide. The story attracted the attention of the Wall Street Journal, the International Herald Tribune and, bizarrely, the North Korea Times, which allocated it four paragraphs.

Among the Scottish establishment, which had long since become disillusioned and upset by The Scotsman's editorial policies, there was a warm reception for the deal. Alex Salmond, leader of the Scottish National Party, said: "The Scotsman had a poor period under the previous owners. Hopefully this is a positive step into the future for important Scottish titles."

And Professor Philip Schlesinger, director of the Stirling Media Research Institute at Stirling University, told BBC Scotland that Salmond spoke for a large section of the political and bureaucratic class north of the border, who had resented the paper's critical voice.

"Johnston has made a smart move," he said.

Under Neil's direction the paper, with a history and tradition of supporting the liberal Left, had espoused a more radical, right-wing style of politics. Hallowed Scottish institutions had been challenged and many people felt that the consensus view of the Establishment had been disregarded.

Bowdler, who lived in Edinburgh and often met with the city's influential business and political leaders, was well aware of the criticisms that had been levelled at The Scotsman in the past. In a shrewd move to pre-empt reaction to the acquisition he took the unusual step of writing to MPs and Members of the Scottish

Parliament to coincide with the official public announcement of the deal.

His letter included an invitation to let him have their reaction, which many of the recipients did by telephone, letter and in person. Among them were Scotland's First Minister Jack McConnell, SNP leader Salmond and the then deputy leader of the Liberal Party, Sir Menzies Campbell, who was also MP for Fife North East.

"I felt it was important that they had direct access to me, or to Johnston Press, to express any views they might have or assuage their concerns," said Bowdler.

"The feedback was very positive. Some people made the point of not being nationalistic, but they were delighted to see The Scotsman back in Scottish ownership. Others said they hoped the paper could recover what they regarded as lost ground.

"To all of them I made the point that the newspaper would not be edited from Manor Place. Johnston Press does not have a corporate political view, a corporate political affiliation to any party or an opinion on major issues. Nor would we be dictating the editorial direction of The Scotsman."

After formally completing the acquisition, Bowdler, Michael Johnston and chief operating officer Danny Cammiade visited the Holyrood Road offices of Scotsman Publications and in a series of meetings addressed staff working on all titles. And to reinforce the company's commitment to editorial independence, Bowdler met individually with his new editors – John McGurk, of The Scotsman, John McLellan of the Evening News, and Iain Martin of Scotland on Sunday – to offer them reassurance about the company's policy of non-interference in editorial affairs.

Magnus Linklater, editor of The Scotsman from 1988 to 1994

McGurk had the rare distinction of having edited all three papers. But his association with Johnston Press was already much closer than was his colleagues . . . his home in Edinburgh was only a few doors away from head office in Manor Place!

Later, Bowdler also met with Magnus Linklater, one of the paper's most distinguished editors of recent times, whose tenure at North Bridge between 1988 and 1994 was commemorated with a suite named after him when the premises were converted to a hotel. He is still a contributor to The Scotsman and a regular columnist with The Times.

Visitors to Edinburgh for more than a century were made aware of The Scotsman's presence there, even if they did not know much about the newspaper, by its 190ft-

The baroque-style offices at North Bridge, home to The Scotsman for more than 100 years

high, English baroque-style headquarters at North Bridge. Still one of the main features of the city centre skyline, the building, which is now used as a hotel, came to symbolise the paper's power and influence in the life of Scotland. At a cost of £500,000 its turreted exterior was matched by a showcase interior of marble pillars and floors, panelled walls of mahogany and walnut, and ornate ceilings – but staff accommodation was far more frugal.

The North Bridge premises were built in 1904 and were described by the owners as the largest and most magnificent newspaper buildings in the world. But by the end of the 20th century they had become increasingly inefficient to operate on 13 floors, with associated departments often located several floors apart. In 1990 the familiar roar of the North Bridge presses was silenced when a new colour printing plant was opened by the then owners, Thomson Regional Newspapers, at Newhaven Road – this is now known as Caledonian Offset and was included in the Johnston Press acquisition.

In the years that followed more units were added to the Goss Colorliner press to increase its colour capability and in 2001 a Goss Universal heatset press was installed to produce high quality magazines for Scotland on Sunday and The Scotsman.

Shortly after taking over Scotsman Publications, the Barclays authorised a move from North Bridge to new offices at Holyrood – close to the royal palace of Holyrood House and almost next door to the Scottish Parliament building – at a cost of £19 million. The labyrinthine North Bridge building was exchanged for a sleek structure on three storeys, built around a glass-roofed atrium in the form of a "street" complete with living trees.

The Holyrood showpiece, named Barclay House and said to be worth £25 million six years later, was transferred to Johnston Press on a long-term lease.

The birth of The Scotsman on January 25, 1817 – the

birthday of Robert Burns – was an event that shook the Edinburgh establishment to the core. The founders, solicitor William Ritchie and customs official Charles Maclaren,pledged impartiality, firmness and independence – an indignant and indeed belligerent response to what they saw as "unblushing subservience" of local newspapers to the Establishment.

To emphasise its credentials the paper's masthead included a single thistle, the prickly, defiant emblem of Scotland. Nowadays there are three thistles.

The paper declared itself an enemy of privilege and corruption and was so outspoken that one Scottish peer even described it as "incendiary". It is said that city figures dared not be seen buying or reading The Scotsman and had copies smuggled to them!

Co-editor Maclaren was such a firebrand that this led him to fight a duel with the editor of the rival Caledonian Mercury following some stinging journalistic attacks. The two men met at Ravelston Road, a popular duelling ground, where they were both handed a pistol. After retiring 12 paces they turned, exchanged shots and both missed. But neither was prepared to shake hands and they parted without apologies.

By the 1870s, The Scotsman, then a daily, had a sale of 40,000 copies and was available throughout Scotland – its first national newspaper.

The paper has never been afraid to nail its colours to the mast, remaining as prickly as its three thistles symbol – unswervingly supporting the First World War effort, even during the bleakest days; strenuously opposing a national war memorial at Edinburgh Castle because of its visual impact above the battlements; initially backing the policy of appeasement with Hitler; enthusiastically campaigning for devolution and the formation of a Scottish Assembly.

A commentator once described The Scotsman as "one of the best written, best produced and, in many ways, most civilised newspaper in Britain". Tributes poured in when it marked its centenary as a daily paper in 1955, but those who referred to its unchanging character were in for a surprise – two years later news was printed on the front page, followed in later years by the introduction of full colour. In 2004 came the biggest change of all, the transition from broadsheet to compact format of similar size to the original eight-page quarto journal of 1817.

By then Scotsman Publications had undergone two changes of

Founders of The Scotsman Charles Mclaren (far left) and William Ritchie

Copies of The Scotsman
being loaded onto the
train bound for Glasgow
and the West coast

ownership, firstly in 1953 to Roy Thomson, a Canadian millionaire of Scottish descent, who paid £393,750 for the business. His appearance was timely and almost certainly saved The Scotsman from extinction, for behind its aura of quality and permanence was a different story – the paper was facing financial ruin, vigorous competition and declining sales.

Thomson – later Lord Thomson of Fleet – already owned a chain of newspapers in Canada and the United States and had earlier expressed an interest in buying The Scotsman. The owners, direct descendants of the Ritchie family, turned to him in their hour of need.

"Uncle Roy" restored the fortunes of the business, endeared himself to the staff and seemed to upset most of the Edinburgh establishment with his brash, forthright approach. None was more critical of Thomson than his own editor of The Scotsman, Murray Watson, who likened the new owner – "Hi folks, my name's Thomson; call me Roy" – to a vulgar, money-minded, colonial intruder.

A mark of Thomson's success was the profitability of the company when his Thomson Organisation decided to retreat from the British regional newspaper scene – a success story reflected in the £85 million paid by Ellerman Investments in 1995.

Nevertheless, the Barclays reasoned that there was further potential for growth and development, especially as it appeared to them that Scotsman Publications had been overshadowed and somewhat neglected within the Thomson business.

This was one of two Thomson centres in Scotland, but none offered the same value or attraction and the Barclays wasted no time in wrapping up the acquisition. During the next 10 years they invested heavily in the Edinburgh operation and sought to establish The Scotsman as a British national brand with a strong editorial and sales team in London. Ironically, during the same period sales of The Scotsman and other Scottish titles declined at a similar rate to that which English national papers increased their penetration north of the border.

For their £160 million investment a decade later, Johnston Press acquired not only the prestigious Scotsman but also a stable of titles with a combined weekly paid-for circulation of 840,000, weekly free distribution of 254,000 and an award-winning website.

Indeed, Scotsman.com had become something of a trendsetter since its origins in 1996 to become Scotland's first comprehensive online newspaper and a portal for Scotland and all things Scottish on the internet. The site twice won the Newspaper Society's prestigious Best Daily Newspaper on the Internet award and at the time of the acquisition had audited monthly unique users of more than three million and more than 20 million page impressions.

Other printed publications have, inevitably, lived in the shadow of The Scotsman but are success stories in their own right. Scotland on Sunday, which was launched in 1988, won a string of industry awards – but the biggest vote of confidence came from its readers. The quality broadsheet comfortably led the Sunday broadsheet market in Scotland and outpaced its Scottish rival, the Sunday Herald.

The Glasgow Herald group started the latter in 1999 when it became fearful of the inroads Scotland on Sunday was making into its west coast advertising base. But on the second week of the confrontation between the two newspapers Scotland on Sunday sold 134,500 copies – the biggest sale in its history.

The Edinburgh Evening News was another valuable addition to Johnston's portfolio of evening titles. It was founded in 1873 by three sons of a Moray farm manager who all followed different careers before deciding that the city should have its own local newspaper.

Subsequently owned by United Newspapers, the News merged in 1963 with its rival the Evening Dispatch, which had been bought by

The state-of-the-art offices at Holyrood

Lord Thomson along with The Scotsman to form part of Thomson Regional Newspapers. In 1995 the News went full circle when it converted from broadsheet to tabloid – the original format 83 years before when its four pages sold for one halfpenny.

It was during the Thomson era that the Edinburgh Herald and Post free newspaper was started in 1978, as the Edinburgh Advertiser, and by 1991 had expanded to a series of three. A major re-launch involving a new masthead and redesign took place in 2001, when the titles were changed to Herald and Post Edinburgh, Herald and Post Fife and Herald and Post West Lothian. The trio became a quartet in 2004 with the appearance of the Herald and Post Perth.

The flurry of acquisitions in 2005 presented an organisational headache for Johnston executives, who decided on a streamlined divisional structure to reduce the number of people reporting directly to Danny Cammiade.

The changes, which were announced on completion of The Scotsman deal, saw the East Midlands and South Midlands divisions merged to form a new Midlands division with Nick Mills in charge; the North, Northeast and North Midlands/South Yorkshire divisions merged to form an enlarged North division under Chris Green; and all the Scottish operations were combined under Michael Johnston, following his move from the South division. In the reshuffle this was handed on to Gary Fearon, who moved from the disbanded Northeast division at Sunderland to Portsmouth. Chris Pennock, formerly divisional managing director for the South Midlands, was appointed to a newly created post of group newspaper sales and marketing director to oversee group-wide initiatives on daily and weekly newspaper sales and related marketing strategies.

This, then, is almost the end of our story of Johnston Press, but it is by no means the end of the Johnston Press story. When the next chapter comes to be written there is little doubt that the shape and size of the company will have changed considerably, and the fact that DMGT were even willing to consider selling off their Northcliffe empire showed that the process of industry consolidation had almost certainly not yet run its course.

Some market analysts suggested that the industry was reaching its final shape, but no one seriously expects it to remain the same forever. And with almost 100 independently owned newspaper companies in Britain the predatory instincts that have characterised the industry are unlikely to be satisfied yet.

But what of Johnston Press?

It requires a fertile imagination and some inspired crystal ball gazing to answer that question – but change there will be.

If the same conundrum had been put to Archibald Johnston when he bought the Falkirk Herald in 1846 he would never have envisaged the growth of a newspaper publishing group that was to become so influential in the British Isles, with titles throughout Scotland and England, and Ireland. And it would have been beyond anyone's wildest dreams that Johnston Press would have become the second largest regional newspaper publisher in the land, as it did in early 2006 following the acquisition of The Scotsman Publications Ltd.

As we have charted the Johnston story change has been the constant theme – titles bought and sold, but mostly bought, the wee Scottish minnow acquiring much larger fish in the newspaper sea, ever newer technology that revolutionised the way titles were produced.

And that relentless change has not only altered the face of Johnston Press but the industry as a whole. Companies that once seemed unassailable have come and gone, amalgamated, been taken over or simply quit. Remember Westminster Press and the Thomson Organisation?

At the same time other changes in the market place resulted in groups that operated a multi-media

Chris Pennock, who was appointed group newspaper sales and marketing director in a senior management reshuffle policy,including Pearson, Reed Elsevier and Emap, being replaced by groups dedicated solely to local newspaper publication such as Johnston Press and Newsquest.

Consolidation that marked the years either side of the Millennium saw the disappearance of other well-known names. In the last ten years alone the Big Four had increased their combined national share of copies sold or distributed from 37 per cent to 73 per cent.

Nevertheless, regulatory constraints and the watchful eye of the Competition Commission served to put a partial brake on further industry consolidation, although the Communications Act 2003 removed some of the most irksome restrictions and conditions. The new legislation has yet to be put to its first thorough test, but in 2005 Johnston Press successfully dipped a toe in the water with the £100,000 acquisition of the Thorne Gazette, a small free distribution newspaper near Doncaster. This was approved without some of the bureaucratic complexities of previous takeovers.

At the same time Johnston Press, through chief executive Bowdler, and other proprietors continued to seek a relaxation of the narrow way in which the Office of Fair Trading and the Competition Commission viewed the markets in which newspapers operate by effectively excluding the influence of other media on their business activities.

So how does Johnston Press view its own future?

After the Score Press, Irish and Scotsman acquisitions, attention was focused on another development closer to home – the effect of the internet on newspaper revenues and circulations and how the group's websites could be harnessed to offer a complete local package of printed and online services.

The 2005 strategy meeting did not rule out further acquisitions abroad but agreed that for the immediate future more resources should be directed towards the digital publishing activities of the business. "After the false dawn when everyone got terribly excited about dotcom companies, what is now clear is that digital media is absolutely real and a fundamental part of people's lives," chairman Parry told his colleagues.

Far from viewing the internet as a threat, the Johnston board regarded it as an opportunity to further expand its local activities and enrich the lives of communities in which it already had a strong presence. It also accepted that the days when Johnston Press could only claim to be a regional newspaper publishing company were coming to an end.

"We must see ourselves as a regional publishing company," Parry stressed. "That mindset is very important because it then means that we are as comfortable publishing for hand-held devices and computers as we would be publishing physically in print.

"At the same time we absolutely believe in the future of the printed medium, but not in isolation."

Trading projections prepared for the board envisaged a time when an increasing part of Johnston revenue would come from digital publishing. In 2005 the company's revenue from the internet accounted for just one per cent of income, but national statistics indicated steady growth in this area – for example, a study by accountants PricewaterhouseCoopers for the International Advertising Bureau showed that spending on internet advertising in the UK rose by 62 per cent to more than £490 million in the first half of 2005.

Just as the company prided itself on the design and content of its newspapers, so it was looking ahead to producing leading-edge websites that would prove attractive to advertisers as part of a package of outlets, from paid-for newspapers to leaflets, and be a prime source for people seeking a wide range of information.

It was accepted that in the long term more people would turn to electronic devices to access their news and classified advertising. But the outlook for print, and in particular for local newspapers, was regarded as positive. To quote Parry: "Local newspapers will remain a vital and central part of our local publishing mix for years to come."

But there is no doubt that when the sequel to this history of Johnston Press is written it will almost certainly report on a group that is delivering news and information in ways that are far removed from its traditional roots in 19th century Falkirk.

After all, Johnston Press has spent a lifetime living with change, meeting threats, grasping opportunities and relishing challenges. It has never lost heart, or faith in its conviction that Life is Local – a truly remarkable achievement and something of which the company is intensely proud.

> We must see
> ourselves as
> a regional
> publishing
> company...
> we absolutely
> believe in the
> future of the
> printed
> medium, but
> not in isolation

Roger Parry

Index

D

D. MacLeod Ltd, 31, 45, 46, 55
DMGT (Daily Mail and General Trust), 321, 322, 337
Daily Mail and General Trust see *DMGT*
Dakeyne, John Barrington, 290
Days Out UK, 231
Derbyshire Times, 36, 51, 52, 55, 57, 59-64, 76, 81, 90, 93, 97, 143, 160, 203
Derry Journal, 313, 314, 317
Dicks, Christopher, 127
Dickson, Ian, 56, 98, 116
Digital publishing, 218, 303, 306, 338, 339
Dinnington, 144, 221, 230, 297, 298
Doncaster Free Press, 87, 112, 150
Dor, Henri Leopold, 139
Downing, Stephen, 82, 281
Driffield Times, 162, 170, 290
Dubbins, Tony, 86, 97
Dunn and Mason, 115
Dunn and Wilson, (see also *Riley, Dunn and Wilson*), 113-118, 124
Dunn, Hugh, 115

E

East Midland Allied Press (Emap), 95, 119-121, 124-126, 152-177, 181, 197, 232, 234, 253, 273, 292, 302, 304, 305, 307-310, 312, 338
Eastern Counties Newspapers, 180
Edinburgh Evening News 323, 336
Edinburgh Herald and Post, 323, 336
Edmondson, David, 261, 266
Edwards, Mark, 75, 173
Electronic publishing, 304
Ellerman Investments, 324, 327, 328, 335
Elliott, Geoff, 199
Emap, see *East Midland Allied Press*
Evening Dispatch, 336

F

F. Johnston and Co Ltd, 5, 16, 23, 46, 49, 55, 59, 93, 97
F.W. Pawsey and Sons, 123
Falkirk Herald, 10-12, 14, 18-20, 22, 26, 28, 29, 35, 52, 58, 67-69, 71, 117, 132, 283, 337
Faure Walker, Henry, 224, 265
Fearon, Gary, 224, 336

Featham, Bob, 321
Fife Free Press, 37-39, 330
Fish 4, 304, 305
Forbes, Norma, 108, 236
Four Counties Newspapers, 230
Fowler, Lord, 261

G

G.C. Brittain and Sons, 80, 112
Gannett, 228, 229, 233, 247, 248, 250, 251, 253, 254, 259
Geroski, Paul, 279
Gibbs, Bill, 179
Gilson, Mike, 199
Glasgow East News, 231, 330
Glasgow Herald, 325, 327, 335
Gooding, Suzanne (Green, Mrs T.H.), 92, 96, 99, 101, 104
Gordon, Lord, 223, 308
Gould, Graham, 132, 176, 266, 285, 286
GPMU, see *Graphical, Paper and Media Union*
Graf, Philip, 128, 278
Graphical, Paper and Media Union (GPMU), 152
Green, Chris, 224, 266, 337
Green, Mrs T.H., see *Gooding, Suzanne*
Greenhead Books, 117
Grime family, 274
Grime, Alan, 276
Guardian Media Group, 151, 247, 248, 259

H

Hale, Don, 81, 281
Hale, Joe, 118, 122, 124, 146
Halifax Courier Ltd, 111, 129, 134, 298
Halifax Evening Courier, 78, 129, 132, 133, 304
Hampshire Chronicle, 50
Harrogate Advertiser, 166, 246, 267, 273, 274
HCN, see *Home Counties Newspapers*
Heart of England Newspapers, 107, 155, 175
Hedderwick, Alexander, 11
Heidrick and Struggles, 145, 242
Hemel Hempstead Gazette, 161, 167
Hilton, Margaret, 224, 266
Hinton, Les, 296
Hollinger International Inc., 325
Holt, Peter, 29

U

UBS (also see *Phillips and Drew*), 187, 191

"Uncle" Fred, see *Johnston, Fred*

United Newspapers, 53, 54, 57, 143, 167, 170, 172, 245, 268, 271, 272, 335

United Provincial Newspapers (UPN), 243-245, 260, 273, 276

UPN, see *United Provincial Newspapers*

V

Villiers, Charles, 191

W

W.J. Linney Ltd, 52

Waddell, Ken, 18, 20

Wakefield Express, 72, 88, 90, 91, 287

Waley-Cohen, Sir Stephen, 184, 195

Walker, Peter, 173, 176

Watson, Alan, 35

Watson, Murray, 334

Watson, Tony, 269

Websites, 6, 8, 199, 218, 289, 299-305, 322, 323

West Sussex County Times, 72, 92, 94-97, 99, 100, 102-104, 108, 110, 111, 124, 125

Westminster Press, 25, 153, 158, 160, 164, 166, 168, 205, 206, 337

Wetton, Adrian, 266

Whittaker family, 169

Whittaker, Sir Meredith, 169, 170

Wigan Observer, 267, 290

Wilfred Edmunds Ltd, 51, 53-56, 177

William B Harris Ltd, 123

Williamson, Trudi, 138, 140, 176

Wilson, David, 290

Windle, Harry, 51, 63

Winfrey, Francis Charles, 164

Winfrey, Pat, see *Winfrey, Richard Pattinson*

Winfrey, Sir Richard, 121, 164, 170, 174

Winfrey, Richard John, 164

Winfrey, Richard Pattinson (Pat Winfrey), 164, 171, 174

Wood, Edward, 78, 129, 131-133, 136, 137, 140

Wood, Westworth and Co, 94

Woodhouse, Monica, 50, 98

Wormsley, David, 252

Y

Yorkshire Communications Group (YCG), 90, 94

Yorkshire Conservative Newspaper Co. Ltd, 268

Yorkshire Evening Post, 78, 212, 215, 245, 267, 270

Yorkshire Post, 111, 143, 148, 212, 215, 217, 229, 244, 245, 262, 263, 267, 268-271, 326

Yorkshire Post Newspapers Ltd, 268, 271

Yorkshire Weekly Newspaper Group (YWNG), 88-92

Appendix

Johnston Press newspaper titles

As at February 2006

E – Evening   F – Free   M – Morning   S – Sunday   W – Weekly

SCOTLAND

Johnston (Falkirk)
The Falkirk Herald **W**
Linlithgowshire Journal & Gazette **W**
Cumbernauld News & Kilsyth Chronicle **W**
Carluke & Lanark Gazette **W**
Falkirk, Linlithgow & Grangemouth
Advertiser **F**
Cumbernauld & Kilsyth Advertiser **F**
Kirkintilloch & Bishopbriggs Herald **W**
Milngavie & Bearsden Herald **W**
Motherwell Times & Bellshill Speaker **W**
Advertiser (Strathkelvin) **F**
Glasgow East News **F**

Strachan & Livingston
Fife Free Press **W**
East Fife Mail **W**
Glenrothes Gazette **W**
Fife Herald & St. Andrews Citizen **W**
Fife Leader South **F**
Fife Leader North **F**
Kirkcaldy Herald **F**

The Tweeddale Press Group
Southern Reporter **W**
Berwickshire News
& East Lothian Herald **W**
Berwick Advertiser **W**
Berwick Gazette **F**
Hawick News & Scottish Border Chronicle **W**
Selkirk Weekend Advertiser **W**
East Lothian Times **F**
Midlothian Times **F**
Peebles Times **F**
Midlothian Advertiser **W**
East Lothian News **W**

Angus County Press
Brechin Advertiser **W**
Donside/Deeside Piper & Inverurie Herald **W**
The Arbroath Herald & Angus County
Advertiser **W**
Forfar Dispatch and Kirriemuir Herald **W**
Montrose Review **W**
Mearns Leader **W**
Car Mart **F**
Kincardineshire Observer **W**
The Buteman **W**

Galloway Gazette Group Ltd
Galloway Gazette **W**
Carrick Gazette **W**

Stornoway Gazette Ltd
Stornoway Gazette and
West Coast Advertiser **W**
The Hebridean **W**

Scotsman Publications Ltd
The Scotsman **M**
Scotland on Sunday **S**
Edinburgh Evening News **E**
Perth Herald & Post **F**
Edinburgh Herald & Post **F**
West Lothian Herald & Post **F**
Fife Herald & Post **F**

NORTH

Yorkshire Post Newspapers
Yorkshire Post **M**
Yorkshire Evening Post **E**
Yorkshire Sport **W**
Leeds Weekly News **F**
Pudsey Times **F**
The Yeller **F**

Wharfe Valley Times *F*

Ackrill Newspapers
Harrogate Advertiser *W*
Knaresborough Post *W*
Northallerton Thirsk and Bedale Times *W*
Pateley Bridge & Nidderdale Herald *W*
Ripon Gazette *W*
Wetherby News *W*
North Yorkshire News *F*
Harrogate Herald and Champion Shopper
Guide *F*

The Halifax Courier
Halifax Evening Courier *E*
Brighouse Echo *W*
Todmorden News *W*
Hebden Bridge Times *W*
Calderdale News *F*

Yorkshire Weekly Newspaper Group
Wakefield Express *W*
Pontefract & Castleford Express *W*
Selby Times *W*
Morley Observer and Advertiser *W*
Wakefield Extra Series (inc. Rothwell and
Oulton Extra) *F*
Hemsworth & South Elmsall Express *F*
Pontefract & Castleford Extra *F*
Ossett & Horbury Observer *F*
Selby Chronicle *F*
Dewsbury Reporter *W*
Batley News *W*
Morley Observer *W*
Spenborough Guardian *W*
The Weekly Advertiser *F*

Yorkshire Regional Newspapers
Scarborough Evening News *E*

The Malton & Pickering Mercury *W*
Filey Mercury *W*
Whitby Gazette *Bi-weekly*
Bridlington Free Press *W*
Driffield Times *W*
Beverly Guardian *F*
Bridlington Gazette & Herald *F*
Driffield Post *W*
Pocklington Post *W*
Trader & Weekly News *F*

Northeast Press
Hartlepool Mail *E*
Shields Gazette *E*
Sunderland Echo *E*
Hartlepool Star *F*
Seaham & Houghton Star *F*
Morpeth Herald *W*
News Post Leader *F*
North Shields & Whitley Bay
News Guardian *F*
Northumberland Gazette *W*
Peterlee Star *F*
South Tyne Star *F*
Sunderland Star *F*
Washington Star *F*

Sheffield Newspapers
Sheffield & Doncaster Star *E*
Angling Star *W*
Sheffield Telegraph *W*
Sheffield Weekly Gazette *F*
Sheffield Journal *F*

Wilfred Edmunds
Derbyshire Times *W*
Buxton Advertiser *W*
Ripley & Heanor News *W*
Ilkeston Advertiser *W*

Appendix
Johnston Press newspaper titles (continued)

As at February 2006

E – Evening   F – Free   M – Morning   S – Sunday   W – Weekly

Matlock Mercury *W*
Eastwood & Kimberley Advertiser *W*
Belper News *W*
Chesterfield Express *F*
Chesterfield Advertiser *F*
Alfreton & Ripley Echo *F*
Dronfield Advertiser *F*
Bolsover Advertiser *F*
High Peak Courier *F*
Ilkeston Shopper *F*
Eastwood Shopper *F*
Buxton Times *F*
Peak Times *F*
Eckington Leader *F*

North Notts Newspapers
Hucknall Dispatch *W*
Worksop Guardian *W*
Mansfield Chad *W*
Mansfield & Ashfield Observer *F*
Alfreton Chad *F*
Ashfield Chad *W*
Dinnington Guardian *W*
Retford Trader & Guardian *F*
Worksop Trader *F*
Dinnington & Maltby Trader *F*
Retford & Bantry Trader *F*

South Yorkshire Newspapers
Doncaster Free Press *W*
Doncaster Advertiser *F*
South Yorkshire Times *W*
Goole & Howden Courier *F*
Epworth Bells *W*
Gainsborough Standard *W*
Gainsborough News *F*
Thorne Gazette *F*
Northern Farming Gazette *F*

NORTHWEST

Lancashire Evening Post
Lancashire Evening Post *E*
Wigan Evening Post *E*
Chorley Guardian *W*
Leyland Guardian *W*
Garstang Courier *W*
Preston & Leyland Reporter *F*
Longridge News *W*

Lancaster & Morecambe Newspapers
Lancaster Guardian *W*
Morecambe Visitor Series *W*
Lakeland Echo *F*
Lancaster & Morcambe Star Buys
(The Reporter) *F*

Lancashire Publications
Wigan Observer *W*
St Helens, Prescot & Knowsley Reporter *F*
Wigan Reporter & Property Scene *F*
Leigh Reporter *F*
Ashton News *F*
Standish Village News *F*

Blackpool Gazette & Herald
The Blackpool Gazette *E*
Lytham St Annes Express *W*
Blackpool Reporter *F*
Fleetwood Weekly News *W*

East Lancashire Newspapers
Burnley Express *Bi-weekly*
Clitheroe Advertiser & Times *W*
Nelson Leader Series *W*
The Reporter *F*
The Valley *F*

Isle of Man Newspapers
Isle of Man Courier *F*
Isle of Man Examiner *W*
Manx Independent *W*

MIDLANDS

East Midlands Newspapers
Peterborough Evening Telegraph *E*
Peterborough Citizen *F*
Peterborough on Sunday *F*
Town Crier West Cambridgeshire Series *F*
Fenland Citizen *F*
Lynn News *Bi-weekly*
Norfolk Citizen *F*

Welland Valley Newspapers
Stamford Mercury *W*
Spalding Guardian *W*
Lincs Free Press *W*
Harborough Mail *W*
Melton Times *W*
Grantham Journal *W*
Stamford Citizen *F*
Melton Citizen *F*
Grantham Citizen *F*
Rutland Times *W*
Bourne Local *W*

Lincolnshire Newspapers
Lincoln Chronicle *F*
Boston Standard *W*
Louth Leader *W*
Sleaford Standard *W*
Skegness Standard *W*
Market Rasen Mail *W*
Horncastle News *W*
Lincolnshire Citizen *F*

Anglia Newspapers
Bury Free Press *W*
Suffolk Free Press *W*
Diss Express *W*
Newmarket Journal *W*
Haverhill Echo *W*
Bury Citizen *F*

Northamptonshire Newspapers
Chronicle & Echo *E*
Northants Evening Telegraph *E*
Northampton Mercury *F*
Northants Citizen *F*
Northants on Sunday *F*

Premier Newspapers
Milton Keynes Citizen *F*
MK Review *F*
Leighton Buzzard Citizen *F*
Leighton Buzzard Observer *W*
Tuesday Citizen *F*
Luton Herald & Post *F*
Luton News & Dunstable Gazette *W*
Bedfordshire Times & Citizen *F*
Biggleswade Chronicle *W*

Central Counties Newspapers
Bucks Herald *W*
Buckingham & Winslow Advertiser *W*
Hemel Gazette *W*
Brackley & Towcester Advertiser *W*
Berkhamstead Gazette *W*
Bucks Advertiser *F*
Bicester Review *F*
Hemel Herald Express *F*

Heart of England Newspapers
Banbury Guardian *W*
Banbury Citizen *F*

349

Appendix
Johnston Press newspaper titles (continued)

As at February 2006

E – Evening   F – Free   M – Morning   S – Sunday   W – Weekly

Rugby Advertiser *W*
Rugby Review *F*
Daventry Express *W*
Leamington Courier Series *W*
Leamington Review *F*
Kenilworth Weekly News *W*

SOUTH

Portsmouth Publishing & Printing
The News (Portsmouth) *E*
Bognor & Chichester Journal
& Guardian Series *F*
Guardian Home Finder *F*
Chichester, Bognor Regis and Midhurst
& Petworth Observer *W*
Ems Valley Gazette *F*
Hayling Islander *F*
Portsmouth Journal Series *F*
Petersfield & Bordon Post *W*
West Sussex Gazette *W*
Worthing Advertiser *F*
Shoreham Herald *W*
Worthing Guardian *F*
Littlehampton Gazette *W*
Worthing Herald *W*

T. R. Beckett
Hastings Observer *W*
Bexhill Observer *W*
Rye & Battle Observer *W*
Eastbourne Herald *W*
Eastbourne Gazette (inc. Hailsham and
Seaford Gazettes) *W*
Hastings and Bexhill News *F*
Eastbourne Advertiser *F*

Sussex Newspapers
West Sussex County Times *W*

Mid Sussex Times *W*
Crawley Observer *W*
Horsham Advertiser *F*
Mid Sussex Citizen *F*
Weekend Herald *F*
Sussex Express *W*

NORTHERN IRELAND

Mortons Newspapers
Ballymena Times *W*
Coleraine Times Series *W*
East Antrim Advertiser *F*
Larne Times *W*
Lisburn Echo *F*
Ulster Star *W*
Lurgan Mail *W*
Portadown Times *W*
Londonderry Sentinel *W*
North West Echo *F*
Banbridge Leader *W*
Craigavon Echo *F*
Dromore Leader *W*
Mid Ulster Echo *F*
Mid Ulster Mail *W*
Tyrone Times *W*
Farm Week *W*

Century Newspapers
Belfast News Letter *M*
Belfast News *F*
Farming Life *F*

Derry Journal
Derry Journal *Bi-weekly*
Foyle News *W*
Coleraine Journal *W*
Sunday Journal *S*
City News *F*

REPUBLIC OF IRELAND

Leinster Leader Group
The Tallacht Echo *W*
The Leinster Leader *W*
The Dundalk Democrat *W*
The Leinster Express *W*
The Offaly Express *W*
The Limerick Leader *W*
Limerick Chronicle *W*
Longford Leader *W*
Leitrim Observer *W*

Kilkenny People Publishing *W*
Kilkenny People *W*
Nationalist & Munster Advertiser *W*
Tipperary Star *W*

Donegal Democrat
Donegal Democrat *W*
Letterkenny People *F*
Donegal on Sunday *W*

JP VENTURES

Off Road Titles
Trials & Motorcross News *W*
Dirt Bike Rider *Monthly*

Outbound Publishing
Emigrate Australia *Monthly*
Emigrate Canada *Monthly*
Emigrate South Africa *Bi-Monthly*
Emigrate New Zealand *Monthly*
Emigrate America *Bi-Monthly*
World of Property *Bi-Monthly*
Property France Magazine *Bi-Monthly*
Emigrate Magazine *Annual*

Days Out UK
Days Out UK *Annual*

Best Asian Media Ltd
Asian Leader *Fortnightly*
Asian Life *Bi-annual*
Eid Magazine *Annual*

351

Acknowledgements

Life is Local: the History of Johnston Press is the culmination of two years' research and writing that has been pleasurable and absorbing throughout. At times it reminded me of my early days in journalism as a reporter in Halifax – conducting interviews, meeting people, combing through reports and documents and then putting all the information together as a story ready for publication.

The only difference was that this story spanned 200 years, covered the length and breadth of the British Isles and stretched to 100,000 words.

The history of Johnston Press is a fascinating tale and it has indeed been a privilege to tell it. But in so doing I have relied on the help and goodwill of many people who have rallied to the cause at my request – editors, managing directors, librarians, photographers and secretaries who all produced so much archival material that at times I was overwhelmed by the quality and the quantity.

It has also been my pleasure to meet and interview a number of very special people – those with an intimate knowledge of Johnston Press or the companies that have been absorbed over the years. My thanks go to, among others, Freddy Johnston, Tim Bowdler, Sir Robin Miller, Charles Brims, Joe Hale, Roger Parry, Ken Waddell, Ian Scott, Iris McGowran, Iain Bell, Marco Chiappelli, David Briffett, Harry Windle, Derrick Platt, Stuart Paterson, Richard Cooper, Chris Oakley, David Rowell, Edward Wood, Graham Gould, David Crow and John Bradshaw. My sincere apologies to anyone I have inadvertently omitted.

Heartfelt thanks and appreciation are reserved for the two women without whose assistance this book would not have been possible – Jayne Cameron, at head office in Edinburgh, whose efficiency and skill lightened the burden of administration, and my wife Sheila, who became something of a "Johnston widow" for two years but was always available for help, advice and moral support.

Much of the historical detail was sourced from anniversary supplements and booklets published by numerous Johnston newspapers. I also delved deep into the pages of *The men that carry the news*, the story of United Newspapers, by Guy Schofield, *Men of Mark*, the history of Emap, by R.P. Winfrey, *Scotland's Paper* by Albert Morris and *Reporting Yorkshire*, the history of the Yorkshire Post, by Michael Hickling.

Numerous reports prepared by the Competition Commission provided invaluable background and statistical information on the major acquisitions undertaken by Johnston Press. In addition the company freely made available its files and archives in Edinburgh and I was given open access to reports and minute books whenever this was needed.

Finally, thanks are also due to the small group of people who agreed to check through the manuscript for errors, mistakes and omissions, especially my good friend Malcolm Knott. Every effort has been made to trace copyright holders and obtain their permission to use their material, and ensure the book is complete and accurate.

E.R.